HODGES UNIVERSITY
LIBRARY - NAPLES

P9-DJL-736

THE MODERN
American Presidency

THE MODERN
American Presidency

Lewis L. Gould

Foreword by Richard Norton Smith

 University Press of Kansas

© 2003 by the University Press of Kansas

All rights reserved

Published by the University Press of Kansas (Lawrence, Kansas 66049), which was organized by the Kansas Board of Regents and is operated and funded by Emporia State University, Fort Hays State University, Kansas State University, Pittsburg State University, the University of Kansas, and Wichita State University

Library of Congress Cataloging-in-Publication Data

Gould, Lewis L.
    The modern American presidency / Lewis L. Gould ; foreword by Richard Norton Smith.
        p. cm.
    Includes bibliographical references (p.   ) and index.
    ISBN 0-7006-1252-1 (alk. paper)
    1. Presidents—United States—History—20th century.   2. Presidents—United States—Biography.   3. United States—Politics and government—20th century.   4. United States—Politics and government—1897–1901.   I. Title.
    E176.1 .G68 2003
    973.9'092'2—dc21   2002154108

British Library Cataloguing in Publication Data is available.

Printed in the United States of America

10 9 8 7 6 5 4 3 2

The paper used in this publication meets the minimum requirements of the American National Standard for Permanence of Paper for Printed Library Materials z39.48–1984.

CONTENTS

That Theodore Roosevelt is the father of the modern presidency is an article of faith among historians of the executive office. Only the boldest of revisionists would contest the claims of that swashbuckling egoist, whose flair for melodrama helped transform the presidency from chief administrative officer to a kind of permanent morality play — scripted, directed, and performed by the dervish Henry Adams called "pure act." Besides, if TR isn't the genesis of today's highly scripted, image-hungry White House, then who is? George B. Cortelyou?

George B. *who?* He may not be a household name, even in political science circles, but according to Lewis L. Gould it was Cortelyou, working in tandem with President William McKinley, who anticipated much of the modern chief executive's role as newsmaker, agenda setter, public educator, and *uber* celebrity. Seventy years before Richard Nixon scribbled malign notes in the margins of his daily press summary, Cortelyou supplied McKinley with "current clippings." Nearly a century before the Clinton White House operated a War Room reflecting the more or less permanent campaign that has all but engulfed the Oval Office, Cortelyou unveiled a nineteenth-century version. For it was under McKinley that the United States edged onto the world stage, focusing attention on the White House as incubator of American foreign policy.

That winners write history is axiomatic. Gould understands that luck and timing also rank high among the factors influencing posterity's judgment. No one illustrates this better than the last president of the nineteenth century. McKinley had the misfortune to be succeeded by Theodore Roosevelt, whose instinctive grasp of leadership rode the crest of the emerging mass media. "Taft is a far abler man than I," he once wrote of his ill-fated successor, "but he don't know how to play the popular hero and shoot a bear." Ever since, TR and his self-proclaimed "preacher president" cousin Franklin have been canonized as patron saints of executive activism.

By contrast, less aggressive — or more administratively minded — presidents have been largely written off by scholars. It is a rare historian indeed who credits Taft with anticipating the modern Office of Management and Budget or Warren Harding with plans to establish a post–World War I Department of Defense. Gould is such a historian. In fashioning "a work of historical analysis aimed at the elusive target of the general reader," he understands that an American president is more than the dramatist-in-chief. Constitutionally, if not always temperamentally, he is also a manager of events for whom the *prevention* of crisis is as important as crisis management.

In this thoughtful, comprehensive, deeply researched volume, Gould skillfully draws lines of institutional continuity at the expense of what might be called the "fat pope, thin pope" theory of alternating executive styles. He *grounds* the presidency in ways that challenge popular stereotypes. Consider his treatment of Calvin Coolidge, that most prosaic of passive-negative leaders. Do the roots of twenty-first-century White House spin really lie in Coolidge's shrewd use of radio, his frequent press conferences, and his cultivation of Hollywood and other celebrities? Gould believes they do. Likewise, he argues for Dwight Eisenhower as a more naturally gifted bureaucratic innovator than FDR. Ike's military background helped to inspire the National Security Council and the White House Office of Congressional Relations, and his preference for indirect or "hidden-hand" guidance handed the poisoned chalice of visibility to surrogates. Thus, Sherman Adams became the most detested chief of staff until Nixon's H. R. Haldeman, or the first Bush's John Sununu (what *is* it about New Hampshire governors?).

If the presidency observes any law, Gould tells us, it is the law of unintended consequences. Harry Truman and Eisenhower were the least imperial of men (even if the latter displayed little reluctance to use the new CIA for covert operations in Latin America and the Middle East). Yet their response to Cold War pressures restructured the White House along lines that foreshadowed later abuses of power. For example, by citing executive privilege to shield White House staff members from Senator Joseph McCarthy's subpoenas, Eisenhower created a dangerous standard for his successors — Nixon, above all — who lacked his unique prestige earned in war.

Under John F. Kennedy the culture of celebrity took up full-time residence in the White House, aided by a glamorous First Lady, a youthful, telegenic family, and the televised press conference (sourly dismissed by James Reston as "the goofiest idea since the hula hoop"). Mindful of his narrow victory in 1960, Kennedy employed the pollster Lou Harris to help him mold public opinion, thereby advancing the more or less continuous campaign that would reach illegal proportions under Richard Nixon. "You've got to be a little evil to understand those people out there," Gould quotes Nixon. This dark view of humanity coexisted with a mulligan stew of genuine idealism, the imaginative pursuit of decentralized government ("the New Federalism"), and a paradoxical weakness for quick fixes (wage and price controls) and intellectual men on horseback, à la Daniel Patrick Moynihan and John Connally.

"The modern presidency had an uncanny capacity to reveal the character flaw that presidential campaigns, in the case of Nixon and Carter, were designed to mask," writes Gould. "Nixon could not stay within the law, and Carter could not translate piety and commitment into effective leadership." Other writers have sought to explain Ronald Reagan's enigmatic conduct of the presidency ("He knows so little," sighed National Security Adviser Bud McFarlane, "yet accomplishes so much") within a context of Reagan's earlier Hollywood career. Few have done it so succinctly or persuasively as Gould. Supported — some would say managed — by a strong chief of staff, James Baker, and a small army of professionals gifted at packaging the modern presidency for the television audience, Reagan proved to be a conservative innovator. The president's weekly radio address and the "heroes in the balcony," choreographed as part of each year's State of the Union address, had their policy counterparts in dramatic tax and spending cuts and the Strategic Defense Initiative (SDI) that threatened the equilibrium of Cold War terror.

For Reagan admirers who credit the president with personally winning the Cold War through his arms buildup and SDI, Gould has constructed a deft trap: acknowledging that such conclusions may be validated as the records of his administration are opened, the author cannot resist contrasting Reagan's alleged hands-on role in dismantling the Soviet Union to the president's hazy detachment from Iran-Contra. For all this, however, Gould may underestimate the historic legacy of the so-called Reagan Revolution. In politics there is no more sincere form of flattery than imitation, as Bill Clinton's presidency demonstrates. An activist by temperament, a risk taker in his personal life, Clinton proved largely risk averse in the policy arena.

In truth, he found himself operating within a broad Reaganesque consensus, one he appeared to endorse in declaring the era of big government to be at an end. If Clinton was "a mainstream president in his policies," asks Gould, why did the man and his methods prove so polarizing? How Americans felt about the Clintons had a great deal to do with their feelings about the decade of the sixties, a divisive era that the new president and his wife, fairly or not, came to personify. The Clinton years will be remembered for the trivialization of impeachment, Gould asserts. At the same time, he acknowledges, "Presidential scholarship always lags behind presidential actions." It is simply too early for him, or anyone else, to form more than rudimentary assessments of the second George Bush's performance.

Where the office itself is concerned, however, Gould does not hesitate to offer sobering conclusions. "To treat the modern presidency as a success story," he insists, "is to falsify the historical record. As a new century begins, the presidency today is no more capable of grappling with the difficulties of globalization, terrorism, and environmental change than was the law office approach of Grover Cleveland from 1893 to 1897." Carried to extremes, Rooseveltian persuasion, sprinkled with Sorensenian eloquence and Reaganesque image making, has led to the triumph of public relations over public policy. To wage "a long twilight struggle" against global terrorism, writes Gould, "presidents will have to reduce the time they spend on distracting trivia in order to husband their energies for the serious priority of protecting the nation."

One could easily carry this idea further — for as the president becomes a mere celebrity, citizens' expectations sink accordingly. Before Clinton left office, pollsters found it necessary for the first time to ask two questions, one dealing with job performance, the other assessing Clinton personally, in order to gauge popular attitudes. Here is disturbing evidence that the permanent campaign may have produced a permanent cynicism.

All food for thought, stylishly prepared and elegantly served up by one of America's most thoughtful, and thought-provoking, scholars. No one who reads *The Modern American Presidency* is likely to think of the office in quite the same way. George B. Cortelyou, we hardly knew ye.

Richard Norton Smith

Four years ago, Fred Woodward said that he would like to see someone write a history of the emergence of the modern presidency in the twentieth century for general readers. To keep the book to manageable size and within the reach of its potential audience, he suggested that a text of around eighty thousand words would be suitable. With perhaps a sense of bravado, I agreed to take on the task of writing such a book.

Two decades earlier in *The Presidency of William McKinley* (1980), I had contended that William McKinley had been the first modern president because of the way he had enhanced the power of the office during and after the war with Spain in 1898. I had then considered in *The Presidency of Theodore Roosevelt* (1991) the contributions that Theodore Roosevelt had made to the development of the presidency between 1901 and 1909. As I examined the performances of William Howard Taft and Woodrow Wilson in the White House during the decade after Roosevelt, I became more persuaded that the rise of the modern presidency should be traced back to the period between 1897 and 1921.

To the degree that the literature on the presidency in the twentieth century ever got beyond the assertion that Franklin D. Roosevelt was the first modern president, it tended to assign little weight to the administrations of Warren G. Harding, Calvin Coolidge, and Herbert Hoover. Although depicting these executives as dynamic activists would have been a reach, except in the case of Hoover, it became clear that the three Republican presidents had employed techniques of managing the institution, especially in handling the media, that carried over into the Roosevelt years and beyond.

A precise definition of modernity in the American presidency has proved elusive, but the key elements would most likely include a significant increase in the size of the White House staff, a chief of staff to manage the expanded personnel, bureaucratic procedures to handle the interaction with the press, formalized relations with Congress through a White House office, greater power for the president as commander in chief, expanded travel in and out of the United States to build political support, increasing access to and dependence upon both traditional and electronic media, and continuous campaigning to ensure reelection and the success of the president's party.

Inevitably, bureaucracy became the dominant feature of the White House, with interconnected layers of staff to interact with Capitol Hill, the public, other branches of government, foreign countries, the courts, the First Lady, interest groups, legal questions, and a host of unexpected contingencies. Simply understanding how the complex and varied presidency worked, its customs and assumptions, proved a more challenging assignment for both its occupants and eventually for the scholars who studied it.

But the essence of change in the presidency did not reside in the bureaucratic accretion of assistants, offices, and staff labels. What the presidents did in the twentieth century mattered most. They fought and won two world wars and led the country in other regional conflicts. They championed legislation, oversaw the economy, traveled around the world, and articulated American values. They became, in a favorite phrase applied to many of them, "the most powerful men in the world," and their every movement and foible were seen as suitable for analysis, criticism, and dissection. Presidents did not reach this lofty status all at once. The many roles that modern presidents play evolved over the course of the century in response to national and world pressures and events. As the United States became a world power, the president's place in the government had to be more central if the nation was to have coherent leadership.

Other forces thrust the president forward in distinctive respects. When McKinley was in office, the political party shaped the way presidents were selected and governance was conducted. After 1900, however, the intense partisanship of the late nineteenth century receded. Reformers pushed for procedural changes — the direct primary, direct election of senators, limits on patronage — that reduced the clout of the parties. The degree to which parties had been central to the designation of presidential candidates diminished. Aspirants for the White House had to gain the nomination on their own and win reelection with personal organizations that they created and maintained.

One little-noticed feature of the twentieth-century presidency was the extent to which the institution absorbed for its own purposes the style and methods of celebrity and show business. While much attention has been properly focused on presidential press relations, the emergence of presidential stardom and its effects on the institution have needed more study, and in the chapters that follow I attempt to address that issue. To win election and reelection now requires mastery of the arts of movies and television, but these time-consuming rituals, though necessary from a political perspective, produce a corresponding loss of concentration on the business of governing the country. A key theme of this book is that presidential celebrity is a major element of the modern presidency and a long-term weakness as well.

The character of the late-twentieth-century presidency also developed from laudable attempts to remedy past problems that in turn led to unintended consequences. The most striking example is the Twenty-second Amendment, limiting presidents to two elected terms. Designed to prevent another Franklin D. Roosevelt and his four terms, the amendment codified the two-term tradition. Yet the change imposed a particular version of the presidency on the Constitution that took away the rights of voters to select an individual for a third term if they wished. More important, it created an environment in which the first term was seen only as a prelude to the productive second term that would validate presidential greatness. The Twenty-second Amendment, however, drained presidential power in the second term from what had become in effect a lame-duck president. The result was a series of anticlimactic or disastrous second terms in the post–World War II era.

One major conclusion of this account of the rise of the modern presidency is that, with the possible exception of Franklin D. Roosevelt, most chief executives would have had a better historical reputation if they had contented themselves with a single elected term and retired at the end of it. The notion that a one-term president is ipso facto a failure has been another distorting element in the conduct of the institution. The pressures of reelection do not bring out the best in presidents. The phenomenon of the continuing campaign acts like an acid on any impulse the incumbent may have to make unpopular but necessary decisions for the American people.

Even the most ambitious and successful presidents now have only eight years to impose their vision on the nation and the government. The rigors of campaigning leave most candidates exhausted at the end of the process. Presidents-elect then have to step into a job that is highly structured and physically draining but that puts a premium on symbolism over serious thought. The days are filled with the pomp and circumstance of glorified busywork that takes time from what modern presidents most need, the opportunity to think about what they are doing.

To suggest that presidents participate in fewer campaign appearances, photo opportunities, and staged events is not to argue that they ought to become isolated figures dispensing decisions from a cloistered White House. Campaigning and communicating will always be part of what a president does. Over the course of the twentieth century, however, the notion grew that presidents were somehow about the people's serious business when they pursued reelection, raised money for their party, and staged media occasions at a rate that cut into time for understanding the complex issues and hard policy choices the nation faced. Presidents rarely increased their intellectual capital while in office; by the late twentieth century any pretense of doing so had been all but abandoned.

In the writings about twentieth-century presidents, there is the tacit assumption that the way the institution turned out was best for the nation. A talented group of politicians occupied the presidency over the past one hundred years, all of them doing what they believed to be best for the United States. It is no denigration of their patriotism and commitment to say that most of them fell well short of the challenges of an impossible job. To treat the modern presidency as a success story is to falsify the historical record. As a new century begins, the presidency today is no more capable of grappling with the difficulties of globalization, terrorism, and environmental change than was the law-office approach of Grover Cleveland from 1893 to 1897.

This is a work of historical synthesis aimed at the elusive target of the general reader. It does not pretend to be a narrative account of every twentieth-century president or administration in full. When primary sources were readily available and pertinent, I used them, but much of the narrative necessarily depends on memoirs, previous accounts of key presidencies, and the valuable work of other historians and political scientists. Citation of all the relevant works on each president would have made for a book two or three times the size of this one. Omission of a book or article should not be read as evidence of criticism of that scholar's work. Some key titles have no doubt been missed. The industry of writing about presidents never sleeps.

The book could not have been written without the aid of the volumes in the American Presidency series of the University Press of Kansas. As an author in that series, I know how rigorous are the editorial procedures the participants must traverse. Diverse in their points of view about their presidents, the books in the series provide a narrative sweep of how the United States was governed in the past century in ways that make these volumes an intellectual resource on their own terms.

I am grateful to Fred Woodward for asking me to write this book and for guiding it with such an expert hand. His willingness to take time out from his many responsibilities to encourage my work attests to his kindness and skill. My colleague, Bud Lasby, provided a close, informed reading of the whole text and gave me valuable thoughts about Harry Truman and civil rights that went into that chapter directly. Another colleague, Robert A. Divine, was very generous over the years with opportunities to write about presidents and First Ladies in his editing projects. My former students, graduates and undergraduates, prompted me to think about the modern presidency throughout my teaching career. I owe particular debts to Thomas Clarkin, Stacy Cordery, Byron Hulsey, Mark Young, and Nancy Beck Young for sources and insights.

Some years ago, Professor Ephraim Smith shared with me documents and articles he had collected about George B. Cortelyou that proved valuable in assessing Cortelyou's influence on the presidency. Bob Lester invited me to be a consultant in the effort by Lexis-Nexis to place presidential materials on-line, and that assignment provided important background research for this book. Don Carleton, director of the Center for American History at the University of Texas at Austin, gave enthusiastic assistance to the book, and Linda Peterson was very helpful in selecting illustrations from the center's collections. I am grateful to Dirck Halstead, David Kennerly, and Bruce Roberts for permission to use their excellent photographs. Chris Hiers provided a superb cover illustration. The readers for the University Press of Kansas, Richard Ellis and Richard Norton Smith, gave me thoughtful criticisms, many of which I have incorporated into the final version. Richard Norton Smith also kindly contributed the foreword to the book. Neither they nor any of the other people mentioned are accountable for the shortcomings of this book, which are my responsibility.

Patricia Schaub was a valuable aide with the research for the book. Dr. Larry Breedlove kept me in good health to finish the task, as did Christine Eubank, Claire Hyder, and Ellen Smith. Rick Levinson provided timely comments about the overall approach of the book. Karen Gould was patient and supportive, as always.

1

The Age of Cortelyou
William McKinley and Theodore Roosevelt

Although disputes exist about when the modern presidency began, it had not yet appeared during the second administration of Grover Cleveland, from 1893 to 1897. In his approach to the office, Cleveland operated as the Buffalo, New York, attorney he had been before he entered politics in the early 1880s. The White House had no staff in the modern sense of the word. Cleveland worked with a single secretary, Henry T. Thurber, and a half-dozen clerks to conduct the nation's business. By the end of his term, with his presidency in disarray after the congressional elections of 1894, Cleveland's daily mail had dwindled to a trickle, and the pace of work slowed at the Executive Mansion.[1]

The president's failure to deal effectively with the economic hard times arising from the Panic of 1893 left him with a divided Democratic party and a large residue of popular discontent in the South and the West. Threats against Cleveland's life intensified security at the White House. By 1896, guards and rules kept the reclusive Cleveland out of public view, and the White House seemed a forbidding fortress. The president had no liking for reporters, and he sought to frustrate their efforts to learn what was taking place inside the government. "News-gathering," wrote David S. Barry, a veteran reporter, was pursued "much after the fashion in which highwaymen rob a stage coach." There were no facilities inside the mansion where journalists could work, and reporters waited outside in all kinds of weather to interview any important Washington figures who came to see Cleveland.[2]

The White House itself was a ramshackle building that was showing its age by the end of the nineteenth century. One observer said in March 1897 that "the perfect inadequacy of the executive offices to the present demands is apparent at a glance, nor is the lack of room less obvious at the social functions which custom as well as reasons of state impose upon the President." In the midst of a severe economic downturn, there was no money for refurbishing the building and little thought of renovating the working areas to accommodate a more vigorous executive. On the verge of assuming world responsibilities, the presidency was understaffed, and the facilities at the disposal of the nation's chief executive were minimal.[3]

That was how the American people wanted their president treated. He was "Our Fellow-Citizen of the White House," not a dominant presence set apart from the rest of the country. The president was expected to hold regular public receptions where citizens could get in line to shake his hand and offer quick comments on his performance in office. At the same time, the chief executive could walk around Washington in relative safety on his own, without an impressive retinue of guards and handlers. The president was far from the national celebrity he would soon become. Pictures of William McKinley in 1901, for example, show the president sitting in his carriage with an aide but with few protectors anywhere in view. Although Abraham Lincoln and James A. Garfield had both been assassinated, there did not seem to be any credible threat of a repetition of such a tragedy as the nineteenth century neared its close.[4]

The dominant political trends of the day reinforced the impression of presidential irrelevance. Politicians saw the presidency as at most an equal branch of government with the Congress. For the Republicans, their roots in the traditions of the Whig party disposed them to regard a powerful executive with suspicion. As Senator John Sherman of Ohio put it, "The executive department of a republic like ours should be subordinate to the legislative department." Although the record of Abraham Lincoln belied this position, Republicans saw the Civil War as justifying the need for a strong president in such perilous times but not thereafter.[5]

The Democrats, for their part, regarded presidential activism as largely negative in character and designed to prevent the busybody Republicans from spending too much and intruding on the private affairs of the average citizen. The precedent of Andrew Jackson ran through the Democracy, and Cleveland had been only the most recent example of a president who sought to prevent bad policies from being adopted. Even then, Democrats were suspicious of presidential strength. "The truth is," wrote the *Richmond Times* in 1897, "all this idea of prerogative in the President is wholly out of place in our Constitution."[6]

Two aspects of American life set the presidency in 1897 apart from the institution as it existed more than one hundred years later. The late nineteenth century was still in the heyday of the strong party system of American politics, which had dominated since before the Civil War. The electorate was more involved in partisan affairs, and allegiances to the Democrats and Republicans were intense. Newspapers covered the doings of politicians with a far greater thoroughness than in contemporary society because of the assumption that public affairs were a central preoccupation of most informed citizens. Voters demonstrated that commitment by a higher participation in elections. In 1896, for example, some 75 percent of the eligible voters in northern states had gone to the polls when William Jennings Bryan faced off against McKinley.

Presidents operated in a world of frequent elections, important party conventions, and a system of government patronage that defined their options and watched their activities. The chief executive was expected to conform to the mores of his party and to give heed to the counsel of Republican or Democratic elders. As a result, the president was not a lone wolf or free agent but had to conduct himself within the limits of existing partisan procedures.

This system seemed as strong as ever in 1897, but in fact it had already begun to erode by the time McKinley took office. As the problems of an industrial society mounted, voices were heard contending that partisanship was not the answer to the nation's difficulties. Bosses, caucuses, and patronage seemed inefficient ways in which to manage the nation's affairs. The discontent with politics would soon emerge during the Progressive Era, as steps occurred to limit the influence of parties through the direct primary, the referendum, and the regulatory agency. The gradual decline in the power and scope of the parties would be one of the shaping influences on how presidents functioned as the twentieth century proceeded.

Another key shift in the environment of the presidency was taking place almost imperceptibly as the nineteenth century ended. In 1896 the McKinley presidential campaign had shown a crude motion picture of the candidate in a few major cities. The phonograph was just coming into use, and inventors would soon perfect the radio as a means of transmitting voices across long distances. Newspapers were becoming more pictorial as the reproduction of photographs changed the way that readers experienced the news. It was much too early to speak of a mass media in the United States, but the various elements were coming into being. As technology accelerated, the capacity to shape attitudes, divert Americans, and affect the behavior of politicians would become a dominant fact of how presidents conducted themselves in office.

Under McKinley and later in the administration of Theodore Roosevelt, management of the press from the White House would evolve as a key tool of modern presidents. But the efforts of chief executives to stay abreast of the transformations wrought by media technology would always lag behind the pace of change in the way events were presented to the American people. Presidents would find themselves enmeshed in a culture that admired celebrity and insisted on continuous entertainment. Feeding the voracious appetite of a media-conscious culture would require that presidents take on many of the trappings of stardom themselves. In the process, the customs of show business and the lure of personality would infect the workings of the presidency in ways that had a corrupting influence on the manner of leadership in the White House.

Discussing the growth of the modern presidency has usually conveyed a benign, positive sense of an institution evolving to meet the challenges of more difficult times. Less attention has been given to the trivializing impact of balancing stardom and substance. Much of the expansion of the presidency has been policy driven, but much of it as well has been to feed the curiosity of the public about the personal character of the occupants of the White House. As the interaction between the presidency and the mass media has evolved, the effect has been to reduce the time available to the chief executive for the serious business of governing the nation. The amount of triviality has increased, but the more important impact has been to introduce continuous campaigning as a major activity of presidents. While that endeavor seems to be related to the seriousness of the office, in fact it has become a kind of mental busywork that seems more important than it really is.

Such problems seemed improbable at the end of the nineteenth century. Although the presidency was in a weakened state in March 1897, the previous generation had seen the beginnings of a revival of the office from the low point of Andrew Johnson's disastrous administration and the two ineffective terms of Ulysses S. Grant. Presidents Rutherford B. Hayes, James A. Garfield, and Benjamin Harrison had made initial steps toward revitalizing the institution. Hayes from 1877 to 1881 had asserted presidential prerogatives over

The framer of the modern presidency, William McKinley, shown here at his desk in the White House, was an innovative executive behind his conventional demeanor and conservative economic policies. (Courtesy of the Library of Congress.)

appointments and the civil service. Having limited himself to a single term, however, his efforts lost momentum as his presidency ended. Garfield continued the struggle with lawmakers in his own party and had made some progress toward establishing his rights to select federal officers before he was assassinated in July 1881 and died two and a half months later. Garfield's death represented a missed opportunity for the revival of the presidency during the Gilded Age.[7]

After Cleveland's first term, from 1885 to 1889, another Republican, Benjamin Harrison, defeated the incumbent in 1888 and took office in March 1889. The new president wooed members of Congress with consultation and White House dinners. An effective speaker before large crowds, Harrison traveled across the country to push his programs and to publicize his office. He also established procedures to make the White House function on a more orderly basis. In his personal dealings with politicians, Harrison was frosty and aloof. His activism, like that of his party, did not go down well with the voters, and the Republicans suffered dramatic losses of congressional seats in the elections of 1890. Harrison served out his term but lost his reelection bid to Cleveland in 1892. Cleveland in turn finished out his rocky second term in March 1897 and gave way to the Republican victor in the 1896 election, William McKinley.[8]

McKinley had served in the House from 1876 to 1891, representing the district that included Canton, Ohio, and Stark County. He rose to be the chairman of the House Ways and Means Committee and made himself an expert on the intricacies of the tariff issue. He wrote the protectionist McKinley Tariff of 1890 that set the stage for Republican losses in the congressional elections. Defeated in the Democratic landslide that same year, he ran for governor of Ohio successfully in 1891 and was reelected in 1893. Soon he was being mentioned as a contender for the presidency in 1896. Popular with his fellow Republicans, he was an easy winner in the contest for the party's presidential nomination in 1896 and then beat the Democrat William Jennings Bryan in the November election, which turned on the gold standard versus the inflationary doctrine of "free silver."[9]

Despite a growing body of historical writing that has demonstrated McKinley's strength as president, the stereotype that he was weak and irresolute has persisted. As a result, his important role in launching the modern presidency has remained obscure. Because he wrote so little about his motives, his perceptions about the need to reinvigorate the presidency and his intention to do so have not been understood. His misfortune in having the energetic and charismatic Theodore Roosevelt succeed him in 1901 also overshadowed McKinley's contributions. Generations of historians and political scientists have simply repeated clichés about McKinley without a close examination of his performance in office.

Having watched his predecessors from Hayes to Cleveland in action, the fifty-four-year-old McKinley came back to Washington intent on reestablishing the president as a national leader. Like other chief executives, he learned on the job, too. The need to wage a two-ocean war instructed him on the wisdom of a more organized White House in 1898 and 1899. Nonetheless, these refinements grew from a basic inclination to be an activist president that he had nurtured during his years in Congress and as the governor of Ohio. His contemporaries understood how McKinley had reinvigorated the presidency, even if subsequent writers did not.

One key area where McKinley built on the precedents of the past was in his use of presidential travels to create popular support for his policy initiatives. Hayes had been called "Rutherford the Rover" for his propensity to leave the White House on extended speaking trips. Harrison also went out among the people on several long speaking tours, where his effective speaking style pleased large audiences. McKinley liked the process of crisscrossing the nation and welcomed the chance it gave him to personalize the presidency. He made several speaking swings during his early months in office to offer a contrast to Cleveland's reclusive style.[10]

But McKinley's real innovation in presidential travel came in autumn 1898 when he used the process to implement his program of territorial acquisition, following the war with Spain. Invited to attend a celebration of the fighting's end in Nebraska, he capitalized on the cross-country journey to make his case to the people through the nation's heartland. Not since Andrew Johnson's disastrous "swing around the circle" at the height of the Reconstruction battle with Congress in 1866 had a president traveled during a congressional election campaign. The political reverses that Johnson suffered suggested that it would not be wise for a president to repeat the experiment.[11]

In 1898, however, McKinley did not conduct a political tour as such, and he made no direct appeals for Republican votes. The sight of the president speaking from a train or in a packed auditorium on behalf of retaining the lands obtained in the recent fighting made for a compelling spectacle. "We have had great glory out of the war, and in its settlements we must be guided only by the demands of right and conscience and duty," he said at Arcola, Illinois, on 15 October 1898. He did not have to remind his listeners that the Republicans had won the Civil War and had capitalized in the past on such patriotic appeals. The trip minimized Republican losses in the 1898 elections and built support for McKinley's decision to acquire the Philippine Islands from Spain in the peace talks then being conducted in Paris. The president sent word to his emissaries in late October that all of the archipelago should become the property of the United States.[12]

Once the peace treaty had been signed in December 1898, McKinley returned to the stump with a tour through the South. Though sectional friendship was the keynote of his speeches, he also renewed his theme of accepting the territorial results of the war. The audiences were enthusiastic and his theme appealing. At the same time, the presence of the president reminded wavering southern Democratic senators that the peace treaty would be voted on during the coming weeks. The subtle use of what would become the bully pulpit under Theodore Roosevelt would be a hallmark of McKinley's style.[13]

McKinley returned to the public in 1899 to defend his policy in the Philippines. In 1900 he stayed off the campaign trail in deference to the custom that an incumbent president did not make an active appeal for votes. But in his second term he planned more ambitious travel that would have extended the reach of presidential power. He told the French ambassador in summer 1901 that he intended to travel to Cuba and thus to break the informal rule that kept the chief executive inside the nation's borders during his term of office. Earlier that year McKinley had made a cross-country speaking tour, and his next stop was at the Pan-American Exposition in Buffalo, New York, in September 1901. His last speech on 5 September 1901 was designed to pressure the Senate gently to act on his reciprocal trade treaties when Congress reconvened later in the year. The president's assassination on 6 September interrupted that initiative, but McKinley had been a forerunner of presidents who traveled to aid their legislative programs.[14]

McKinley's propensity to move about the country meant that the White House had to develop procedures to accommodate press coverage of these presidential events. That in turn demanded a greater degree of staff work, both to set up the trips and to make the executive branch function smoothly dur-

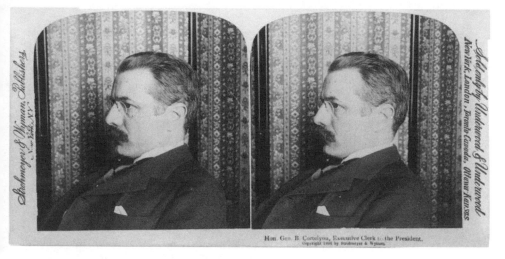

These stereopticon slides of George B. Cortelyou, taken in 1898, capture him on the eve of his greatest influence on modernizing the presidency and White House practices. (Courtesy of the Library of Congress.)

ing the president's absence from Washington. By 1898 and 1899 more and more of these duties fell not on McKinley's secretary, John Addison Porter, but on Porter's assistant, George B. Cortelyou. The emergence of Cortelyou to a position of authority in the McKinley White House represented a key step in the initial development of the modern presidency.[15]

In a significant sense, all the president's men and women of the twentieth century stood in the shadow of George B. Cortelyou and his services to McKinley and Theodore Roosevelt between 1897 and 1903. The techniques that Cortelyou developed and put in place were refined and elaborated by his successors, but the essential principles on which the management of the presidency rested belonged to the efficient, retiring Cortelyou.

George Bruce Cortelyou was thirty-three when he became a stenographer and executive clerk to President Cleveland in 1895. A native of New York City who had been born into a prosperous family, Cortelyou had attended college in Massachusetts and later trained in stenography. He worked first in the New York Post Office, next at the New York Customs House, and then joined the Post Office Department in Washington, D.C., as the secretary to the fourth assistant postmaster general.[16]

Cortelyou's skill as an organizer and his tireless productivity led Cleveland to recommend that McKinley retain him. John Addison Porter, whom McKinley first appointed as his secretary, was a pretentious Connecticut Republican "who felt himself too large for the petty details of his position." Prone to bad health, Porter was often absent and, within a year, Cortelyou was doing most of the work of the presidential secretary. Discreet and polite, he treated all presidential callers with exquisite courtesy and respect. He saved his own views for the president and became McKinley's closest daily adviser. In his shorthand memoranda that he wrote on a regular basis, Cortelyou kept a valuable record of the administration's decisions during the war with Spain and the negotiations over the Philippines that followed. He did not receive the official title of secretary until 1900, after Porter had departed, but the job and its responsibilities had long been his.[17]

The bespectacled, square-faced Cortelyou helped McKinley in a number of key areas that became part of modern presidential practice. The amount of correspondence that McKinley received expanded dramatically because of the war with Spain. For letters and memoranda that McKinley needed to see, Cortelyou directed his six "verbatim reporters" to note in the upper left-hand corner the proposed action to deal with such documents. The notations guided the formation of replies and provided a history of actions taken. Cortelyou also devised a system that routed to the various departments letters that required their action but did not need McKinley's attention. Though a dry subject, systematic record-keeping would be a key element enabling presidents to manage their work. Cortelyou's system was a step toward more elaborate procedures that enabled a president's staff to follow the ever-growing amount of paper that poured into the White House each day.[18]

Cortelyou's influence was also evident as he facilitated McKinley's efforts to improve relations with the Washington press corps. Unlike his predecessor, McKinley enjoyed the company of reporters and did not regard them as adversaries. Within three weeks of his inauguration, he had a reception for the journalists, where he remembered their names and faces. It was he, and not Theodore Roosevelt, who arranged in 1897 for journalists to have their own working space inside the White House on the second floor. There, outside the president's office, the reporters assigned to cover McKinley were given a long table with seats assigned to the major newspapers and news services. John Addison Porter, and later Cortelyou, came out and talked frequently with the journalists. Regular briefings occurred at noon and at four in the afternoon. The groundwork for a press room in the White House and later for presidential press conferences had been done.[19]

At the White House, Cortelyou worked out procedures for releasing presidential speeches, the annual message, and statements in advance for the convenience of the newspapers. Although McKinley did not meet with reporters as a group, he did sit for interviews, with the ground rules that he could not be quoted directly. An elaborate ritual of phrases told the discerning reader that McKinley was speaking — "the president is said to believe," "it can be stated with confidence," and so on. As a reporter noted some twelve years after McKinley's death, "while apparently not courting publicity," McKinley "contrived to put out, by various shrewd processes of indirection, whatever news would best serve the ends of the administration." Cortelyou was the gatekeeper for the president in such cases, and unofficial Washington knew "that the only sure means of access to President McKinley was Mr. Cortelyou."[20]

Late in the twentieth century, President Richard Nixon and his successors would set up procedures to provide summaries of press comments about the president, his programs, and his standing with the public. As a member of President Cleveland's staff, Cortelyou noted how newspaper articles that attacked the president were discarded. When he went to work for McKinley in 1897, he began the compilation of "current comment," which provided the president with clippings from many newspapers. Cortelyou supervised the work of the clerks, who daily surveyed important editorial opinion. Letters from McKinley to key editors and influential Republicans could then be based on what McKinley had read. When critics suggested during the negotiations leading up to the war with Spain that McKinley was getting only the side of the news that favored the administration, Cortelyou wrote in his shorthand diary that "the President sees everything, whether in the shape of mail, telegrams, or newspapers that can indicate the drift of public opinion." Compared to some of his twentieth-century successors, whose press summaries told presidents what they wanted the incumbent to hear, Cortelyou was as objective as possible.[21]

Another innovation in presidential operations that came in the McKinley years was the increased reliance on the telephone within the Executive Mansion. The administration installed fifteen telephone lines that ran to the eight executive departments as well as to the House and Senate. With his cable box at hand, McKinley had a greater capacity to supervise policy than any president before him. McKinley also used a crude version of the dictaphone to leave messages and instructions for his aides. The discreet president, who rarely wrote when he could talk privately, found the telephone a congenial way to transmit messages and orders with a minimum of written records. Nonetheless, Cortelyou left some interesting examples of McKinley's telephone interchanges in his papers.[22]

Porter and Cortelyou took over an office on the second floor of the White House when the Spanish-American War began and transformed it into what was known as the War Room. The president could send telegrams over the twenty telegraph wires that linked him with the major cable lines between the United States and the Caribbean. The War Room never closed, and the president went there frequently to monitor events. By 1898 and 1899 a precursor of the White House Situation Room had already taken shape.[23]

When the president traveled, news interest in his doings increased still more. Cortelyou recognized that McKinley's train had to become "an executive office during a presidential trip." With the six stenographers who accompanied him, Cortelyou saw to it that reporters had an accurate text of what McKinley had said within a few minutes after the president finished speaking. In one instance, the stenographers transcribed a five-minute speech and gave it to journalists before the presidential train left the station. The traveling White House generated human-interest anecdotes about McKinley's daily activities and the people whom he met, which the reporters wove into their copy. The resulting coverage, even from journalists whose newspapers opposed McKinley, usually put the president in a favorable light.[24]

Cortelyou and McKinley made an effective team. The secretary was present during the troubled days before the Spanish-American War began, and he functioned more and more as a chief of staff than simply as a copyist for the president. McKinley knew that he could rely on Cortelyou's absolute discretion, and he leaned on his aide to see that his orders were carried out. Much of McKinley's strength as president grew from his wise use of Cortelyou's executive talents. Though the two men left scant records of their collaboration beyond the day-to-day business of the White House, Cortelyou shared McKinley's interest in the revival of the presidential office. The president and his personal secretary moved with the same quiet purpose to establish the institutional basis for the modern presidency.

The demands of the war with Spain in 1898 and the imperial expansion that followed required the presidency to monitor events on a twenty-four-hour basis. The War Room of the McKinley presidency anticipated the more elaborate Situation Rooms of the twentieth century. (Courtesy of the Library of Congress.)

As a wartime president, McKinley capitalized on the foreign policy crises to stretch the powers of his office beyond the limits that had constrained his predecessors. He set up military governments in Cuba and the Philippines based on his authority as commander in chief, and these institutions functioned for several years without congressional oversight. His actions rested on what his Secretary of War Elihu Root called "a military power derived from his authority under the Constitution as Commander-in-Chief of the Army and Navy."[25]

Although historians and political scientists have credited Theodore Roosevelt with the initial use of academic experts and presidential commissions to make and advance executive policy, McKinley actually began the practice with eleven major commissions that he appointed between 1897 and 1901. McKinley used "the independent action of the executive" and, for example, paid for the two Philippine commissions that he dispatched to the islands from monies appropriated for the executive branch. Congressional oversight of these panels was thus forestalled. A newspaper critical of such techniques wrote in 1900: "President McKinley is much given to administering the government by commission, and in this way is enabled to escape direct responsibility and reward friends. Very few of his commissions were created by authority of law, but were made up under what is claimed to be the war power of the president."[26]

During the later years of his administration, McKinley was even more aggressive in wielding the war power in foreign policy. In 1900 he sent troops into China as part of the international relief expedition during the Boxer Rebellion, doing so "on his own sole authority as Commander-in-Chief." At the time, there were reservations about McKinley's initiative because Congress was not in session and China was a sovereign nation with which the United States was not at war. The *Philadelphia Times* said that it represented "an absolute declaration of war by the executive without the authority or knowledge of Congress, and it is without excuse because it is not a necessity." McKinley's conduct set a precedent that other chief executives would follow during the twentieth century. Arthur Schlesinger Jr. called it "a crucial shift in the presidential employment of force overseas."[27]

By the time McKinley's second term began in March 1901, the size of the presidential apparatus in the White House had expanded. Cortelyou supervised thirty clerks who handled the more than one hundred thousand pieces of mail that came to the White House each year. The routines that he had set up for dealing with these papers worked smoothly. It was still possible for the staff to group the documents chronologically and file them alphabetically on that basis. In a similar manner, relations with the press had become more systematized. The result was that the White House had become by 1901 the nation's major center for political news. The Congress was left in an important, but more subordinate, role.[28]

The transformation of the presidency that occurred during the McKinley era aroused contemporary comment from Americans worried about the growth of presidential authority. Perry Belmont, a Democratic critic, wrote in March 1900 that "since the inauguration of President McKinley there has been an enormous extension of Executive power." Four years later, noting how McKinley and Theodore Roosevelt had wielded the war power, a scholarly student of military government said, "In America we were supposed to have started out with an executive with carefully defined powers, but we are now developing one with prerogatives which must be the envy of crowned heads."[29]

The McKinley presidency was not "a collection of specialized bureaucracies with hundreds of professional staffers," but neither was it any longer "a small, personalized office." Under the guidance of Cortelyou and McKinley, the White House had set up the foundation on which the presidency would grow in the twentieth century. Cortelyou functioned as both a kind of chief of staff and a press secretary. In time, it would prove logical to divide these functions. Similarly, the fivefold growth in support staff from six clerks to thirty pointed toward even larger bureaucracies. Though no one would mistake McKinley's presidential train for Air Force One, they performed similar operations. McKinley was his own best lobbyist with Congress, but that task too could be delegated to aides in the future. By all the standards that the American government would later know the modern presidency, McKinley and Cortelyou between 1897 and 1901 were showing the way for their successors.[30]

William McKinley's contributions to the modern presidency faded away for several reasons. He had the bad luck to be assassinated and to have his death occur in the first year of the twentieth century. That made him a transitional figure who usually fell on the nineteenth-century side of American history and political science textbook chapters. Moreover, he was a Republican, and the modern presidency, except for Theodore Roosevelt, would be associated more with Democratic chief executives. But McKinley's major misfortune, from the point of view of his standing as an innovative president, was to be followed by the irrepressible and colorful Roosevelt. Artful dullness was part of McKinley's political style, but it left his reputation vulnerable to a charismatic successor.

Theodore Roosevelt always had a good sense of timing as president, but coming into the office as he did in September 1901 meant that he would always be identified with the arrival of a new century and a sense of historical novelty and freshness. Fifteen years McKinley's junior and the youngest president in the nation's history, Roosevelt seemed modern and forward-looking as the twentieth century understood the term. With his stodgy clothes and formal manner, McKinley symbolized a historical period that already appeared to be old just a few months after his murder. That judgment has carried over into appraisals of how Roosevelt performed in the White House.

With the possible exceptions of Andrew Jackson and Ulysses S. Grant, Theodore Roosevelt was the first president to enter the White House as a celebrity in his own right. Unlike those two predecessors, however, Roosevelt also had youth and personal excitement on his side. By 1901 the capacity of the popular press to disseminate images about a figure such as Roosevelt was more advanced than in Jackson's time and even for Grant three decades earlier. Ever since he had entered the New York Assembly in 1881, Roosevelt had attracted intense newspaper publicity. His career included an abundance of colorful incidents and rollicking controversies. He had punched cattle on his ranch in the Dakotas, made an unsuccessful run for mayor of New York in 1886, been head of the city's police commission from 1895 to 1897, and served as assistant secretary of the navy under McKinley. In 1898, he led his regiment of Rough Riders up Kettle Hill against the Spanish in Cuba. On the basis of that military triumph, he had won the New York governor's race in 1898. Following his efforts to provide minimal regulation for the state's corporations, he had been "kicked upstairs" to the vice presidential nomination in 1900. A year later he was president. For two decades, "Teddy"(a nickname he disliked and that his friends never used) had been a familiar presence on the nation's front pages. Name recognition would never be a problem for the new president.[31]

When the concept of the modern presidency is moved back to the early twentieth century, Theodore Roosevelt is seen as its embodiment. In a public sense he surely was. Between 1901 and 1909 he led the nation through the skillful handling of visible techniques that his successors have emulated. Roosevelt was the first president to make conscious use of his whole family as part of his political image. While his high-spirited daughter Alice was often a distraction because of her antics, his other five children provided diversion for the press and underlined Roosevelt's status as a father and family man. His wife Edith set a moral tone for Washington society and expanded the role of the First Lady with her musicales and weekly receptions for society women of the city and the nation at large. Early in his administration, Roosevelt decided to abandon the title of Executive Mansion for his residence; henceforth, it was to be known as the White House.[32]

The Roosevelts faced the problem of a deteriorating White House when they moved in. As a result, they embarked on a hasty renovation process that was completed in a mere six months in 1902. The changes, shaped by architect Charles Follen McKim, were significant. New executive offices were installed in what became known as the West Wing; the East Wing was reserved for social events. Within the West Wing or the Executive Office, there was now a press room near the front entrance. The building itself contained an abundance of rooms that could accommodate an expanded presidential staff. Much of the work of the Roosevelt administration was carried on in the new facility. Because of the speed with which the renovation was done, however, other presidents would confront problems of space and decay in the decades ahead.[33]

Within the workings of the White House itself, Roosevelt's approach to his duties was less bureaucratic and systematic than McKinley's had been. For example, Roosevelt disliked the telephone and used the instrument with less frequency than McKinley did. Roosevelt relished interacting with reporters personally, and the procedures that Cortelyou had established were often bypassed in favor of a more personal intervention. William Allen White noted that "he talked state secrets in a loud voice to statesmen in the presidential workroom, so that reporters could hear." As a result, there was a more frenetic, improvised quality to the Roosevelt presidency that accounted for much of the fun and fascination with which the American people viewed his administration.[34]

When Theodore Roosevelt is called "the first modern president," it is important to be careful in defining his contributions to the evolution of the office. In some respects, he was a conventional chief executive. Unlike Woodrow Wilson, it did not occur to him to deliver any of his annual messages or other communications to Congress in person. He observed the tradition of written documents that had been in existence since Thomas Jefferson began them in 1801. Nor did he break the custom that incumbent presidents did not campaign themselves, for either election or reelection. In 1904, Roosevelt stayed off the stump and allowed surrogates to make the case for a full elective term. Further, he deferred to the tradition that a president should serve only two terms. Mindful of McKinley's rejection of a third-term boomlet in summer 1901, Roosevelt sought to fend off Democratic charges that he wished per-

Theodore Roosevelt's vigor, energy, and charisma made him the first modern celebrity president, as this photograph of him speaking in 1902 illustrates. (Courtesy of the Theodore Roosevelt Collection, Harvard College Library.)

petual power. On election night in 1904, he told the press that he would not
be a candidate for another term four years later. It was a decision he came to
regret for its impact on his fortunes in 1908 and 1912, but the announcement
illustrated how much Roosevelt remained within the accepted limits that his
predecessors had established.[35]

With almost three years to go before the Republican party would make its
nomination for president in 1904, Theodore Roosevelt in September 1901 had
time in the slower paced world of his day to formulate policies to make his
presidency a success. The party system remained strong in the nation's public life, and the incumbent was not expected either to raise money or to pursue his nomination through personal campaigning. Although the press was
intensely interested in politics, the more leisurely news cycle had not yet resulted in the permanent campaign that would shape the lives of presidents at
the end of the twentieth century. Congress did not meet in perpetual sessions,
either. Roosevelt, for example, had three months in office before Congress
reconvened for its regular session in December 1901, and there was little sentiment for a special session after McKinley's death.[36]

When he became president, Roosevelt promised to carry on "absolutely
unbroken" McKinley's policies, and he largely did so. For Roosevelt, continuity was the ticket to the Republican nomination in 1904 and the presidency
in his own right. While the modern presidency evolved as presidents sought
to distinguish themselves from their predecessors, in Roosevelt's case he had
to graft his own style onto the procedures that were established when he arrived in September 1901. In significant respects, Roosevelt's first three years
represented a second term for McKinley. The prosecution of the Northern
Securities Company under the Sherman Antitrust Act in 1902 was in line with
conduct that McKinley had been contemplating. Mediation in the Anthracite Coal Strike of 1902 built on what McKinley and his close ally, Senator
Marcus A. Hanna of Ohio, had done when a similar walkout threatened the
coal industry in 1900. In foreign policy, the acquisition of the Panama Canal
Zone carried out the larger aims of the McKinley administration to control
the Caribbean Sea in the interests of the United States.[37]

Roosevelt's distinctive contribution in his first term was in the manner in
which he made and proclaimed these decisions. He understood that democ-
racies need to be entertained in peace as well as in war, and so he did not make
policy in the sober tones of the late nineteenth century. The Northern Secu-

rities case became a well-publicized confrontation between big business and an active president out to protect the rights of small entrepreneurs and the consumer. Thus, the president pitted himself against predatory corporations in the public arena even as he sought accommodations with business leaders in private. In the case of the Anthracite Coal Strike during autumn 1902, he positioned himself between capital and labor to provide American society with what he later called the Square Deal. These episodes, and others that followed, became moral melodramas in which citizens rooted for and against what Roosevelt was doing.[38]

George B. Cortelyou stayed on in the Roosevelt White House for the first year of the new administration to provide support and counsel to the president and his personal secretary, William Loeb of New York. Roosevelt shared the high opinion of Cortelyou's abilities that McKinley had had. In spring 1902, when talk of a cabinet shuffle circulated, Roosevelt told newsmen: "Whenever a vacancy shall occur in the Cabinet, it is my purpose to appoint Mr. Cortelyou if he will accept, and I want that distinctly understood." Roosevelt had seen how Cortelyou managed the crisis arising from McKinley's death and how adeptly the secretary had handled press relations at that time.[39]

It became evident in 1902, however, that it was time for Cortelyou to assume duties in the cabinet. As a discerning reporter noted, "Mr. Roosevelt has no systematic regularity about his methods either at work or at play." Roosevelt spoke freely to some reporters whose stories he liked and dismissed others with a curt nod. Cortelyou "softened the rough word and contemptuous shoulder shrug, explained the harsh criticism and made everybody feel that under the President's rugged exterior beat a sympathetic heart." When Cortelyou left the White House to become secretary of commerce and labor early in 1903, he took those qualities with him. He was, however, the first presidential assistant to emerge from the White House as a celebrity in his own right, with a political career based on his service to the president.[40]

Before he left, Cortelyou codified procedures for the refurbished White House in a fourteen-page booklet, "White House and Executive Office: Organization and Rules." There he set out the precise duties of the clerks and the secretaries, specified the hours and procedures when the White House would be open, and instructed employees regarding the style of documents and the appearance of their desks. Most important, Cortelyou worked out the lines of authority running down from the president's secretary to the assistant secretaries and through the rest of the White House staff. By summer 1902, that force included twenty-seven secretaries, five doorkeepers, and seven messengers. Another dozen to fifteen servants assisted the president and his family. From that point on, the number of people in the White House rose steadily.[41]

Theodore Roosevelt had an unerring instinct for the spotlight and spent a good deal of his time cultivating the White House press corps to advance his policies. Newsmen appreciated the separate quarters that they gained in 1902, and Roosevelt represented a powerful and consistent source of exciting news. Although he did not hold press conferences, he often admitted cooperative reporters to his regular early-afternoon shaving sessions with the White House barber. As the razor flashed, the president would explain his views to the scribes who were then in his favor. "I wish I had time to tell you all the funny things he said," wrote one reporter after a shaving session with Roosevelt. "He talked a blue streak even while the barber was shaving him." The reporters who were close to Roosevelt received the derisive title of cuckoos from their envious colleagues in the White House press corps.[42]

In dealing with the press, Roosevelt sometimes went beyond simply courting reporters and indulged in direct management and dissemination of the news. During 1905 he arranged for a ghostwritten column, "The President," to appear in the *Ladies' Home Journal*. That same year, a presidential directive announced to the major press associations that "hereafter no information will be given to anyone about anything that has occurred at a Cabinet meeting." Cabinet members were warned of their "moral obligation" to keep the deliberations secret and that they should not be moved "by weakness or good nature" into leaks to newsmen. On several other occasions, Roosevelt sought to quell unauthorized leaks from his administration. He had about as much success as other chief executives would find in trying to eliminate embarrassing or damaging revelations.[43]

By the middle of Roosevelt's second term, complaints intensified among newsmen about the president's desire to manage what the public heard about his performance. "It is becoming more difficult to get uncolored news," wrote one disgruntled scribe, "yet the press agency feature of the executive departments was never so active." Correspondents understood that "you must not print news objectionable to or censorious of the administration, especially from the White House, or you will get disliked, and will probably suffer for it."[44]

Roosevelt took a number of steps against journalists who crossed him. They might be placed in what the president called the Ananias Club, named after a biblical liar. In other cases, Roosevelt called or wrote their publishers to have offending reporters removed from duty at the White House. In 1906 he turned against the crusading journalists in the nation's magazines when he compared them in a major speech to the character in John Bunyan's *Pilgrim's Progress* who raked the muck on the floor rather than looking at the heavenly sky above. The label "muckrakers" proved enduring and indicated that the president, like many of his successors, had a thin skin when it came to press scrutiny.[45]

Then, in 1909, Roosevelt insisted that the Justice Department sue Joseph Pulitzer and the *New York World* for libel when the publisher and his news-paper alleged corruption in the financing of the Panama Canal through a $40 million payment to a French company. The suit was eventually thrown out, but a dangerous precedent had been established. From banning Socialist newspapers from the mails to his litigation against the *World,* Roosevelt also set an example for future presidents in his cramped approach to the freedom of the press.[46]

During his nearly eight years in office, Roosevelt showed in other areas the most admirable and the least attractive aspects of the emerging modern presidency. On the positive side, he used what he called in 1909 the bully pulpit to rally support for his efforts in his second term to regulate railroads, secure pure food and drug legislation, and obtain federal inspection of meatpacking plants. Acting as the steward of the general welfare, he launched modern conservation with executive orders that created national parks, wildlife refuges, and national monuments. In national resources, Roosevelt demonstrated how an activist president could set a national agenda.[47]

To implement the stewardship theory of the presidency, Roosevelt believed that the chief executive must be able to do whatever was not expressly forbidden in the Constitution. For him, the idea of implied powers offered the chance to innovate and reform. As his friend Gifford Pinchot put it, Roosevelt "used the whole Government of the United States consciously, and with the most conspicuous success, as a means of doing good to the people of this country." Roosevelt's confidence that he knew with certainty what the good of the country required was endearing to many members of his generation. Since the basis of such decisions was Roosevelt's personal sense of right and wrong, it meant that the actions of the federal government often occurred because of the individual discretion of the executive rather than on the basis of an objective standard.[48]

In foreign policy, Roosevelt also sought an expansive role for the nation. His personal diplomacy and timely use of American naval power helped secure a revolution in Panama that brought the United States the zone it needed to build a canal across the isthmus. He mediated a settlement of the Russo-Japanese War and sent a delegation to the Algeciras Conference in 1906 to resolve the fate of Morocco and to defuse a European crisis. As commander in chief, he sent the Great White Fleet on a round-the-world cruise in 1907 and 1908 to impress Japan and the world with American naval power. His policy, Roosevelt said, was to follow the African adage: "Speak softly but carry a big stick." Mindful of the suspicion of foreign entanglements that permeated the electorate, he emphasized both aspects of the aphorism. He did not commit the nation beyond what the political will of Congress and the voters would sustain. Despite his reputation as a diplomatic blusterer, he did not send American troops into combat, outside the preexisting insurrection in the Philippines, during his administration. Though he governed an empire, Roosevelt in foreign policy knew that he was a circumscribed imperial president.[49]

As he conducted foreign policy and shaped his relations with Congress over foreign affairs, Roosevelt often departed from orderly procedures and the accepted methods of treaty making. To shape policy, he relied on informal contacts abroad and often on private agents to influence other nations. When the U.S. Senate balked at some of his initiatives, as in the Dominican Republic in 1904 and 1905, he was quite willing to work out executive agreements that did not require congressional action. Such arrangements also became common in his relations with Japan, including the Taft-Katsura Agreement of 1905 and the Root-Takahira Agreement of 1908. Roosevelt had a case that legislative approval was sometimes too slow and awkward, but there was a large potential for misuse of these devices as well.[50]

As an administrator of domestic policy, Roosevelt had little patience with bureaucratic traditions that required him to go through the secretaries of the various departments to get things done. He cultivated subordinates below cabinet level and often bypassed their superiors. The practice kept government officials on their toes, but at the same time it could result in presidential meddling rather than in orderly policy making.

To manage his domestic relations with Congress, Roosevelt acted in some ways that his successors emulated. The effort to pass the Hepburn Act to strengthen the power of the Interstate Commerce Commission over the railroads in 1905 and 1906 provides a case in point. To rally support for the reform, Roosevelt made a series of public speeches during his travels around the nation in 1905. He used some well-timed Justice Department prosecutions over rebating to dramatize railroad abuses, and he cooperated with friendly reporters to have studies of questionable railroad practices appear in middle-class magazines. When the Hepburn bill was before the Senate in 1906, he plunged into the legislative process in a manner that made the president an equal and visible player in shaping the final outcome along the lines that the White House desired. Roosevelt then behaved in a similar manner in the struggle over meat inspection and the Pure Food and Drug Act. By 1906 it was clear that future presidents would have to be legislative leaders and not just a distant presence apart from Congress.[51]

Roosevelt's dealings with Congress underscored, however, that modern presidents could not simply bend lawmakers to their will. Over the course of his presidency, relations with Capitol Hill deteriorated. Roosevelt sent too many peremptory messages on too many subjects. Congressional patience with the practice wore thin. Roosevelt made disparaging remarks about lawmakers as well, and his words made their way to the House and Senate. Congressional resistance to executive interference, led by Speaker Joseph G. Cannon, characterized the last years of Roosevelt's administration. "That fellow at the other end of the Avenue," said Cannon, "wants everything, from the birth of Christ to the death of the devil." The president never delegated relations with Congress to aides or friendly lawmakers. He was the chief legislator. Yet reliance on his own personality and influence did not prove sustainable over time because of his innate suspicion of the motives of the members of Congress.[52]

The issue of the Secret Service in 1908 and 1909 illustrates how Roosevelt's efforts to enlist the agency, located in the Treasury Department, as a general investigative arm of the executive branch aroused suspicions of undue presidential power. Roosevelt believed that the best way to ferret out wrongdoing in and out of government was through a detective agency responsible to the Justice Department and the president. When Congress questioned the wisdom of this innovation, Roosevelt sent them a special message, asking, "Does

Congress desire that the Government shall have at its disposal the most efficient instrument for the detection of criminals and the prevention and pun-
ishment of crime, or does it not?" When the matter was put that way, Roosevelt
easily won the public relations war with Capitol Hill. Nonetheless, the critics
of the president had a point that giving the chief executive a personal detective service opened up problems of potential abuse.[53]

The Brownsville episode of 1906 suggested how Roosevelt might act if
his discretion was unfettered. Black soldiers in that Texas border town were
accused of attacking townspeople and firing indiscriminately in retaliation
for racial slights. Though no evidence directly linked the African-American
troops to the incident, Roosevelt discharged the soldiers without a trial or
a hearing. He insisted that their failure to confess their crime was proof of
their guilt and joint responsibility for what had happened. The incident
provoked a congressional investigation, led by a foe of Roosevelt's, Senator
Joseph B. Foraker of Ohio. Though the probe cast serious doubt on the guilt
of the soldiers, Roosevelt did not waver in his judgment that the men were
responsible. To prove their guilt, he hired personal investigators to pursue
evidence of wrongdoing. These operatives employed bribes and manufac-
tured some evidence to satisfy the president's wants. Using private detectives
to support a presidential finding against soldiers was a broad interpretation
of how the chief executive might perform as the steward of the American
people.[54]

Roosevelt's energy as president led him to address the issue of how well
the executive branch carried out its functions. He had been interested in the
subject since his days as governor of New York, when he sought reorganization of the state's canals, prisons, and factory inspections. Both Elihu Root
in the War Department and Gifford Pinchot in the Forest Service pursued
administrative reforms. To achieve change, Roosevelt knew, he would have
to find a means to look at government operations without involving a hostile Congress in the inquiry.

The result was the Committee on Departmental Methods, or the Keep
Commission, named after its chair, Charles Hallam Keep of the Treasury
Department. Created in June 1905, the five-person panel was told to find out
"what changes are needed to place the conduct of the executive business of
the government in all its branches on the most economical and effective basis
in light of the best modern business practice." The commission did valuable

work, and it asserted the principle that the president was in charge of all the work of the executive agencies. In that sense, the commission was the precursor of periodic efforts to reform the workings of government throughout the twentieth century.[55]

What the Keep Commission did not do was to look at the actual operation of the presidency and the way the chief executive carried out his duties. Roosevelt did not believe that the presidency needed to respond in a more bureaucratic and managerial manner. Nor was he an admirer of orderly procedures and clear lines of authority. His personal energy enabled him to conduct a large amount of business without the need of an array of staff members. Yet in fact Roosevelt directed a kind of informal staff in his Tennis Cabinet that joined him on the White House tennis courts and afterward talked about policies. Men such as Pinchot, James R. Garfield of the Department of the Interior, Charles P. Neill of the Bureau of Labor, and Herbert Knox Smith of the Bureau of Corporations composed the nucleus of a personal staff. Some Washington critics dubbed them "the incense swingers" because of their devotion to the president. Since the group met Roosevelt's needs, he did not grasp the importance of creating more regular arrangements for rendering presidential decisions.[56]

Like William McKinley, Roosevelt blended elements of what would become the modern presidency with a deference to the traditional procedures of being president. In his use of publicity, relations with the press, and deft handling of his family as a political asset, he became a model for future presidential success. His treatment of Congress showed how legislative goals might be achieved but also indicated that a preaching president could soon wear out his welcome with the congressional congregation. As a diplomatist, he pushed the boundaries of presidential leadership on the world stage. His victories quieted adverse reaction in Congress, though reservations about his unchecked executive discretion lingered.

Where Roosevelt proved less innovative was in the manner of running his own office. He did not expand on the bureaucratizing changes of McKinley and Cortelyou. If anything, he scaled them back. Instead of dividing responsibility for press relations and the care of Congress, Roosevelt did most of the work himself. There was no change in managing the flow of paper. Despite a series of governmental deficits toward the end of his term, Roosevelt felt no impulse to investigate budget matters systematically.

WELL BEGUN AND WELL DONE

"Stepping Out of the White House." The publicity surrounding the shift from Roosevelt to Taft in 1909 masked the tension between the two men that would lead to their split in 1912. (From Albert Shaw, A Cartoon History of Roosevelt's Career *[1910].)*

Roosevelt performed a kind of high-wire act as president between 1901 and 1909. He behaved as modern presidents would but without a net. Even his hyperactive body felt the strain of assuming so much responsibility for himself by the end of his presidency. His White House boxing matches had blinded him in one eye, and he had gained a good deal of weight in the eight years of power. Theodore Roosevelt did establish the modern presidency as a powerful concept in the minds of the American people. Setting up the executive machinery to make the idea work in practice would fall to Roosevelt's successors.

2

The Lawyer and the Professor
William Howard Taft and Woodrow Wilson

In the evolution of the modern presidency, Woodrow Wilson receives an honored place as an exponent of strong leadership during his two terms. Fighting a war to victory caused Wilson to strengthen the scope and authority of his office. For William Howard Taft and his single term from 1909 to 1913, the appraisal is more mixed. Taking office after Theodore Roosevelt and serving only one troubled term, Taft is usually seen as more in the mold of Warren G. Harding and Calvin Coolidge, other Republican presidents who fell short of greatness in office. Yet both Taft and Wilson also shaped their presidencies in reaction to Theodore Roosevelt's example. In so doing, they developed practices that extended the creation of the modern presidency.

Both Taft and Wilson found themselves conducting the presidency as the system of partisan politics that had been dominant in the late nineteenth century experienced further declines. At the same time, the emerging mass media influenced how presidential news was covered and the presidency interpreted. Taft never mastered these changing elements. Wilson had some success during his first term but found his second administration more problematic. By the time he gave way to Warren G. Harding in March 1921, Wilson's presidential leadership had been repudiated by the American people.

The procedural reforms of the Progressive Era gathered momentum during these two administrations, and the net result was a tangible decline in the shaping role of parties in political affairs. During the Taft years, the direct election of U.S. Senators was achieved through a constitutional amendment. Woman suffrage became a stronger national campaign, as state after state adopted some form of it, and the advocates of national change pressed for their constitutional amendment. In choosing presidential candidates, the direct primary became more common, and the changes embodied in the initiative, referendum, and recall also appeared in some states. Popular sentiment against parties intensified. As one progressive put it in 1910, "The people are inclined to be suspicious of any partisan organization. It suggests exclusiveness, possibly some sinister purpose and at least the chaining of big men to little or corrupt men. There is a loss of moral force in party action."[1]

At the same time, the Taft presidency operated in the context of the expansion of the news media's attention to that office and the growth of mass entertainment as a competitor for the public's interest. The number of daily newspapers in the nation's major cities remained high, and their ability to depict the president through photographs became more sophisticated. Taft did not like intense news coverage and made little secret of his disdain for the new way of following a president around.[2]

The emergence of the motion picture signaled a permanent shift in how Americans would interact with their chief executives. By the second year of Taft's administration, for example, there were reported to be twenty thousand nickelodeon theaters operating in the United States, and an estimated quarter-million customers attended these establishments every day. Short films of fifteen or twenty minutes were giving way to more extended features with a plot and recognizable characters. The star system was just around the corner, and magazines covered the culture of these celebrities for an emerging audience. It did not take long for politicians to recognize the value of the movies as a way of delivering a partisan message, and within a few years newsreels would feature political messages. Roosevelt had sensed that presidents could benefit from being in the spotlight as other celebrities were, but both Taft and Wilson approached the new world of mass entertainment gingerly. Their presidencies did not come to terms with the changes overtaking American culture.[3]

Though it is not possible to make Taft a success in the White House, he endeavored, even more than Theodore Roosevelt had, to reform the inner workings of his office. He established a commission on government efficiency that laid the foundation for the president to function as a more effective manager of the executive branch. In the process, he promoted the idea that the federal government needed a budget process to create sound financial decision making. These innovations did not reach completion under Taft, but they did point to future presidential initiatives in the same direction during the 1920s and 1930s. In some respects, Taft represented a throwback to the nineteenth century in his conception of presidential power and manipulation of public opinion. Yet in his quest for efficiency and predictability, he looked forward to the managerial style of the presidency in ways that Roosevelt had not done.

William Howard Taft brought a different conception of the role of the president to the White House when he took over from Roosevelt on 4 March 1909. A former federal judge, colonial administrator in the Philippines, and secretary of war, Taft came out of the law and its formalized training. Roosevelt used the three-hundred-pound Ohioan as a troubleshooter in the cabinet. When he traveled as president, Roosevelt said that he had left Taft back in Washington "sitting on the lid." The portly Taft became the butt of numerous fat jokes during his tenure in the Philippines and in the cabinet. When he cabled Secretary of War Elihu Root in 1903 that he "stood up well" after a twenty-five-mile horseback ride, Root fired back: "How is the horse?" Taft released the wire to the press himself. Roosevelt and Taft were close during the Roosevelt presidency, but crucial differences of temperament and political ideology lurked just below the amicable surface of their relationship.[4]

Fifty-one years old when he took office, Taft had campaigned in 1908 as the heir of Roosevelt and was pledged to carry out the policies that his predecessor had advanced. Conservative Republicans worried that Taft would be too close to Roosevelt. Careful attention to Taft's speeches, however, would have alerted political observers to the potential differences between the two men. What the government needed, Taft said in October 1908, was "not to be spectacular in the enactment of great statutes laying down new codes of morals or asserting a new standard of business integrity." Instead, the next president would require "the men and machinery" to go forward with what Roosevelt had started.[5]

These statements grew from Taft's view of presidential power and its proper exercise. He believed that the chief executive should remain within the boundaries of the law rather than move beyond them. He thought Theodore Roosevelt had done just that on too many occasions through reliance on the implied powers of his office. The realm of conserving natural resources was one specific area where he believed that Roosevelt had unduly stretched the law. Taft had little patience with Roosevelt's doctrine of an unwritten "residuum" of power

In the reworking of the White House in 1909, the Oval Office in the Executive Office Building became the focus of presidential decision making. (White House Collection.)

in the presidency that allowed the chief executive to take action when Congress and the courts had not preempted him. Such a doctrine in Taft's mind invited presidential overreaching and potential misconduct. "It might lead," Taft said after he left the White House, "under emergencies to results of an arbitrary character, doing irremediable justice to private right."[6]

From his days in the Roosevelt cabinet, Taft also disliked the way Roosevelt had circumvented departmental secretaries and dealt with sympathetic junior officials to get his way. As he told his wife in October 1909, "The whole administration under Roosevelt was demoralized by his system of dealing directly with subordinates." In office, Taft sought to establish clear lines of authority within the federal government, running from the White House to the various branches of the executive. Such a task did not prove easy to accomplish in four years.[7]

Taft had a tough act to follow in Roosevelt, and it soon became evident that the new president lacked many of the skills that made Roosevelt such a master of the public side of his office. The presidency was the first major elective office that Taft had held, and he did not have an instinctive feel for political management. Under the stimulus of the 1908 presidential campaign, he had performed well as a candidate. Once inaugurated, however, he put aside the techniques of the hustings, became less attentive to the press, and seemed to regard the public's interest in his performance as intrusive and inappropriate.

Taft also came to the presidency anxious not to repeat what he saw as Roosevelt's mistakes and to put his own stamp on the office. His family, and especially his wife, Helen Herron Taft, believed that it was imperative for him to "be his own king." To that end, the new First Lady made stylistic changes in the look and management of the White House. These included the use of liveried African-American servants and a revamped decor of the Executive Mansion to underline the point that a new and more sophisticated regime had arrived. Naturally, the implied rebuke to Roosevelt and his wife did not sit well with the former president.[8]

For his part, President Taft sought to be legalistic where Roosevelt had been freewheeling. Taft also reacted to the adroit ways in which his predecessor had manipulated the press to advance his own agenda. Taft intended to let his actions be his best advertisement for the merits of his programs. He was right in that he could not be another Roosevelt and was wise not to try. Yet he went too far in the other direction and abandoned many of the techniques of the modern presidency that might have been adapted to his own personal style. As one Washington observer noted, Taft's "bump of politics was a deep hole." Roosevelt was equally succinct: "Taft is a far abler man than I but he don't know how to play the popular hero and shoot a bear."[9]

One cause for Taft's inattention to these matters was the serious illness of his wife, which she experienced in April 1909. Until that time, the First Lady had been both a spouse and a de facto presidential aide. Mrs. Taft had played a large role in the selection of the cabinet, and she expected to become a close adviser of her husband. She had a well-developed sense of public relations and an equally deep suspicion of Theodore Roosevelt's motives. Though her sickness was not the sole cause of Taft's early mistakes as president, her absence removed a cautionary voice on which the president had long depended.[10]

When Taft took office, the total number of White House personnel who assisted the president had reached eighty people. Seventy or so individuals worked as clerks, telephone operators, and messengers. Eight others held what could be called staff positions. There was the president's secretary; a military aide, Archibald W. Butt; and five clerks with specific duties for appointments, accounts, and legislative business. Mrs. Taft also had a social secretary. The president struggled with the problem of finding a satisfactory secretary during the first two years of his administration. Fred W. Carpenter, who came over with him from the War Department, was not up to the task. His successor, the Chicago businessman Charles Dyer Norton, shared the president's zeal to reform and rationalize White House decision making. Unfortunately, Norton's political skills were not as good as he thought they were, and he blundered during the 1910 campaign. He was replaced in 1911. Only with the arrival of Charles Dewey Hilles did Taft finally have an accomplished performer in this demanding post. Hilles effectively oversaw Taft's successful campaign for renomination in 1912 and then left to run the presidential campaign.[11]

The Washington press corps found, to their dismay, that the friendly, accessible Taft of the War Department and the campaign trail had vanished. In his place was a president who was convinced that his deeds would provide the best possible publicity for the administration. As he told the Kansas editor William Allen White on 20 March 1909, "I have confidence in the sound judgment of the people based on what is done rather than what is proclaimed or what is suspected from appearances." When journalists turned up at the White House in the early days of the administration, they found the president's secretary, Fred W. Carpenter, inclined to turn them away. Reporters seeking an audience with Taft might have to wait several days for admission to see the president. As a result, the stream of news from the White House slowed to a trickle. In the ensuing vacuum, journalists went to Taft's opponents for stories and lively quotations and found them in abundance. Roosevelt's friends were quite willing to convey derogatory anecdotes about Taft and to make the case for another Roosevelt presidency in 1912.[12]

Many of the practices that had eased the way for reporters under McKinley and Roosevelt were abandoned, once Taft settled in at the White House. The president procrastinated about writing his speeches, and advance copies were unavailable to the news services. Often he prepared his remarks on his way to the speech itself or simply delivered what he wanted to say "off-hand, without any notes." That method suited him, but it drove the newspapermen covering him to distraction. In the case of his address defending the Payne-Aldrich Tariff in Winona, Minnesota, in September 1909, Taft's hastily prepared remarks called the controversial measure "the best tariff bill that the Republican party ever passed." The phrase, which could have been explained if advance texts had been ready, pleased party regulars but outraged Republican progressives. More carefully considered wording would have better served Taft's interests. The demands of frequent presidential speeches, many of them ceremonial as the chief executive became more visible, were taxing the ability of any president to produce them on a regular basis.[13]

Taft also lacked Roosevelt's sure touch with public opinion. Although he played tennis avidly, Roosevelt did not do so publicly, and there were few newspaper photographs of the pudgy president on the White House court. Taft, on the other hand, loved to play golf and went to posh country clubs to enjoy a round with the rich men who were members there. The press and photographers trailed Taft around the course to record the chief executive at play. The resulting pictures of the rotund president on the links with millionaires struck a sour note at a time of reform, when golf seemed the preserve of the rich. Taft also enjoyed the process of travel and spent time journeying around the country. The absence of a definite purpose for such junkets raised questions in the press about the president's commitment to his official duties. That was unfair. Taft worked hard at his job but was unable to convey the sense of personal energy and positive achievement that had been a hallmark of the Roosevelt years.[14]

With a divided Republican party to lead, Taft sought to achieve legislation that would make the changes Roosevelt had pursued "permanent in the form of law." Yet his predecessor had left him with the thorny and contentious issue of tariff revision to resolve first. Meanwhile, other subjects such as conservation and railroad regulation pressed for attention. Even before he took office, Taft concluded that he had no choice but to cooperate with the conservative Republican leadership in Congress, Speaker Joseph G. Cannon and Senate leader Nelson W. Aldrich. A coalition with the Democrats was not viable, and the Republican progressives, while vocal, lacked the votes with which to build working majorities in the House and Senate. With the agreement of Roosevelt, Taft signaled that he would not challenge the existing

More and more the president was expected in the early twentieth century to make public appearances where cameras could catch him. Here William Howard Taft strikes a presidential pose at a June 1910 baseball game in Washington, D.C. (Courtesy of the Library of Congress.)

structure of partisan control on Capitol Hill. Though necessary, that decision soured relations with the party's progressive wing almost at once.[15]

Accustomed to Roosevelt's noisy brawls with lawmakers and disillusioned with the details of party warfare, voters reacted tepidly to Taft's legislative strategy in 1909 and 1910. The president did little to explain himself publicly on many of the disputed issues, and he lacked Roosevelt's capacity to sum up an issue in a pithy phrase. For example, Taft did secure passage of the Payne-Aldrich Tariff with lower customs duties on some raw materials, which represented as much as he could do. Despite an apparently secure Republican majority in the Senate, Aldrich found himself without the votes to pass a tariff measure that did not include concessions to special interests on industrial products, cotton, and wool. The necessary deals that Aldrich struck outraged midwestern progressives such as Jonathan P. Dolliver of Iowa and Robert M. La Follette of Wisconsin. They wanted Taft to veto the bill, but the president refused. The vocal criticisms of the progressives left the enduring impression of a president being led by reactionaries in Congress. Dolliver quipped that Taft was "an amiable island surrounded by men who know exactly what they want." Behind the scenes during summer 1909 Taft was a leader in securing most of the rate reductions that the bill contained, but he had already lost a key battle in the war of presidential perception. Thereafter, Taft was linked in the public mind with Cannon and Aldrich.[16]

Equally damaging was the controversy between Taft's secretary of the interior, Richard A. Ballinger, and the chief forester and key Roosevelt lieutenant, Gifford Pinchot. The dispute turned on coal lands in Alaska, but the central issue was whether Taft would carry on Roosevelt's policy of conservation through the broad use of executive discretion. Taft believed that the rule of law (as he defined it) should prevail and that Roosevelt had been too willing to employ the prerogatives of his office for seemingly desirable conservation goals. What began as a bureaucratic turf war spilled out into the popular press as a controversy between one president and another. The fracas resulted in the ouster of Pinchot early in 1910, when he attacked Ballinger publicly. The president had to fire Pinchot for insubordination. Taft came out the loser in the political dustup, and the episode further eroded his links with Roosevelt, who got the news while he was on his African safari.[17]

There then followed what would become a familiar ritual of congressional hearings into the controversy, in which the Taft administration performed badly in the battle for public approval. Once again, Taft displayed little sense of the public relations dimensions of his position, and his political enemies created the impression that the administration was insensitive to conservation matters and beholden to special interests. Even the ultimate replacement of Ballinger by a proconservation secretary of the interior in 1911 could not lift the cloud that the war with Pinchot had created.

Taft rebounded during 1910 with a constructive program of legislative enactments that included the Mann-Elkins Act to regulate the railroads, postal savings, and a conservation law. Yet by then neither the progressives nor the public gave the president much credit for his success with Congress. Once Theodore Roosevelt returned from the African hunting trip in early June, Taft found that the feud with his predecessor dominated the headlines. Efforts to reconcile the two men worked temporarily, but the animosity festered for the next two years. The Republicans suffered losses in the congressional elections of 1910, and Taft's prospects for reelection dimmed.[18]

The president attempted a major legislative initiative in 1911, with his proposal for tariff reciprocity with Canada. Although he pushed the executive agreement through Congress, voters in Canada rejected the pact and Taft incurred another humiliating defeat. By late 1911, the worsening relationship with Roosevelt broke down completely when the Justice Department filed suit against United States Steel. The indictment contained language critical of Roosevelt's antitrust policies as president.

Early in 1912, Roosevelt became a candidate for the Republican nomination. A bitter primary battle ensued, with Taft and Roosevelt exchanging insults in key states. The Republican National Convention became a political donnybrook. Roosevelt bolted the party amid charges that the nomination had been stolen from him. With his control of the party machinery and support from Republican conservatives, Taft demonstrated that an incumbent president, no matter how unpopular, could secure his party's nomination, even in the face of a charismatic challenger such as Roosevelt.[19]

That Taft had to campaign personally and enter several primaries marked what proved to be another key shift in presidential behavior. The nineteenth-century convention that incumbent presidents did not seek reelection personally was naturally fragile and likely to be abandoned when political survival was on the line. After he won the Republican nomination in 1912, Taft recognized that his cause was hopeless and remained on the sidelines in the fall. Nonetheless, a significant change in the unwritten lore of the presidency was taking place.

This story of Taft's political collapse and defeat at the hands of Roosevelt and Woodrow Wilson in 1912 is part of the folklore of American presidential politics. On that level, Taft hardly seems part of the evolution of the modern presidency and therefore belongs to the pre-McKinley pattern of the nineteenth century. So much attention has been focused on the erosion of the Taft-Roosevelt friendship that the president's contributions to the management of the White House and his efforts to introduce greater efficiency have largely remained the province of a few political scientists and historians. Yet Taft and his staff pursued important alterations that would in time enable the White House to function with enhanced effectiveness during the first half of the twentieth century.

One area was seemingly mundane but in fact crucial to the president's ability to get the information needed to complete the work of the office. By

1909, the daily flow of mail into the White House had reached such proportions that the older system of Personal and Official Correspondence, begun under Roosevelt and administered by C. E. Ingling and his fellow clerks, was outmoded. The White House filing staff developed a numerical system of case files that were classified either by name or by subject. Records relating to politics, for example, were assigned the number 300 and were then grouped under that heading, subdivided by states. The numerical system offered more opportunity to categorize documents with precision, but it meant that a relentless multiplication of case files took place. Some files might have only a few selected documents; others might comprise hundreds of pages and be small archives in and of themselves. From its inception during the Taft years until the end of the Eisenhower administration, the case file system endured and became the method by which successive presidents managed the expanding documentary record of their institution.[20]

Circumstances and personal inclination impelled Taft to consider other methods of improving presidential organization and efficiency. He disliked Roosevelt's improvised methods of running the White House and wanted to see orderly procedures that would enhance the president's ability to have his instructions implemented. By 1909 Taft also faced the recurring problems of government deficits. In 1908 the deficit stood at more than $57 million; a year later it had risen above $89 million. The problem was that the federal government had no budget mechanism to balance revenues and spending. Moreover, the president lacked any means to establish what the government ought to spend each year, and Congress retained control of the appropriations process. Both the White House and Capitol Hill recognized the dimensions of the issue in 1909, but the lawmakers did not want the president to take over their long-standing control of the purse strings.[21]

Congress did grant Taft funds in 1909 to explore ways in which governmental expenditures might be cut and "greater efficiency and economy" achieved. The president construed his mandate broadly and asked his secretary, Charles D. Norton, to look into administrative changes during summer 1910. Relying on his background in insurance and the expertise he had acquired while at Treasury, Norton set about his work with enthusiasm. From the start, the premise was that the president should control the study, with neither the cabinet nor Congress able to block its implementation. To run the project, Taft and Norton selected Dr. Frederick Cleveland, a member of the Bureau of Municipal Research in New York City. The five-person group that he headed was called the Commission on Economy and Efficiency. Its goal became to reshape the president's capacity to direct and oversee the executive branch of the government. As Cleveland said, there was no system by which "information can get to the President or to the head of a Department in a regular and systematic manner."[22]

While the commission made a number of suggestions to promote cost cutting and efficiency, the key changes it proposed involved combining agencies to achieve a specific purpose and making them more responsive to the president than to Congress. To that end, Cleveland and his colleagues recommended consolidation of agencies in the Treasury Department and looked toward combining the Navy and War Departments into a single Defense Department. With a budget set by the executive and a coherent hierarchy of departments, the president would be responsible for initiating policy and then carrying it out. Taft set about creating a budget system on his own in 1911, with instructions that the agencies and departments should follow it in formulating their spending requests.[23]

Congress responded with an amendment to a 1912 appropriations bill that forbade the president from doing what Taft had done and that instructed the executive agencies not to cooperate in the executive's program. Further, the lawmakers trimmed appropriations for the commission and reduced its size to three members. Although the president instructed the executive departments to cooperate with the commission, their reaction was often slow, as the cabinet secretaries recognized that the commission's work threatened their power. To meet these rebukes to his authority from Congress and within his own administration, Taft answered with an assertion of presidential power that actually went a long way toward adopting the doctrine of implied presidential discretion that Roosevelt had advocated. Taft claimed that "it is entirely competent for the President to submit a budget." Moreover, he did not believe Congress had the power to prevent him from doing so.[24]

In practical terms, Taft never got to test his claims since his administration ran out in March 1913. The incoming Congress, dominated by Democrats in both houses, had little interest in following the recommendations of a repudiated Republican. Efforts to enlist Woodrow Wilson in the effort to keep the commission alive also collapsed when the new president said that the commission had little relevance to his administration. The political reaction to the Cleveland commission indicated that the process of shifting power to the executive branch in an institutional manner during the first third of the twentieth century was a complex and often controversial undertaking.[25]

Taft's one-term presidency came to be regarded as only an interregnum between the activism of Theodore Roosevelt and the strong presidency of Woodrow Wilson. In important respects, this impression was an accurate one. Taft made little use of the practices that Cortelyou had instituted a decade earlier to manage president-press relations. Taft also put aside the techniques that had enabled Roosevelt to dominate the news during his years in office. He actually achieved a good deal in terms of antitrust prosecutions and substantive legislation on railroad regulation, postal savings, and conservation. But because he did not act in the mold of a presidential activist and instead pursued moderate ends, he pleased neither faction of his own party. His campaign for efficiency and presidential autonomy was an important legacy for the future but not one that added to his historical reputation.

Woodrow Wilson, on the other hand, fared well in appraisals of American presidents during most of the twentieth century, and his ranking among the great chief executives seems secure. Yet there is more ambiguity about Wilson's record in the White House than is often recognized. His domestic achievements are large — the establishment of the Federal Reserve System in 1913, the Underwood Tariff during the same year, the Clayton Antitrust Act in 1914, and the Federal Trade Commission that came at the same time. Two years later, during the run-up to the presidential campaign of 1916, Wilson obtained from Congress the Adamson Act, to provide an eight-hour day for railroad workers; the Federal Farm Loan Act; and a law to regulate child labor. In terms of substantive legislation, he has one of the most impressive records of any president in American history.

In foreign affairs, Wilson was also a central figure in the evolution of American diplomacy and the guiding principles of the nation's foreign policy. His handling of the vexing issues of neutrality between 1914 and 1917, the participation with the Allies in the coalition that defeated Germany and the Central Powers, and his unsuccessful fight for the League of Nations have been examined for their revelations of a strong executive using the power of the presidency to make his country a major power on the world scene.

Yet there is a contradiction at the heart of Wilson's presidency that is rarely examined. When he left office in March 1921, he was a sick, broken man.

Moreover, he was deeply unpopular with the American people, and he had brought the presidency to one of its low points in the twentieth century as a result. The White House was seen as a kind of gloomy prison where an infirm Wilson clung to power as the nation turned to the Republicans and the presidential candidacy of Warren G. Harding. As H. L. Mencken wrote in September 1920, "The heaviest burden that the Democratic party has to carry in this campaign is the burden of Dr. Wilson's unpopularity." Because the tide of historical events in the 1930s and 1940s seemed to vindicate Wilson's pleas for internationalism, the wounds he inflicted on his party and his office by 1921 have been played down and largely forgotten. Yet these developments set the stage for how the three Republicans in the 1920s approached changes in the workings of the presidency.[26]

Wilson enjoyed a meteoric rise to the White House. In 1909 he was the well-regarded president of Princeton University who had been identified with educational reform at that prestigious institution. He had been the subject of some modest speculation as a Democratic presidential candidate in 1908, but he never threatened Bryan's hold on the nomination. By age fifty-two, Wilson had written a number of scholarly and popular books on American history and government, and he had ambitions for higher office that he had shared with only a few friends. Wilson made his initial reputation with *Congressional Government*, published in 1885 during the period of ascendancy for the legislative branch. Following the war with Spain and McKinley's and Roosevelt's expansion of presidential power, Wilson came to see the office as having a greater potential for leadership. As he wrote in 1908, a president whom the nation trusted "can not only lead it, but form it to his own views."[27]

Events soon shaped themselves to make Wilson's political dreams become a reality. His tenure at Princeton ended over bitter disputes with alumni and trustees about eating clubs and the future of the institution, which led to his enforced departure in 1910. Meanwhile, New Jersey Democrats, facing a divided Republican party, looked for a fresh face to heal their own internal wounds. Wilson became their gubernatorial nominee and won the election. As a southerner who had carried an industrial state, he was immediately considered as a potential nominee in 1912 for the Democrats, who sought a new name after the defeat of William Jennings Bryan in 1908.[28]

Wilson pushed a reform program through the New Jersey legislature in 1911, which added to his allure among Democratic progressives. He plunged into the presidential race and, following a difficult struggle with Speaker of the House James Beauchamp "Champ" Clark of Missouri, won the nomination after forty-six ballots at the convention in Baltimore in late June 1912. Facing the Progressive party of Theodore Roosevelt and the weakened Republicans under Taft, Wilson articulated a program, the "New Freedom," which promised tariff reform and action against the trusts to restore competition. Roosevelt offered the "New Nationalism," which envisioned a stronger regulatory state and enhanced government power. The two men waged one of the most substantive presidential campaigns in American history around these competing visions of the future of reform. With the Democrats united, Wilson won a decisive victory in the electoral college and entered the White House with 43 percent of the popular vote. His party captured secure control of both houses of Congress as well.[29]

Wilson had long been infatuated with the British system and its prime ministerial style of government. His view of the presidency borrowed much from that overseas precedent. He was less concerned about the institutional workings of the office, and he had no interest in extending the life of the efficiency commission that Taft had appointed. Instead, Wilson ran the presidency in his first term like a small faculty office, with only one major staff assistant, his secretary Joseph P. Tumulty. His circle of advisers was limited, including the enigmatic and unpaid Texan, Edward M. House, who served Wilson as a kind of roving diplomat. Wilson showed that it was still possible to be a strong president without becoming a modern one.[30]

Wilson was responsible for some major innovations that increased the popular standing of the presidency. When he prepared his message on tariff reform for delivery to the Congress in April 1913, he broke the precedent that had existed since Thomas Jefferson in 1801 and decided to appear in person before Congress. Although one wife of a congressman said the change was "not epoch making," Wilson's appearance indeed marked a crucial shift in how the president related to both Congress and the public. The State of the Union address in the past, for example, had been a tedious experience of listening to clerks reading what the presidents had said, but now the occasion would become a media event. Until the advent of radio and sound motion pictures, the full potential of a presidential speech to a national audience would not be realized, but the decisive first step had been taken toward the semitheatrical occasion that these addresses have become.[31]

Woodrow Wilson's decision to deliver his tariff message in person to Congress in 1913 broke a long-standing tradition and caused one cartoonist, Clifford Berryman, to wonder why Theodore Roosevelt had not had the same idea. (Courtesy of U.S. Senate Collection, Center for Legislative Archives, National Archives.)

Another innovation that Wilson adopted was to hold regular press conferences with the reporters assigned to the White House. The change was the idea of Wilson's secretary, Tumulty, who told members of the press corps, "You boys are great personages in public affairs, and in Washington I will look after the publicity of this administration myself." Tumulty had begun working for Wilson during his first gubernatorial campaign in New Jersey. An affable young man in his early thirties, Tumulty used his Irish wit and charm to present his boss in the most favorable light. He styled himself the "publicity director" for the White House.[32]

The press conferences began on 15 March 1913, with Wilson pledging to one hundred reporters to hold these meetings weekly and, when possible, twice a week. At first the sessions were quite successful, as reporters asked questions about the issues of the day. Wilson proved to be skillful in dealing with the queries from journalists who assembled in the East Room. The ground rules specified that the president could not be quoted directly without his permission. Wilson prepared thoroughly for the conferences, and the process helped him, as it would other presidents, to think through his policies. He showed an adeptness with the language that enabled him to respond with effective comments that made news. The president also used the occasion to dispel rumors about administration policies.[33]

Despite the relative success of the press conferences, Wilson abandoned them in July 1915 on the grounds that issues of foreign policy arising from American neutrality required more of his attention. They were restarted after the 1916 election and then dropped again for ostensible reasons of national security. Like many of his successors, Wilson chafed at the ritual of being questioned by reporters who were either his political opponents or in his mind his intellectual inferiors. He and Tumulty thus looked for ways to get the news to the people that would not filter it through the Washington press. The entry of the United States into World War I and the creation of the Committee on Public Information in 1917 supplied an institutional means to accomplish these ends.[34]

The spreading power of the mass media affected Wilson's conduct of the presidency even as he sought to keep himself and his family out of the glare of publicity. In 1916 the Democratic National Committee made a film, "The President and His Cabinet in Action," and another motion picture attacking Wilson's Republican rival Charles Evans Hughes. The Republicans had their

The motion picture camera came into increasing use in presidential elections, and these frames of Woodrow Wilson are taken from a Democratic film that audiences saw in 1916. (From World's Work *[October 1916], author's collection.)*

own campaign features about their candidate. Aspirants for the White House were now seen as real people in motion by hundreds of thousands of movie-goers. Wilson marched in preparedness parades, went to baseball games, and provided ample chances to photographers on his speaking tours. These informal moments would soon become staged events, as future presidents and their aides sought to maximize their impact on the public.[35]

Wilson's approach to the duties of the presidency itself stemmed from two related elements. First, since he believed his mind was superior to the minds of his political associates, enemies, and reporters, he rarely saw the need to consult others in detail on substantive matters. Knowing what course he wished to take, he used his own typewriter to draft messages, write speeches, and prepare memoranda. Staff help beyond Tumulty was rarely required. The other issue turned on Wilson's health. Because of recurring problems that included hypertension and blindness in one eye after 1906, he was placed on a low-stress regimen that included daily exercise such as golf and frequent rests during the day. With his well-organized mind and ability to write quickly, he turned out an impressive number of presidential decisions and writings in a few hours each day during his first term. During World War I his work-day lengthened to accommodate the demands of the crisis.[36]

Circumstances facilitated the enactment of Wilson's agenda as a new and activist president in 1913. The Taft-Roosevelt split crippled the GOP's congressional candidates and resulted in the election of many new House Democrats in 1912. These freshman lawmakers looked to Wilson for guidance on policy questions. The Democrats were also eager to refute the persistent Republican charge that they were incapable of running the country after the mistakes of the Grover Cleveland era. As a result, Wilson's priorities of tariff reform and the creation of the Federal Reserve System faced few stringent legislative obstacles in 1913. His constant attention to the progress of these measures was required, but their eventual passage was assured, once a Democratic consensus emerged between Capitol Hill and the White House. Achievement then built on achievement as the New Freedom became a reality under Wilson's direction in 1913 and 1914.[37]

Some aspects of the president's strength in office produced dubious results. The Democratic victory in 1912 brought southerners into the government to the point where one reporter observed, "The South is in the Saddle." As a southerner himself, Wilson readily agreed when his cabinet officials such as Treasury Secretary William G. McAdoo and Postmaster General Albert S. Burleson solidified racial segregation within the federal government and especially in Washington. Neither Roosevelt nor Taft had been champions of racial justice, but Wilson let his prejudices toward African Americans shape national policy in an adverse way.[38]

In both foreign and domestic affairs during his first term, Wilson was able to wield presidential power to advance his own agenda and to confound his political enemies. In 1914 he secured passage of the Clayton Antitrust Act, which reflected his ideas of vigorous antitrust enforcement from the 1912 campaign, and the Federal Trade Commission Act, which borrowed liberally from the idea of a regulatory agency that Theodore Roosevelt had advocated as part of his New Nationalism in 1912. Also in 1914, after the outbreak of World War I, the Democrats employed the argument of supporting Wilson's neutrality policy and standing behind the president to counter Republican attacks on his handling of the economy and the impact of New Freedom programs. The slogan "War in the East! Peace in the West! Thank God for Wilson!" foreshadowed the campaign theme in 1916, "He kept us out of war."[39]

During the period of American neutrality, from August 1914 to April 1917, Wilson expanded the role of chief executive to meet challenges to his authority from within his own party. Early in 1916, when his program to increase the nation's military power through preparedness for the army and navy was in trouble among Democrats in Congress, he went on a speaking tour to pressure lawmakers to support his views. Although the junket enhanced the president's popularity, it did not translate into an immediate triumph. Still, future presidents would emulate Wilson's example.[40]

Shortly after these events, a legislative revolt among Democrats loomed over the issue of Americans traveling on the merchant ships of warring nations. The Gore-McLemore Resolution warning citizens against such journeys represented a direct threat to presidential control of foreign policy. Wilson used persuasion and patronage to beat back the attempt to constrict his authority in foreign affairs.[41]

In the 1916 presidential campaign, Wilson faced the challenge of a reunited Republican party under the leadership of their nominee, the former U.S. Supreme Court justice Charles Evans Hughes. Aware of the precedent that an incumbent president did not actively campaign for reelection, Wilson nonetheless decided that he could not win if he only let other Democrats make the case for him. At first, in an effective variant of the front-porch campaigns of the late nineteenth century, he made a number of regular speeches from his summer home, Shadow Lawn, in New Jersey. Then in early October, he went as far west as Omaha, Nebraska, for a campaign address, and he made additional speeches in Indiana, Illinois, and Ohio during the rest of the month. An appearance in New York was part of the wrap-up to the active campaign. Wilson's trenchant attacks on Hughes and the Republicans, combined with his message that "I am not expecting this country to get into war," proved crucial in what turned out to be one of the closest elections in the nation's history.[42]

The erosion of the taboo against a president taking a visible part in the reelection effort in 1916 foreshadowed the permanent campaigns of the late twentieth century. By the end of the 1920s and into the 1930s, a president would be expected to defend his record in person and to campaign as actively as the challenger. These developments occurred as the role of the political parties in presidential elections narrowed and the shaping of electoral strategy shifted toward the White House. Wilson won the contest against Hughes in large measure because of his ability as an incumbent to frame the issues in a manner that the Republican candidate found difficult to answer. Even though the president and the Democrats lacked the financial resources of the Republicans, incumbency and Wilson's emphasis on peace, prosperity, and reform won him 277 electoral votes to Hughes's 254.[43]

Throughout his political career through 1916, Woodrow Wilson had enjoyed a run of superb political luck as candidate and president. The joke in Washington in 1916 was that if Wilson "was to fall out of a sixteen story building . . . he would hit on a feather bed." Following his reelection triumph, however, he encountered persistent difficulties that plagued his presidency for the next four years. As other twentieth-century presidents would discover, winning a second term was often the beginning of unexpected problems and historic disappointments.[44]

The dominant early feature of Wilson's second term was the entry into World War I, which occurred in April 1917. The president led the nation to victory in Europe nineteen months later, and he used all the explicit and latent powers of his office to achieve that triumph. During the period of American belligerency, Congress strengthened presidential power over the economy, foreign policy, the military, and public opinion. Though the institutional base of the presidency remained thin, Wilson and his advisers improvised a structure in 1917 and 1918 that mobilized the American economy and put the nation's soldiers overseas to help the Allies defeat Germany on the western front. Wilson's use of his enhanced authority, however, boomeranged on the president and his party, and the result was a turning away from executive power as he had exercised it.[45]

The manner in which the conflict was fought and won involved political costs that resulted in defeat for Wilson and the Democrats in the 1918 congressional elections. The fragile coalition that had brought him reelection in 1916 fell apart. That failure in turn hampered his attempt to transform success on the battlefield into a more permanent peace through the creation of the League of Nations, with the United States as a member. As a result of these developments, the presidency experienced a period when the strength that Theodore Roosevelt and Woodrow Wilson had asserted came into question.

Woodrow Wilson's key political decision about the management of World War I was to make it largely a Democratic undertaking. Some prominent Republicans received appointments to public posts well away from the centers of power. William Howard Taft served on the National War Labor Board, and Elihu Root went on a diplomatic mission to Russia. Wilson did not name anyone from the Grand Old Party to his cabinet, and there was a popular perception that openly Republican soldiers such as General Leonard Wood were denied overseas duty to prevent the emergence of Republican war heroes. Wilson was probably correct in rejecting the offer of Theodore Roosevelt to raise a division for service in France, but the episode convinced Republicans that members of their party were not wanted in the conduct of the war at the highest levels.[46]

The president's unhappiness with his political opponents grew from his contempt for their philosophy and his rankling memories of the dirty 1916 campaign. Rumors had circulated about Wilson's alleged infidelity during his first marriage and the passionate courtship that led to his second marriage to Edith Galt in December 1915. Wilson said in a private letter that the 1916 "campaign was indeed one of the most virulent and bitter, and I must believe, one of the most unfair on the part of the Republican opposition that the country has ever seen." Not having to face the voters again if he observed the two-term tradition, he gave little attention to the relative narrowness of his own reelection victory.[47]

Despite their two victories in 1912 and 1916, the Democrats remained a sectional and minority party with a shaky hold on power outside the Solid South. The 1916 election left them with a narrow margin in the House. Their eleven-vote majority was more substantial in the Senate on paper, but a number of Democrats in the upper house disliked Wilson intensely. Their defection could put the party's majority in jeopardy on key issues. Wilson's political position was therefore weaker than he realized in April 1917. Unless he managed presidential decisions with attention to the even balance of the parties, he could tip the advantage to the Republicans. This kind of juggling act was not something that came naturally to him during his second term in the midst of a war.[48]

While the increasingly conservative Republicans were united in their dislike of Wilson, the Democrats experienced the internal strains that would plague them during the 1920s. Some southern and western congressional leaders had opposed entry into the war and were lukewarm about pursuing the conflict. On issues such as prohibition of alcohol and woman suffrage, the Democrats were divided still more between their dry strongholds in the South and their urban machines in the Northeast and Middle West. Despite his efforts to find an accommodation among the competing factions of his party, Wilson's forceful exertion of presidential power heightened internal discord for Democrats in 1917 and 1918.[49]

Wilson's commitment to a partisan course in fighting the war at home meant that he usually tilted toward the southern wing of the Democrats on Capitol Hill. In the case of agricultural products such as wheat and cotton, the president asked for and received the authority to fix prices on those commodities. He imposed a price of $2.20 per bushel on wheat in summer 1917 but left the price of cotton unregulated in deference to the power of the South in Congress. Republicans revived the arguments of the Civil War era about southern dominance in Congress, a strategy that produced GOP gains among wheat growers in the plains states who had leaned toward Wilson in 1916. Tax policy during the war also bore more heavily on the Republican Northeast than it did on rural taxpayers in the South and West.[50]

In other significant areas, Wilson's executive activism produced political losses for his party. Convinced that there was opposition to his policies both from antiwar sentiment and also from the conservative press, the president established the Committee on Public Information, led by George Creel, to distribute information about the war effort that provided the government's side of events. This attempt to institutionalize a ministry of information in the federal government achieved some positive results during 1917 and 1918, but its attempts to undermine ostensible German sentiment in the United States became part of the excesses of the domestic record of the Wilson administration.[51]

President Wilson seemed to have a tin ear on the question of civil liberties in wartime. He allowed Postmaster General Burleson to bar dissenting periodicals from the mails. Only once did he overturn one of Burleson's decisions, and then the postmaster general ignored the request. For the most part, Wilson went along with his subordinate's repressive policies. Similarly, Wilson accepted the reliance that his attorney general, Thomas Watt Gregory, placed on private vigilantes through the American Protective League to find and punish antiwar sentiments. The result of these tactics was increasing unhappiness among Wilson's progressive and liberal allies with the harsh policies of the administration.[52]

By 1918 the Democrats had gotten themselves into such political difficulty that even Wilson's prestige could not extricate them, as it had done in 1914. His popularity had begun to slip, and the idealism that had appealed to so many people during his first term now rang hollow in light of the administration's treatment of its political opponents and those who disliked the war. In late October 1918, Wilson asked for the election of a Democratic Congress to uphold his leadership in making peace with the soon-to-be-defeated Germans. Instead, the voters returned a Republican House of Representatives and a Senate with a narrow Republican majority in what amounted to a political repudiation of the president and his leadership.[53]

Following this political rebuke that left him with an opposition Congress, Wilson did little to accommodate the new political reality. With the war ended through the Armistice, he allowed the transition from war to peace to occur in the economy with a minimum of government supervision. The result was a period of labor unrest, racial violence, and an anticommunist Red Scare. These developments intensified the power of conservative opinion and helped the Republicans as they prepared for the 1920 elections. A strong president in wartime, he became passive after the fighting ended as he pursued his foreign policy goals.[54]

In the world arena, Wilson acted as if his authority were unchallenged. He expected that a Republican Senate, led by Henry Cabot Lodge, would accept a peace treaty that included the League of Nations without serious consultation. From this assumption flowed a number of crucial presidential blunders. First, Wilson decided to go to the Peace Conference himself. Though Roosevelt and Taft had each left the continental United States during their presidencies for short periods, Wilson's trip signaled that chief executives could become globe-trotters in foreign policy. Where Wilson erred was in not taking a major Republican leader with him to Paris. Hatred for Lodge and a lack of respect for Taft and Elihu Root moved the president, who overlooked the idea that the key point was approval of the eventual treaty, not his personal likes and dislikes.[55]

The Treaty of Versailles, with the League of Nations, probably represented the best diplomatic settlement of World War I that Wilson could have achieved, but the president missed opportunity after opportunity to use his influence with the press and public in Paris to lay the groundwork for a Senate endorsement of the final product. Secrecy at the Peace Conference grew out of Wilson's abiding distrust of the press, and the consequence was a lack of popular understanding in the United States of what took place in Paris. In the vacuum that resulted, Republicans filled the newspapers with attacks on the League of Nations and its primary architect.[56]

When he returned from France in July 1919, Wilson continued the tactics with Congress that he had relied on in the past. He informed lawmakers of his work in shaping the treaty, but he did not engage in genuine consultation or negotiation. As it became clear in late summer that the treaty was in trouble in the Senate, the president turned to a familiar strategy of a speaking tour to arouse public opinion and sway undecided senators. While observers doubted that his approach would change many minds, Wilson embarked on an exhausting cross-country trip in September 1919. His comments did not sway senators and may have cost him some votes in that arena. The illness that he suffered, followed by his crippling stroke, prevented any conclusive judgment on the effectiveness of the president's attempts. The tone of Wilson's speeches before his collapse did not suggest that many opposing senators would have been moved to change their votes.[57]

Following the failure of his health, Wilson refused to compromise on the League, and the Senate rejected the pact, first in November 1919 and in a revised form in March 1920. The failure of the United States to enter the League was largely blamed on Wilson's intransigence toward the Republicans in

Congress. As one Democrat put it, "The Wilson League of Nations is about the most effective millstone that any party, bent on suicide, has tied about its neck to date."[58]

Wilson's second term thus ended with a rejection of his leadership, as the president lay an invalid in the White House. Compounding the negative impact on the presidency was the manner in which Wilson's health problems were handled. His wife and his doctor, Cary T. Grayson, released as little information to the press about the president's condition as they could. Their tactics amounted to a cover-up of Wilson's much reduced capacity to govern the nation effectively. Gossip circulated about the president's mental condition and rumors held that Mrs. Wilson was almost the real chief executive of the country.[59]

As a result of the deceit of Wilson's entourage, public confidence in his presidency receded during 1920. The White House, closed since the beginning of the war in April 1917, seemed an aloof and forbidding place. So detached from reality had Wilson become that he made an abortive effort to secure a third nomination from the Democrats in spring 1920. If the Democrats needed him, he told friends, he would "accept the nomination even if I thought it would cost me my life." The Democrats did not adopt such a suicidal course and chose James M. Cox of Ohio instead, naming Franklin D. Roosevelt as his running mate. By October 1920, as the Democrats lurched toward defeat, the secretary of the interior, Franklin K. Lane, said that "Wilson is as unpopular as he once was popular."[60]

The theme of unhappiness with presidential power ran through the Republican campaign for the White House. "We undertake to end executive autocracy," the GOP platform declared, and "restore to the people their constitutional government." The drafters of the document further complained that Wilson "clings tenaciously to his autocratic wartime powers." In his keynote address to the national convention, Henry Cabot Lodge said, "Mr. Wilson stands for a theory of administration and government which is not American." The Kansas editor William Allen White recalled the ebbing of popular interest in presidential activism. "After eight years of Wilson and the four short years of breathing space with Taft before Wilson, and seven years of Roosevelt," the nation was "tired of issues, sick at heart of ideals and weary of being noble."[61]

The voters went to the polls on 20 November and swept Warren G. Harding into office with nearly 61 percent of the vote. After eight years in power under

Wilson, the Democrats had been decisively rejected. In the repudiation of Wilson also lay a rejection of the strong presidency that he and Theodore Roosevelt had embodied. A British journalist caught the changed mood of the country toward the presidency: "The healthy influence of Theodore Roosevelt so noticeable a decade ago has died down after a period of ineffective leadership which is now to be succeeded by a Government of self-interest." As Wilson left office, the editors of the *Outlook* wrote, "History will soften the verdict rendered by the votes last November on the Administration of Woodrow Wilson, but is not likely to reverse it."[62]

History proved kinder to Wilson than the contemporary assessments of March 1921. His domestic programs foreshadowed aspects of the New Deal, just as his foreign policies seemed prescient after the rise of the dictators in the 1930s. His institutional breakthroughs — addressing Congress in person, regular press conferences for a time, and speaking tours to advance policy programs — became staples of future presidencies. Political failure faded and presidential innovation remained as Wilson's legacy. Vindication did not come, however, until the nation faced another economic crisis as ominous as World War I. Until then, three Republican presidents turned away from the Wilsonian example in public and yet made their own contributions to the modern presidency, away from the glare of the national spotlight.

3

The Modern Presidency Recedes
Warren G. Harding, Calvin Coolidge, & Herbert Hoover

The election of Warren G. Harding in 1920 began twelve years of Republican control of the presidency. Harding and his two successors, Calvin Coolidge and Herbert Hoover, are not usually associated with the emergence of the modern presidency. Instead, they are regarded as conservatives who failed to use the powers of the institution in the forceful manner of Franklin D. Roosevelt during the New Deal. Indeed, their performances are usually seen as actual detriments to the forward progress of the president. As a result, they rarely appear as significant actors in the evolution of the institution except in a negative sense.

Yet lumping these three presidents together obscures each man's contribution to the evolution of the modern presidency before 1933. Under Harding, the president began to have a defined role in the budget process as a consequence of the enactment of the Budget Act of 1921. With Harding's employment of the first speechwriter in the person of the longtime Washington reporter Judson Welliver in 1921, the capacity of the chief executive to communicate his views and to fulfill the ceremonial roles of his position would be permanently enhanced. Though seemingly dour and taciturn, Calvin Coolidge used the new reach of the mass media and the glamour of his wife, Grace Coolidge, to ensure his election in 1924 and then to popularize his presidency. Herbert Hoover expanded the White House staff in a formal way and established other institutional changes to make the presidency more efficient. The depression and the failure of his administration overshadowed the changes that he made. Though the activism of these three men in policy areas varied, each one contributed in interesting ways to the inner history of the presidency.

Each of these three presidents also illustrated the declining role of political parties in the selection of a president and the increasing need to accommodate the mass media in the process of governance. Harding's designation as the Republican presidential nominee in 1920 was not the result of the dictates of senatorial party bosses or machinations in a smoke-filled room. He emerged from a crowded field as a candidate who could be presented to the voters in a way that maximized the use of the instruments of publicity. Following Harding's death, Coolidge inherited the mechanisms of the Republican party, which he easily adapted to his own purposes despite having no real base in the Grand Old Party. Even Herbert Hoover was viewed with suspicion by party regulars because of his progressive background and service in the Wilson administration. His electoral appeal in 1928 overcame these doubts.

The relative success or failure of the Republican presidents also depended to an ever larger extent on their capacity to master the increasingly important mass media in the 1920s. Building on the techniques used in his campaign, Harding relied on the film industry and major newspapers to project a sense of an open, accessible administration after the seclusion of Wilson's second term. Calvin Coolidge was the most adept of the three men in his use of press agentry and image making to create popular support for his programs. In contrast, Herbert Hoover's impressive capacity to manage the press as secretary of commerce and as a presidential candidate deserted him once he was in the White House. Hoover returned to the style of Taft and Wilson, which separated governing from campaigning. It proved a terrible mistake in the midst of the Great Depression.

When Warren G. Harding came into office in March 1921, the desire for a simpler and more open president after Woodrow Wilson's academic aloofness ran across the political spectrum. The left-wing journal the *Nation* applauded Harding's request for an inauguration without a ball and an elaborate parade. They also praised his return to "American methods of government." Where Wilson had been so formal and distant to visitors whose advice he did not want or need, Harding would restore "the historical tradition of an accessible president." Other newspapers praised his willingness to recapture the simpler style of presidential behavior and to return to the concept of the first citizen in the White House.[1]

As president-elect in November 1920, Warren G. Harding attracted news coverage
even on a fishing trip to South Texas. Pathe News provided pictures of the recreation
of the soon-to-be president. (From the Robert Runyon Collection, courtesy of the
Center for American History, University of Texas at Austin.)

Harding has not fared well at the hands of presidential historians, who
generally depict him as a genial boob who was in over his head in the White
House. Nonetheless, his election as president in 1920 had not been an electoral fluke. A newspaper editor from Ohio and a staunch Republican regular, Harding had served one term in the U.S. Senate after 1914 without any
particular distinction in terms of legislation or influence with his colleagues.
Yet these same mediocre qualities helped make him an attractive presidential hopeful when the party's front-runners deadlocked at the national convention: Leonard Wood and Frank O. Lowden canceled each other out in the
race for the nomination.

In a year when the Republicans were certain of victory, Harding came from a key midwestern state, was well liked throughout the party, and campaigned with slogans such as a promise of a return to older values, which appealed to an electorate weary of Wilsonian reform and the higher taxes that went with social change. These attributes helped Harding secure the nomination when the Republicans met in Chicago in June 1920. He was, said one party regular, the "best of the second-raters" that Republicans had to offer. On the campaign trail, Harding's pledge of "normalcy" and an end to "nostrums" struck a responsive chord with the voters. The candidate's intellectual weaknesses and personal indiscretions did not play any role in the outcome of the presidential contest. Harding was not Woodrow Wilson, and in 1920 that was all that mattered to the American electorate. That he would not be an active executive in the White House added to his allure as a presidential candidate.[2]

The new president and his wife, Florence Kling Harding, threw open the White House to guests and tourists. On the first day, guards were removed, the public circulated more freely on the grounds, and Mrs. Harding greeted some of the tourists personally. The new First Lady made sure that reporters were able to record what she did and what she said, to feed public interest about the new occupants of the White House. After the forbidding Executive Mansion of the second Wilson term, the Hardings were a welcome change in Washington. When a maid began pulling curtains so that the public crowds could not see inside the mansion on 4 March 1921, Florence Harding said, "Let 'em look in if they want. It's their White House!"[3]

The fresh spirit of the early days of the Harding administration did not mask the daunting problems that had been inherited from Woodrow Wilson. It was, said a Republican newspaper, "the biggest task that ever fell to the lot of a new Administration." Another editor said that Harding faced "the most appalling mess." On the domestic scene, chronic unemployment, mounting inflation, and the spiraling cost of government vied for attention. Overseas, the failure of the United States to join the League of Nations meant that the country was still technically at war with Germany and its allies. Labor unrest, rising immigration, and the emergence of such organizations as the Ku Klux Klan illustrated the volatility of the period.[4]

To deal with these problems, Harding relied on his cabinet, composed of what the president called "the best minds" he could enlist to serve the government. These included Charles Evans Hughes as secretary of state, Herbert

Hoover as secretary of commerce, and the financier, Andrew Mellon, as secretary of the treasury. The other members of the official family were less talented, as time would show. Harry Daugherty at the Justice Department and Albert B. Fall at Interior would be the most notable failures. As president, Harding gave his cabinet officers wide latitude to run their departments in his brief presidency. The White House did not at first endeavor to shape policy directly throughout the government.

The new president continued the practice of having a single secretary, George Christian, who oversaw White House operations. Christian had been a neighbor of the Hardings in their hometown of Marion, Ohio, and Harding had brought him to Washington to serve as his private secretary in the Senate. To help Christian, Harding added Charles Hard, one of the campaign speechwriters, as an assistant.

Harding resumed the practice of regular press conferences that Woodrow Wilson had abandoned and did so in a much more congenial spirit than his predecessor had displayed. The ground rules of not quoting the president directly were still in effect, but otherwise these sessions went well. Harding considered the questions that the fifty or so newsmen put to him twice weekly. The president, said one journalist, "knows what is news and has an attractive way of communicating it to the press."[5]

Harding's openness produced problems when his impulse for candor got the better of his presidential discretion. In December 1921 the president revealed an aspect of the negotiations at the Washington Disarmament Conference that should have been kept secret, in response to a question from a reporter. A diplomatic embarrassment ensued. After that gaffe, the White House insisted that all questions be submitted in writing in advance. Nonetheless, the reporters liked Harding and did not try to embarrass him. They also did not reveal to the public any of the president's alleged sexual indiscretions or his disregard for the prohibition laws when he entertained friends at the White House.[6]

The Harding administration also saw an enhanced use of the mass media to publicize the institution. Harding posed for countless still and newspaper photographers in many informal settings. Taft and Wilson had resisted such requests. Florence Harding was even more energetic in setting up human-interest moments for the eager press. The interest in having photographic images of the first family grew to such an extent that the White House News Photographers Association was created.[7]

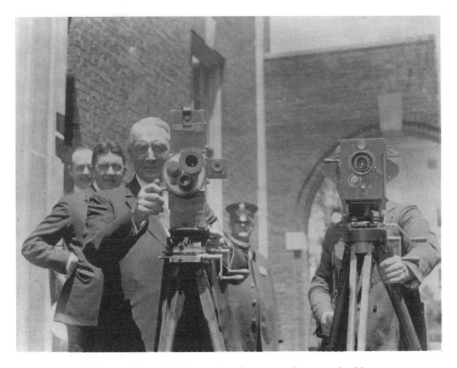

By the onset of the Harding administration, the newsreel camera had become an indispensable part of following the activities of the president. Warren G. Harding poses with one here. (Courtesy of the Library of Congress.)

Another significant change of the Harding years produced a transformation in how the presidency operated. Though previous chief executives had often drawn on friends and political allies for speech ideas in individual cases, the usual custom had been for the president to prepare his own speeches. Roosevelt, Taft, and Wilson had by and large written their own public comments or used a basic text with a few variations for particular audiences. By 1920, however, the number of presidential speaking occasions was increasing as news coverage of the White House became more intense. Preparing remarks for every minor occasion was becoming a major drain on the president's time. Though he was a former newspaper editor, Harding did not find such textual work congenial, and he labored for prolonged periods over major addresses. Having had speeches written for him during

The first official speechwriter, Judson Welliver, shaped words for Warren G. Harding and then for Calvin Coolidge. He was pictured himself in the American Monthly Review of Reviews *(September 1925), from which this photograph was taken.*

the 1920 campaign, he naturally looked to that practice when he thought about having a similar resource available to him in the White House.

The man he selected was a former Iowa journalist, Judson Welliver, who had drafted speeches and managed campaign ideas for Harding in 1920. Welliver was forty-nine years old and had been a familiar face on the Washington scene since the presidency of Theodore Roosevelt. He had many friends in the influential Iowa Republican delegation. Roosevelt had sent him abroad on one fact-finding commission, and Welliver had been generally sympathetic to political reform after 1909. In 1912 he had supported the Progressive party but had not entirely abandoned his Republican roots. After working for several newspapers during the Wilson years, he joined the Harding campaign as one of a number of speechwriters. He relished hardball tactics and crafted devastating attacks on Harding's opponent, Governor James M. Cox of Ohio. He stayed on as a presidential speechwriter with the titles of literary clerk and special employee at a lucrative salary of seventy-five hundred dollars per year.[8]

Welliver has gained a modest degree of posthumous fame because of the creation of the modern Judson Welliver Society, an organization of former White House speechwriters founded by William Safire. Just how much actual speechwriting Welliver did for the president remains unclear. One Harding biographer suggests that his work consisted of composing brief remarks for the president to give on ceremonial occasions while Harding himself continued to write the major addresses of his presidency. For these formal comments, the president would give Welliver a sense of what he wished to say and then left him alone to provide the final product. In any event, Welliver served through the entire Harding presidency and carried on for two years of Calvin Coolidge's term as well. His duties included political work for the White House, and he had good contacts within the business community.[9]

The employment of Welliver and the turn to speechwriting for the president was a necessary step to meet the mounting demands on the time and energy of the chief executive. At the same time, it also put the occupant of the White House at a remove from the words he said. Although gifted speechwriters could impart eloquence to a presidential statement, in the future most of what presidents said would be the product of the minds of others. Presidents relinquished some part of the mental discipline of thinking through an issue for themselves and deciding how best to make a case for a particular policy in exchange for the convenience of having packaged speeches readily available.

The Harding presidency has not been noted for its substantive accomplishments but for its record of scandal and corruption. The wrongdoing in the Veterans Bureau and the Justice Department, not to mention the Teapot Dome affair, has cast a permanent cloud over the president's record. Though Harding bears responsibility for these ethical lapses in that they happened during his administration, he was not personally involved in any of the misdeeds. Too trusting by nature and surrounded by what he once called "my god-damned friends," he failed to set the firm tone of honesty that the presidency required.[10]

In terms of the evolution of the presidency, however, the tawdry aspects of the Harding years are less significant than the way the White House resumed the organizational initiatives launched under William Howard Taft and the Cleveland commission. The key achievement in this regard was the creation of the Bureau of the Budget in 1921 through passage of the Budget and Accounting Act. The roots of this measure went back to the Taft years, and the Republicans had made the argument for budget legislation during the Wilson era as the deficits from fighting World War I accumulated. The need for budget procedures had been an important Republican theme in the

1918 congressional elections that had returned the party to control of the legislative branch. The Republican platform in 1920 called for an executive budget "as a necessary instrument for sound and business-like administration of the national finances."[11]

The Republican Congress enacted such a measure in 1920, but President Wilson vetoed it because it infringed on his power to remove the comptroller general, who would administer the budget process. With a Republican administration in office, Congress passed the bill once again, and President Harding signed it into law. The new bureau was located in the Treasury Department, but it reported directly to the president. This arrangement was awkward and would limit the effectiveness of the new bureau for some years. Nonetheless, as one contemporary observer noted, the "executive budget does enormously increase the control of the executive over the entire government, because it makes the executive, and not the legislative, the policy-determining organ."[12]

The director of the Bureau of the Budget was Charles G. Dawes, who was president of a Chicago bank. More important, as a young man Dawes had raised funds for the McKinley campaign in 1896 and had served in that administration as comptroller of the currency. The desire for orderly government that McKinley and Cortelyou had advanced came naturally to Dawes in his new job. A friendly reporter put Dawes's view of the task into print: "Our Presidents as general managers of the biggest business in the world have heretofore, in matters of administration, been doing too little."[13]

The Bureau of the Budget was only the first step in a program of executive reorganization that got under way during the brief Harding administration. The new president wanted to see a Department of Public Welfare and a Department of Public Works emerge from changes in the structure of the federal government. Congress had created a Joint Committee on Reorganization in December 1920, and Harding had asked to have a presidential representative on the panel. When that request was agreed to, Harding named a progressive Republican from his home state, Walter F. Brown. As the key White House aide for reorganization, Brown and the head of the Bureau of Efficiency in the Civil Service Commission, Herbert F. Brown (no relation), created a document for the Harding cabinet that outlined the existing institutional weakness of the presidency:

The President's staff consists wholly of a small number of personal secretaries and clerks. The time of the staff is taken up with the consideration of legislative business, the preparation of commissions, appointment matters, and so on. Under these conditions the President . . . is unable to function as an administrative officer.[14]

Helping the two Browns in their reorganizing impulse was Secretary of Commerce Herbert Hoover, who actively sought greater power for the presidency. Within the administration, an ambitious reorganization campaign evolved during 1921 and 1922. Under the proposed changes, Hoover's Commerce Department would have been a big winner in terms of gaining power after agencies were shuffled around. Harding also envisioned a union of the Navy and War Departments into a Department of Defense and the creation of an Education and Welfare Department.[15]

When these proposals were submitted to the cabinet in early 1922, infighting within the administration broke out and continued for most of the year as officials sought to protect their particular turf. Nonetheless, the president persuaded his cabinet officials to approve the reorganization proposal in mid-December 1922. Republican losses in the congressional elections a month earlier imparted a greater sense of urgency to accomplish reorganization from the White House. The new plan then went to the Joint Committee on Reorganization early in 1923. The legislation would strengthen presidential power by moving the Bureau of the Budget to the White House and shifting the General Accounting Office from Congress to the Treasury Department. Further, departments would be reorganized according to the programmatic purposes they served. Moreover, the president would receive ongoing authority to set in motion other reorganization procedures in the future as he saw fit.[16]

The Harding plan went to Congress in early 1923 with an uncertain future ahead. To push these changes through would have taken sustained presidential leadership. Whether Harding was up to that task remained problematic, but the president's sudden death from a heart attack in August 1923 rendered the issue moot. His successor, Calvin Coolidge, had little interest in executive reorganization, and the Harding plan was shelved.

Given Harding's mediocre record in other aspects of his administration, it is questionable whether he would have pushed effectively for the changes in the presidency that the reorganization plan contemplated. In any case, the scandals of his presidency and his administrative ineptitude as a leader have received more attention. Harding slipped into the ranks of failed chief executives, and the prestige of his office suffered as a consequence. It did not fare much better under his successor, Calvin Coolidge. As a result, Coolidge's ability to capitalize on the publicity resources available to twentieth-century presidents was also overshadowed. Yet both men pointed the way toward the practices and procedures that shaped the modern presidency.

Because of his well-cultivated reputation as a dour, taciturn New Englander, Calvin Coolidge's adept use of the mass media in the White House has not been regarded as part of the evolution of the modern presidency. Like Harding and Hoover, Coolidge has been viewed as a foil for the more charismatic Franklin D. Roosevelt. Anecdotes abound regarding Coolidge's passivity in the White House and his reluctance to advance legislative initiatives during the Roaring Twenties. Yet a review of his presidency indicates that what a later generation would call spin was a well-developed technique during the 1920s. Constant attention to the management of the press developed as one of the hallmarks of the Coolidge years, and most of the strategies that the president employed would be seen as innovations when they reappeared between 1933 and the end of the twentieth century.

John Calvin Coolidge had just turned fifty-one on 4 July 1923, a month before the death of Warren G. Harding thrust him into the presidency. On his way up through Massachusetts politics between 1906 and 1919, Coolidge showed a mastery of the system and a skill at creating a pleasing public image. He burst on the national scene as governor of Massachusetts during the Boston Police Strike in 1919, when he told Samuel Gompers of the American Federation of Labor in a public letter that "there is no right to strike against the public safety by anybody, anywhere, anytime." Yet even this personal touch was probably the result of artful crafting from one of the governor's informal speechwriters. According to a well-informed Massachusetts reporter, Robert Lincoln O'Brien, Coolidge was already relying on Attorney General Henry A. Wyman. The words Wyman wrote "sounded good" to Coolidge, and "he finally issued them under his name." Two or three other ghostwriters worked for Coolidge during his vice presidency.[17]

When he took over from Harding, Coolidge did not do much to change the organizational structure of the White House as he found it. He replaced Harding's secretary with a former Virginia congressman, C. Bascom Slemp, and he retained Judson Welliver as a speechwriter for two years. In his commitment to Republican ideology, Coolidge was more of a conservative than Harding had been, and he lacked any of his predecessor's interest in reshaping the federal government along more efficient lines. The new president wanted an honest administration that helped business and lowered taxes, and he saw no need to innovate in organizing the presidency. He recognized that a supportive and kindly press would be of significant assistance in accomplishing his goals. In the process, the press would further his plans to be elected in his own right in November 1924.[18]

To win the Republican nomination, Coolidge had to manage the delicate feat of distinguishing himself from Harding without repudiating the policies of his predecessor. He did so by gradually easing out lackluster Harding appointees, such as Attorney General Harry Daugherty, and distancing himself from the emerging scandals of the previous administration, such as Teapot Dome over oil reserves in the West. Part of the reason that Coolidge cultivated his image as a frugal, terse New Englander was to emphasize the contrast with Harding's rather raffish personal style in the White House. The press readily fell in with the new president's persona.[19]

Coolidge did not plan on being an activist president. To a significant degree, he represented a conservatism that wanted to reverse or mute the impact of the progressive changes that had occurred since the turn of the century. Though Harding was no advocate of political or social reform, he had addressed racial issues in a cautious way, and his reorganization plans would have reshaped the federal government in the interests of efficiency. In contrast, Coolidge had little interest in using the power of the presidency to advance a social agenda. Thus his only major contribution to the development of the modern presidency came in the area of public relations. There he elaborated on what Harding had done and pushed forward with press manipulation in notable ways.

The White House correspondents who had liked Harding wanted to work in a cooperative fashion with Coolidge. From the outset, the new president did his best to accommodate the journalists. He continued the practice of regular news conferences and even increased them over the number that Harding had held. Coolidge held five hundred and twenty press conferences during the sixty-seven months of his presidency, or an average of eight such gatherings per month. In the era before radio and television, these occasions were much easier to stage. The correspondents simply came into the

Calvin Coolidge paid close attention to press relations. Here he lays a cornerstone for the building of the National Press Club in 1929. (Courtesy of the Library of Congress.)

president's office and listened to what Coolidge had to say. To a significant degree, he made the press conference a Washington institution that future presidents could not repudiate.[20]

In these regular meetings, Coolidge was much more outgoing and detailed in his remarks than his popular image as a tight-lipped executive suggested. He took into the session only those written questions he intended to answer, but he made sure that he provided enough substance in his responses so that the reporters could build effective stories around what he had said. The practice of not quoting the president directly was still in force, though the attribution of remarks to a "presidential spokesman" was a fiction that everyone recognized as a clumsy and obsolete artifice. Frederick Essary of a Baltimore newspaper, who covered Coolidge's first meeting with reporters, said that the president "was communicative almost to the point of garrulousness. And he has been since." Essary conceded that Coolidge was "not particularly pointed in imparting actual information, but he is far from reserved."[21]

One contemporary analyst said that Coolidge's attitude toward the press embodied "either an extraordinary design or a monumental ingenuousness." Given the amount of attention to the press that is evident in Coolidge's presidential papers, it seems logical to recognize that the president knew just what he was doing. His policies might have looked back to a more conservative nation, but in his management of the press Coolidge and his aides exceeded even Theodore Roosevelt and Harding in their careful wooing of reporters and sensitivity to their journalistic needs.[22]

Although the press was eager to see Coolidge succeed in 1923, any slips could have disrupted the carefully crafted relationship and produced a difficult situation such as Taft and Wilson had confronted. The White House went out of its way to treat reporters in a manner that involved them in the working of the new administration. Coolidge endorsed the presence of the White House Correspondents Association and made sure that friendly reporters knew that he would see them alone without any trouble when they had specific questions. The president's staff spent a great deal of time ensuring that copies of key speeches were available in advance to the press while also cracking down on newspapers that violated the release deadlines.[23]

Coolidge was eager to cooperate with reporters when he traveled around the country. The size of the press entourage that accompanied him on his summer vacations during the 1920s swelled until it included thirty or so correspondents, along with motion picture and still photographers. One commentator labeled Coolidge "the most photographed man who ever occupied the White House." The president did his best to see that the correspondents were treated well on these junkets and invited them and their spouses to social occasions.[24]

By the time Coolidge took office in August 1923, the rise of the mass media provided presidents with the means to project their personalities to the American people without relying exclusively on newspapers. Previous twentieth-century presidents had done so within the limits of the motion picture camera and radio before 1920. As Harding showed in his campaign and presidency, it was now possible to make the chief executive a media celebrity on a new and more elaborate scale. Coolidge did more to exploit these possibilities as the 1920s progressed.[25]

One vehicle was radio, and Coolidge went on the air frequently. The new medium suited his voice, which was not that of the old-style orator who had to reach the back of the hall without amplification. His secretary, C. Bascom Slemp, made arrangements to have radio stations broadcast Coolidge's State of the Union messages. The president also allowed the stations to broadcast the Republican National Convention live in 1924, the first time that had happened. The president's acceptance speech, which came several weeks after the convention, was also carried live on radio. At the end of the campaign, Coolidge made another radio appearance to reach an audience that may have been as high as 20 million. Franklin D. Roosevelt's use of radio in the White House, justly praised by historians, built upon the precedents that Coolidge and later Herbert Hoover established.

Presidential involvement with show business was another area in which Coolidge pushed back the boundaries of acceptability. Acting at the suggestion of the advertising executive Edward L. Bernays, Coolidge in 1924 held a White House breakfast with a group of actors to achieve what Bernays called "nationwide front-page publicity." The performers, led by Al Jolson, had their meal with the Coolidges. The group then gathered on the White House lawn while Jolson and Grace Coolidge led them in singing the president's campaign song, "Keep Coolidge."[26]

Although Wilson and Harding had both seen movies at the White House, Coolidge was a devotee of the new popular art. Films were shown on the presidential yacht, the *Mayflower,* and at the various summer retreats of the Coolidges. At the White House *The Big Parade* was screened, complete with a forty-four-piece orchestra imported from New York. Meanwhile, the aura of such White House visitors as Mary Pickford and Ramon Novarro rubbed off on Coolidge. With his usual shrewdness, the president created a film persona that made him as recognizable a figure in the nation's theaters as the film celebrities with whom he consorted.[27]

In return for this access to stars, Coolidge helped movie lobbyist Will H. Hays stave off efforts to censor motion pictures for their excessive sex and violence. In 1923 Coolidge said that "the possibilities of the motion picture are just being realized." The White House issued a statement in 1926 that the president recognized that "the character of the films has improved and he now hears very little complaint about them." Both Coolidge and Hollywood understood that they could be mutually helpful to each other. That relationship would emerge as a significant aspect of the modern presidency as the movies and later television pervaded American life.[28]

Another key element in Coolidge's careful campaign to control his personal image was his use of his wife, Grace, as a foil to his dour public persona. Will Rogers said that she was "chuck plumb full of magnetism." The stylish, well-dressed First Lady was not allowed to have a public role or to speak out on issues. But she was active in parades, ceremonial occasions, and movie premieres. As Florence Harding had done, she greeted groups at the White House, but she expanded the number of those occasions. Mrs. Coolidge also held musicales at the White House at which such artists as John McCormack and Sergei Rachmaninoff performed. From Christmas carols on the White House lawn to pushing a button to open the Women's World's Fair in Chicago in 1925, Grace Coolidge served the celebrity purposes of her husband's presidency with efficiency and skill.[29]

The Coolidges found that, despite the renovations that had been made in the White House itself two decades earlier under Theodore Roosevelt, the mansion was once again in desperate need of repair. The renovations made in 1902 had not been constructed with care; subsequent additions had increased the stress on the building's attic and upper floors. From mid-March 1927 through early September, the president and his wife moved out and the work proceeded. For the moment, the White House had been preserved, but within twenty years its physical condition and its capacity to serve modern presidents would again become a subject of concern.

Later presidents put the public relations aspects of their office at the service of their political and policy agendas. Simply because Calvin Coolidge was a more passive chief executive does not mean that his attention to the media details did not abet a larger purpose, however negative its goals may have been. To the extent that his handling of the press, movies, and radio succeeded, they sustained his personal popularity. That, in turn, allowed him to pursue his conservative ends without a large degree of controversy. One reason that Coolidge has faded from historical memory to the extent he has stems from his adroit use of the mechanisms of celebrity then available to a president. Once these instruments became technologically outmoded, his image making seemed obsolete as well.

Calvin Coolidge was not an admirer of the Republican who succeeded him in the White House. "That man has offered me unsolicited advice for six years, all of it bad!" Coolidge said in 1928 to a member of his cabinet about Herbert Hoover. Part of the president's displeasure with Hoover arose from the latter's restless activism and involvement with policy issues, many of them outside his area of responsibility as the secretary of commerce. Hoover brought many of the same qualities to the White House, but his failure to deal with the Great Depression has obscured the degree to which he sought to be a modern president himself.[30]

Hoover's reputation as the last of the premodern presidents is largely a function of his political failure and the fact that Franklin D. Roosevelt succeeded him. Examination of Hoover's efforts to reform the presidency along the lines that had been developing since the McKinley-Roosevelt era indicates that he had as ambitious an agenda for institutional change as anyone could have wished. A broadened staff, a wider array of issues to be addressed, activism at home and abroad — such were the goals that Hoover sought to implement before the Great Depression overtook his plans. The old debate about the relative degree of continuity between Hoover and Roosevelt in their economic answers to the hard times could be applied equally to how they engaged the task of being president. That Hoover lacked the attractive personality and vast political skills of Roosevelt is evident. All of this suggests that in the presidency, modernity is important, but it is far from everything.

Herbert Hoover had been an activist all his adult life. Born in 1874 and orphaned as a child, he had worked his way through Stanford as a member of that university's first class. After graduation in 1895, he embarked on a successful career in mining. By the time he was forty, he had earned enough money to enable him to devote the rest of his life to public service. He made a reputation in providing relief to starving Belgians between 1914 and 1917, as director of the Food Administration in World War I, and as secretary of commerce under Harding and Coolidge. In these roles and especially in the cabinet, he had reached out to gather more responsibilities for his department and executive leadership. He believed that his management skills and professional knowledge of how to make institutions work suited him for the many tasks he pursued. In the 1920s his deft performance won accolades from public and press, an approval that he often evoked through management of public relations and self-created publicity for his work.[31]

Hoover was the natural choice for the Republicans after Coolidge said in 1927 that he did not choose to run for a second full term in 1928. Though Coolidge was not thrilled that his party had selected "the boy wonder" to be his successor, Hoover had a strong appeal to the electorate at a time when

"General Prosperity was on my side." The candidate even promised that the nation might be "in sight of the day when poverty will be banished from this nation." If any president could realize such a lofty goal, it seemed to be Hoover, who had succeeded at everything he undertook. Once he won the presidency in 1928 over Al Smith, it was natural for him to assume that he could run the White House with the same efficiency and success that he had displayed in so many other roles. Expectations were high that the Great Engineer could manage the presidency with productivity and beneficial results.[32]

Some changes in how the presidency operated clearly would be necessary to fulfill the assignment the American people had asked him to discharge. One long-overdue reform was to expand the size of the staff that served the presidency. No longer could a president rely on a single key staff member, even one as skilled and efficient as George B. Cortelyou had been. Hoover asked Congress to give him an additional two secretaries and an administrative assistant in 1929, and lawmakers readily complied. As one favorable press account of the new administration put it, Hoover "proceeds precisely as an engineer or an efficiency expert would in attacking a complicated job."[33]

Though Hoover's change represented a small but important step toward providing the president with a larger staff, it was not in and of itself the key to a more productive White House. Like other presidents who followed him, he designed the staff hierarchy more for his personal convenience and loyalty than for clear administrative arrangements. The initial organizational scheme reflected his penchant for clarity and designated areas of responsibility. As time progressed, however, and the problems of the administration multiplied, the neat divisions among press secretaries and policy assistants broke down. Hoover did not designate anyone as a kind of chief of staff. Rivalries emerged for the president's favor. Backbiting and internecine leaking erupted as Hoover's standing with the public collapsed in 1931 and 1932.[34]

Hoover's presidency illustrated that no matter how modern the chief executive was in the specific staff arrangements that were laid out at the beginning of an administration, they were no better than the political skills of the president himself and the individuals who served him. Hoover erred in assuming that an inherently political position could be carried out in a nonpartisan manner, especially at a time of the deepest economic crisis the United States had yet confronted.

As presidents emerged as political celebrities, the creation of attractive photo opportunities became a staple part of their daily routine. Here President Hoover welcomes Children of the American Revolution to the White House on 21 April 1932. (Courtesy of the Library of Congress.)

One area where Hoover expected to excel in the presidency was in his relations with the Washington press. Ever since his return to the United States from his relief work in Europe, he had enjoyed a harmonious connection with reporters. In the Department of Commerce from 1921 to 1929, Hoover and his aides flooded newsmen with press releases, official publications, photo opportunities, and the appearance of access. In moments of crisis, such as the Mississippi flood of 1927, Hoover took to the radio to explain to Americans how relief efforts were going forward. Hoover himself held twice-weekly press conferences that led one correspondent to conclude, "He was the best 'grapevine' in Washington, and a perfect gold mine of 'graveyard stuff.'"[35]

Both the president and the First Lady were willing to employ modern technology to get their message across. The usual view that reliance on radio as a way of selling presidential programs began with the Roosevelts is incorrect. President Hoover permitted radio to cover his speeches once a month, and in that format he gave seventy to eighty radio addresses in all. Yet because of his inability to connect with his audiences, the speeches were far from effective in making his case. Lou Hoover herself appeared up to a dozen times on the radio in an effort to sell her programs of voluntarism as an answer to the misery of the depression. On the whole, she enjoyed a better reception from her listeners than did her husband. Hoover did not grasp how a president could use the radio to make a personal connection with the American people. When a newspaperman told Hoover "to get on the radio and talk to the nation," he could "tell by the expression on his face that it was not the kind of role he liked to play."[36]

By the time Hoover took office as president in March 1929, however, the nature of the press corps that covered the chief executive had begun to change. Greater specialization and professionalism made the White House reporters more intent on having the ability to question the president and discover the facts about policy making and political infighting within an administration. For someone who was attuned to social changes and the development of the mass media in the 1920s, Hoover proved to be out of touch with the way the White House press contingent had been evolving under Harding and Coolidge.[37]

Hoover got off to a promising start with the newsmen in 1929. He named one of his new aides, George Akerson, as his designated press secretary. The new president also liberalized the rules about quoting the chief executive directly. In ways that harked back to the techniques of William McKinley and George B. Cortelyou, Hoover showed up at the Gridiron dinner and otherwise cultivated publishers and reporters. He held seventy-nine press conferences during his first year in office. Perhaps most important for the White House scribes, the new administration upgraded the press room so that each reporter could have an individual desk and a typewriter.[38]

This initial honeymoon did not last. Hoover had no intention of sharing real news with the correspondents, and his press conferences, while frequent, were rarely productive of useful stories. The Hoovers closed off their private lives to the media. Bess Furman, a Washington reporter, disguised herself as a Girl Scout to attend one of Mrs. Hoover's Christmas events and thus penetrated the aura of secrecy that surrounded the first family. Once the depression began, the White House again assumed some of the aloofness that had marked Woodrow Wilson's second term.[39]

Above all, Hoover, despite his mastery of the technical aspects of media coverage, had not learned or would not accept the new, informal rules of presidential–press interaction. He resented personal interest stories, chafed at perceived slights and inaccuracies in news reports, and played favorites among the reporters. As one newspaperman wrote in 1931, Hoover's "incredible sensitiveness to unfavorable publicity arises from a peculiar but not illogical cause. Knowing that the newspapers made him, he assumes they can with equal ease destroy him. In this he is mistaken."[40]

Hoover implemented other presidential practices that historians would later hail as evidence of modern techniques in his successors. He relied on academic and professional experts in a series of commissions to investigate social problems in the United States, including modern social trends and the thorny issue of prohibition enforcement. The president had plans for similar panels to address other questions involving the nation's future. After six months in office, in mid-September 1929, one newspaper noted that "Washington is a center of news these days" because "a quick-witted and aggressive Executive is plainly on the job." Many plans were under way for a productive administration when the stock market crashed later in the month.[41]

Following the crash and for reasons more complicated than just the decline in stock prices, the Great Depression fastened itself on the United States. Despite his administrative talents and hard work, Herbert Hoover proved to be incapable of convincing the American people that he understood how the presidency could be a place of leadership in dealing with the crisis. The man whose energy and determination had brought food and relief to starving millions in Belgium and the Soviet Union during and after World War I could not summon up the same skills to alleviate the plight of his fellow Americans. He retreated into the White House, and his oft-repeated statements about the imminence of recovery failed to inspire confidence or a faith in the future. The devices of the modern presidency, some of which he had helped to develop, were there for him to use, but he held back from exploiting them to the full.

Embittered by the press, Hoover abandoned his efforts to influence reporters. He regarded Congress as an obstacle to recovery, not a potential partner in the enterprise of meeting the nation's needs. The lawmakers were parti-

Herbert Hoover preferred to make his speeches by radio when campaigning for president. He stands before a bank of microphones in his railroad car as he tries to keep his faltering hopes of reelection alive in 1932. (Courtesy of the Herbert Hoover Presidential Library-Museum.)

san and sometimes irresponsible, but they were the instruments available for a president to employ. Worried about what Congress might do to thwart his plans, he failed to regard that branch as a constitutionally necessary part of whatever program he devised to fight the depression. He also lacked the capacity to become what the occasion demanded, "a public man who could rise to the great crisis in a great way." Soon Hoover was the butt of jokes and unfair stories, which further wounded his spirit. For a man who had risen so quickly in politics and public life to almost universal acclaim, it was a shattering contrast.[42]

Despite his dedicated efforts to deal with the Great Depression, Hoover became a kind of modern-day Grover Cleveland, apparently out of touch with the misery that the American people were experiencing on a daily basis. He found the presidency a prison and a burden in 1931 and 1932, but he soldiered on doggedly at his task. He failed to understand what he had known during the 1920s: the modern presidency was as much about the appearance of being a leader as it was about the actual qualities that the executive displayed in office. A once productive alliance with the press turned into bitter hatred on the president's part, and the relationship turned sour permanently. An uncomprehending Hoover lived for thirty more years and never quite grasped why his efforts to advance the leadership abilities of the presidency had turned into such a personal humiliation for him and for his administration.

4

The Modern Presidency Revives and Grows
Franklin D. Roosevelt

When Franklin D. Roosevelt took office on 4 March 1933, the presidency was at another low point in its history. The American economy had reached the bottom of the Great Depression, with the failure of numerous banks and swelling unemployment rolls. Most important, a pervasive sense existed in the nation that the American economic system had broken down. Three years of hard times had tested the will of the people to endure adversity. The incoming First Lady, Eleanor Roosevelt, asked herself: "How much can people take without blowing up?"[1]

Bitterness between the new president and the outgoing administration marked the transition. During the interregnum between the election and the inauguration, Herbert Hoover wanted to induce Roosevelt to sign on to some of his economic policies to deal with the collapse of the banking system. Roosevelt resisted these entreaties to preserve his own freedom of action. As a result, the presidency seemed as immobilized as other American institutions when Roosevelt prepared to take the reins of power.[2]

Herbert Hoover had tried to wield the weapons of the chief executive during the depression, but his failings as a politician and a national leader had undercut his intentions. In the process, the office he held had diminished in both effectiveness and popular interest. He seemed almost removed from the crises, and William Allen White believed that Hoover would be "known as the greatest innocent bystander in history." Yet, as Roosevelt was to demonstrate during the New Deal, the inherent strength of the presidency during a crisis could produce a dramatic revival in the power and authority of the institution.[3]

One of the reigning clichés of presidential scholarship is that Franklin D. Roosevelt created the modern presidency between 1933 and 1945. According to one noted political scientist, Fred I. Greenstein, by 1945 "the presidency itself had undergone a fundamental transformation, replacing Congress as the principal energy source of the political system." Another scholar, James P. Pfiffner, contends that the period "marked the transformation of the presidency from a small personalized office to a collection of specialized bureaucracies with hundreds of professional staffers."[4]

Yet as some of these accounts recognize, the expansion of the presidency under Roosevelt did not come all at once or move in a straight, upward line. During the first six years, for example, Roosevelt's White House looked more like its twentieth-century predecessors than the massive bureaucracy of the contemporary White House. Roosevelt built on, improved, and synthesized the techniques of presidential governance that had been developing since the turn of the century, but in the substance of how he conducted his presidency he rarely went beyond them during his first term and a half. Even when he made institutional changes late in his second term, he never adopted formal bureaucratic structures or achieved organizational efficiency. The Roosevelt presidency looked backward as well as forward in its operations until his death in April 1945.[5]

The new president had not articulated a philosophy of executive leadership in systematic terms before he came to Washington. Such an effort would have been out of character for the pragmatic Roosevelt, who disliked committing himself to grand designs. Fifty-one years old in 1933, Franklin Delano Roosevelt was not a political thinker who believed in or ever developed a coherent philosophy of governance. He resisted such attempts as constraints on his freedom of action. Instead, he drew in an eclectic and effective manner on the various aspects of his own long experience in government.[6]

First, he was a Roosevelt, albeit from the Democratic side of the family, and he shared the activist temperament of Theodore Roosevelt, the uncle of his wife Eleanor. He called TR "the greatest man I ever knew," and he would later say to aides that he wanted to be a preaching president like his cousin. The path that Theodore Roosevelt had taken to the White House Franklin Roosevelt also pursued as assistant secretary of the navy, vice-presidential candidate in 1920, and then election as governor of New York in 1928. The example of vigorous leadership that TR offered during Franklin Roosevelt's formative years remained a powerful force in his memory in the 1930s.[7]

Yet he also recognized that Theodore Roosevelt, while a masterful leader of public opinion from 1901 to 1909, had sometimes provided too much of a good thing in his relations with the institutions of government. He had overdone the practice of submitting congressional messages to an unreceptive Congress, and he had waged too many public battles with opposing lawmakers. Franklin Roosevelt recognized, as TR had not, that a president had to select those occasions when he would confront Congress, and he was careful not to bore the American people with constant calls to action, as his relative had done.

Eight years in Woodrow Wilson's government as assistant secretary of the navy between 1913 and 1921 had given Roosevelt an ideal laboratory in which to test which techniques of presidential leadership had worked and which had failed. During World War I, he had noted the extent to which Wilson had become more imperious and less persuasive with Congress and the public as the demands of the conflict absorbed the president's limited energies. The results of Wilson's inattention to shifts in the popular mood were the election of a Republican Congress in 1918 and the repudiation of the Democrats in 1920 when Roosevelt was the party's vice presidential candidate.[8]

Just as Wilson's failed diplomacy toward the League of Nations influenced Roosevelt's treatment of similar international issues during World War II, the example of how Wilson had operated as a chief executive provided FDR with valuable guidelines for his own administration. The extent to which Wilson allowed himself to become isolated from his constituents and their concerns provided a warning sign to Roosevelt that he kept in mind during his first two terms.

Whether Roosevelt learned anything of use from observing the Republican presidencies of Warren G. Harding, Calvin Coolidge, and especially Herbert Hoover is difficult to determine. At first he demonstrated little interest in the executive reorganization that Harding's administration had advocated. No doubt he recognized that in more adept hands Coolidge's frequent press conferences could be an excellent means of shaping national opinion. And Hoover's inept employment of radio addresses offered Roosevelt a virtual primer on how the new media should not be employed. On the other hand, with someone who could wield radio with adroitness, it provided a personal means of interacting with citizens to the president's advantage. Above all, Roosevelt wanted to present an optimistic face to the voters, in contrast to Hoover's dour impressions during his presidency. Even when delivering bad news to the American people during World War II, Roosevelt always maintained his confident manner.

Two gubernatorial terms in Albany had also honed Roosevelt's approach to executive leadership. Working with a legislature to battle the onset of the depression and communicating with the population of a large and diverse state helped him develop the skills that he transferred to the White House. The hard fight for the Democratic nomination against Alfred E. Smith and others in 1932 gave him a strong sense of the various factions in his contentious party. His decision to fly to the Democratic National Convention in 1932 to deliver his acceptance speech in person attested to his willingness to depart from political customs and to innovate in the conduct of his office. He could have avoided the rigors of campaigning in 1932 since victory was virtually ensured, but he understood that, as an invalid, he had to demonstrate his physical capacity to do the job. Besides, he enjoyed the opportunity to show his positive sense of the nation's future on the stump to the adoring crowds.[9]

Roosevelt's physical condition produced immediate changes in the relationship of the president with his fellow citizens. Paralyzed from the waist down since he had contracted polio during summer 1921, the new president could not walk unaided and required a large entourage of support to move him from place to place during his daily routine. Trips and public appearances necessitated the staging of an event that rivaled the legitimate theater in its handling of the scenery and props. Although Roosevelt never denied that he had this disability, he and his handlers wanted to convey an image of strength and self-reliance about his personality and physical status. They therefore instituted procedures designed to mask the full extent of his illness and its effects from the public. With the complicity of the press corps, the White House created the first true bubble around the president to manage how his image was presented to the nation. Achieving that goal required a larger role for the Secret Service and careful presentation of each presidential event. That in turn necessitated manipulation of the news and the artful creation of what a later generation would call "photo opportunities."[10]

So well done was this operation that few Americans fully comprehended during Roosevelt's administration how disabled he really was in terms of movement and personal freedom. The American people saw him standing when he spoke to Congress or political conventions, and they had scant sense of the dogged physical commitment it took for him to carry off such moments. That such artifice enabled Roosevelt to govern effectively is beyond question. But with the willingness to bend reality for a perceived good cause came also the ability of other chief executives to shape appearances for their own less noble ends. If a large part of the modern presidency relates to the techniques of public relations and ballyhoo, then Franklin D. Roosevelt deserves recognition as a master of those arts. Yet he also must bear some responsibility for their misuse in his own administration and the precedents he provided for even greater masters of presidential illusion who followed him.

Under Roosevelt, the tradition of the New Year's Day public reception also ended. The Hoovers had not held one in January 1933, and the Roosevelts saw no reason to resume a custom that would have required that the president stand on his crutches for several hours. The alternative would have been for citizens of Washington to have seen Roosevelt in his wheelchair. That option made no political sense. The closing of the annual public reception was no doubt overdue, given the demands it imposed on the time and energy of presidents. Nonetheless, the change away from unfettered access to the chief executive represented one more step in the transformation of the president from a first citizen to a political leader set apart from the American people.[11]

One alteration in the White House that stemmed from Roosevelt's paralysis was the installation of a swimming pool in 1933. Funded primarily by the gifts of the people of New York and three other states, the pool was designed and built in less than three months. "This pool will be a big help to me, and it will be about the only air I can get," Roosevelt told the workers who had constructed it. Under the Roosevelts, the family quarters were air-conditioned to avoid the rigors of the stifling Washington summer heat. Slowly the White House in the mid-twentieth century moved toward operation as an all-weather year-round facility for presidents and their families.[12]

To overcome the physical limitations of his situation, Roosevelt relied in large part on the reports of his wife Eleanor, who expanded the role of the First Lady into fresh areas. Other presidents such as Theodore Roosevelt had capitalized on the personal appeal of their family. Even before Mrs. Roosevelt arrived on the scene, Lou Henry Hoover had tried to use her links with the Girl Scouts to mobilize support for voluntary solutions to the depression. Mrs. Hoover also had given radio addresses designed to win support for her

Franklin D. Roosevelt and Jesse Jones in a rare shot of the president on his feet. He leans on Jones for support, and the top of the president's cane is also visible. (Jesse Jones Papers, courtesy of the Center for American History, University of Texas at Austin.)

husband's programs, but in the general failure of his administration her work was relatively unnoticed.[13]

Because of the strains in the Roosevelt marriage arising from his affair with Lucy Mercer in 1918, the president had to employ his wife as kind of informal aide and reporter rather than as an intimate adviser. With her prodigious energies, Eleanor Roosevelt created a new model for a presidential wife as a kind of roving ambassador, ombudsman within the federal government, and launcher of trial balloons. Mrs. Roosevelt kept this activity on a personal level and did not bureaucratize the institution of the First Lady. Her successors would do that, as the wife of the president became an extension of the larger purposes of the administration.

The most dramatic move that Roosevelt took to revive the presidency came when he was sworn in on 4 March 1933. The inaugural address, broadcast nationwide, contained his memorable assertion, "The only thing we have to fear is fear itself." That remark and the sense of new initiatives that he conveyed stimulated national morale and imparted a sense to the nation that the government had an effective leader who would engage the problems of the depression. For the first time since the economic crisis had commenced, the public received a shot of genuine confidence. Most inaugural addresses are deservedly forgotten. Roosevelt's became a milestone in the evolution of the modern presidency, one that few of his successors have matched.[14]

From the outset of his administration, the regular press conference, often held several times during a week, became a hallmark of Roosevelt's presidency. Reporters crowded into his office, stood before his desk bunched together, and fired away with their questions. The impression of a freewheeling interchange was, however, largely an illusion. Although the practice of submitting questions in advance was abandoned, the president did not allow any follow-up queries, or what he termed "cross-examination." Nor, except with Roosevelt's permission, could he as president be quoted directly. Reporters soon found that their capacity to ask meaningful questions was constricted and the advantages all lay with Roosevelt in how the press sessions were orchestrated. As John Gunther, a best-selling author, noted, "I never met anyone who showed greater capacity for avoiding a direct answer while giving the questioner a feeling he *had* been answered."[15]

Roosevelt recognized that these press conferences gave him the best chance to dispense news without having it filtered through the screens of editors and often unfriendly publishers. Although some of the journalists were sympathetic to the president, most of the major newspapers opposed the New Deal and its architect, both in their news columns and on their editorial pages. For a president who could not easily get around on his own, the regular bandying with reporters provided him with a sense of the changes in the popular mood, even if he did not ask them to keep him posted on public opinions as such. Preparations for the press conferences also kept Roosevelt schooled on the issues of the day. As presidents became aware of the potential pitfalls of such conferences and proved less adroit at handling them than Roosevelt was, the total of 997 press conferences that he held in twelve years became one of those presidential records that would never even be approached in the future. Indeed, such openness with the news media would seem more fraught with risk than any president should tolerate.

The media were themselves in the midst of important changes during the 1930s that would in time reshape the cultural context of the presidency. More and more Americans received their news from movie newsreels and the radio in the 1930s. The daily newspaper remained important as a molder of opinion through the end of World War II, but the trend toward mass entertainment was strong and growing. Roosevelt understood the need to keep the public vicariously involved in presidential activities, and, like Coolidge, he capitalized on friendships with radio and movie stars to glamorize his presidency.

Roosevelt was a masterful performer on the radio, and his periodic talks with the American people became legendary as fireside chats. Rather than offering them as frequently as once a week, as was customary by the end of the century in the form of five-minute Saturday morning broadcasts, Roosevelt reserved the technique for special occasions of crisis or legislative deadlock, when he wanted to exert a maximum influence on the popular mind. Far from being informal and spontaneous, these broadcasts were scripted with meticulous care so that every word in the thirty-minute program achieved the maximum political effect. Then Roosevelt turned the force of his personality loose on the audience as he sat before the microphone. The president had "the best voice in radio," according to *Fortune* magazine in 1935. "Until Mr. Roosevelt taught the world how that titanic trombone of tubes and antennae could be played no one had any idea of the possible range of its virtuosity."[16]

The fireside was that of the listener, not the president's. Roosevelt broadcast the chats from the Diplomatic Reception Room in the White House.

FDR's fireside chat broadcasts to the nation were done with professional precision. In this 1942 talk, Roosevelt consults the map as he discusses world strategy with his listeners. (Courtesy of the Library of Congress.)

He was a master of radio and could convey complex ideas in terms that his audience readily understood. A resonant voice and an accessible manner enhanced the effectiveness of the broadcasts. More than any other previous president, Roosevelt had found a way to reach the American people directly, without having his ideas filtered through newspapers or assessed in advance by his political opponents. With television still over the horizon, the burgeoning field of radio was proving a way for presidents to dominate popular attention. In the art of being a political performer through electronic means, Roosevelt was both the first and in many ways the best of all the twentieth-century presidents. There is little doubt that he would have mastered television as well.

Beyond the press's discretion about his paralysis, Roosevelt also benefited from the willingness of the media to preserve his private life from intense public scrutiny. He could not shield all the divorces and scrapes of his sons from view, but his wife's relationship with Lorena Hickok and his own affectionate friendship with his onetime mistress, Lucy Mercer Rutherfurd, were not exposed to the gaze of the nation. These were self-denying ordinances by the working press that would not be present half a century later.[17]

Despite the success he enjoyed in his dealings with the press, Roosevelt did not want to be dependent on the media to measure the currents of public opinion. Instead, he turned to public opinion polls, done for the White House by the Democratic party operative Emil Hurja and later by Hadley Cantril, a private pollster. These surveys gave the White House a means of testing programs and initiatives without consulting other participants in the policy or electoral process. While they increased the autonomy of the president, their availability would tempt other chief executives to use polls not just to track public opinion but also to mold it in a direct way.[18]

In the first five years of the New Deal, Roosevelt did not make major changes in the traditional way the White House was staffed. Though the number of people working for the president increased, their duties tracked the activities of previous White House staffs. Roosevelt did not like formal structures with clear lines of authority, and so he did not increase the size of the White House staff as such. On paper, he had only one secretary to the president, in the person of his old friend and political adviser, Louis Howe; Steve Early, the press secretary, and Marvin McIntyre, the appointments secretary, were listed as assistant secretaries.[19]

Instead, Roosevelt reached out to other departments in the executive branch to provide him with aides for specific projects or pressing issues. During the first years of the New Deal, there were some fifty people formally assigned to other departments who were detailed to the White House for as much as six months to a year. Once their particular task had been completed or when the flow of business slackened, these people could then be returned to their original posts until needed again. This approach suited Roosevelt's ad hoc style of governance and concentrated responsibility in his hands. However, it also meant that the true extent of his logistical support was well hidden from the press, Congress, and public scrutiny.[20]

The increase of daily business that Roosevelt faced between 1933 and 1937 demanded a larger and more efficient staff than he had used during his first term. The number of people who had reasonable claims on direct access to the president was quite large by modern standards. His revitalization of the presidency and the executive in general also meant that more documents came to the White House on a daily basis. Though his day-to-day mail did not grow by the proportions sometimes attributed to it, the flow of paper into the White House increased substantially, and the procedures devised in the Taft administration to keep track of documents showed signs of erosion during the 1930s and 1940s.[21]

Much ink has been spilled over the question of Roosevelt's performance as an administrator. While most accounts recognize that he reveled in a high degree of informal improvisation, some of his defenders maintain that this style gave him ultimate control since all decisions came in the end to his desk. Yet even the prodigious energies of Franklin D. Roosevelt could not assimilate all the information that the White House received. The president's willingness to conduct lengthy appointments in which he often outtalked the person who came to see him represented another drain on his time and attention. There is a good deal of evidence that an efficient gatekeeper would have enabled him to have functioned more effectively in the time available to him in any single working day. The way he performed did result in a flood of productive and needed legislation and ultimately in the transformation of American society through the New Deal. Whether it might have been done in a less chaotic way is now unanswerable.[22]

In his relations with Congress, Franklin D. Roosevelt was not an innovator in the structural sense of creating new mechanisms for dealing with Capitol Hill. He would not have wanted to delegate his authority to an Office of Congressional Relations such as the one that Dwight D. Eisenhower developed. His record of accomplishments in his first term, however, set a level of presidential activism during an economic crisis that created expectations against which all subsequent chief executives have been measured. The Congress that responded with a flurry of laws during the first three months of Roosevelt's presidency wrote the concept of the One Hundred Days indelibly into the consciousness of press and public. Though it was an entirely artificial construct without any substantive significance, the notion that presidents should be evaluated on that chronological basis has proved enduring.[23]

Yet Roosevelt faced conditions that few future presidents would wish to confront. With the economy at its low point of the Great Depression and the banking system on the verge of collapse, lawmakers were ready to dispense with their customary procedures and slower pace to accommodate the needs of the moment in spring 1933. The president simply had to ask for legislation during the first hectic weeks to have it enacted into law. Even when the pace of the economic crisis slowed and partisan opposition reappeared, there was not the public will to return to business as usual on Capitol Hill for several months. In contrast, after the terrorist attacks on the United States in September 2001, bipartisanship lasted for only about six weeks before it broke down.

For Roosevelt himself, the dazzling performance of the One Hundred Days in 1933 proved a mixed blessing. On the positive side, it set his administration off to a dynamic start and established him as the direct opposite of Hoover and his inaction and lack of perception about political realities. The accomplishments instilled in House members and senators a healthy respect for the president's political skill and his touch with the American public. With a Democratic administration in place and secure majorities for the party in both houses of Congress, the executive and legislative branches worked in harmony during the president's first year in office.

Such a level of cooperation, however, could not be maintained indefinitely as the normal interplay of the White House and Capitol Hill reasserted itself in the remaining years of the first term. Roosevelt did not consult as thoroughly with the congressional leadership as he might have, and the lawmakers, especially the southern Democrats, resented the White House aides on whom the president relied as intermediaries with Capitol Hill. With all sides interested in seeing Roosevelt reelected in 1936, these problems did not prove unduly troublesome during the first term, but they became more acute in the second when the country and Congress turned to a more conservative position on New Deal policies. As Roosevelt's ill-fated purge of southern Democrats in 1938 would show, the White House was limited in the amount of pressure it could exert on dissenting lawmakers, once the political climate turned against Roosevelt.[24]

Part of the problem that the president encountered with the Democrats was the diminishing clout and relevance of the parties themselves. Voter participation in elections and politics ebbed during the middle of the century, and the capacity of the president and the Democratic leadership to enforce discipline also eroded. The political machines in the large cities retained their power until World War II, and the population shifts to the suburbs rendered them less important in the years after Roosevelt's death.

Roosevelt's larger insensitivity to congressional feelings became evident in the fight that he launched in 1937 to enlarge the Supreme Court. The scheme to add more liberal justices would have been controversial under any circumstances, but the secrecy with which the president framed the initiative and his unwillingness to consult the Democratic congressional leadership ensured a frosty reception for his ideas on Capitol Hill. From that point on in his presidency, the White House faced a much more intransigent Congress. Although he had served in the New York State Senate, it is not clear that he understood how peremptory his policies appeared to lawmakers in both parties.[25]

One key to success as a modern president is effective leadership of the political party. Roosevelt revitalized and transformed the Democrats in an electoral sense from a chronic minority to the majority party that won seven of nine presidential elections between 1932 and 1968. The New Deal coalition of African Americans, ethnic groups in the major cities, and organized labor constituted Roosevelt's enduring achievement. He succeeded in uniting the fractious Democrats behind his own leadership in four successive presidential elections. What he could not do was reconcile the divergent elements of the party and achieve the ideological consistency for the Democrats that he sought.[26]

Roosevelt's major effort to remake the party came in 1938 after his reverses in the 1937 Supreme Court battle. His purge of conservatives in the South was a failure, and from that point on the president took his party as he found it. By the time World War II arrived, any credible impulse to restructure the Democratic party had evaporated. As a result, the internal fissures among Democrats remained to plague Harry Truman, John F. Kennedy, and Lyndon Johnson.

In another key area of presidential leadership, Roosevelt came up short. Although his evenhanded economic policies and the example of his wife helped move black Americans away from their Republican roots and into the Democratic column, the president himself was a hesitant and vacillating presence so far as civil rights were concerned. Mindful of the power of southern Democrats to hamper or block altogether his legislative initiatives, he moved with caution on antilynching legislation and other civil rights measures. Nor did he do much himself to integrate the armed forces during World War II, and the war for freedom was fought almost exclusively by a segregated military. What gains were made in civil rights came largely from the demands of African Americans themselves or the prodding of the First Lady. His political calculations were reasonable and in his mind prudent. But Roosevelt failed to exploit the leadership possibilities of the modern presidency to educate his fellow citizens about the burdens of race on society, black and white. The reluctance to do so became a major blot on his record in office.[27]

By Roosevelt's second term, the growing demands on the White House staff and his desire for greater control of the federal government convinced him that the presidency had to be reorganized. The structure of a few personal secretaries and aides borrowed from other departments needed more rationality and order. Similarly, the welter of councils and boards that the president had set up to address economic issues required more coordination. The Bureau of the Budget in particular needed to be made more responsive to the president's wishes. The White House thus set in motion plans for an expansion of the size of the bureaucracy that served Roosevelt. It was evident that if he were to meet the mounting domestic and foreign challenges of his second term, he required more than the improvised administrative structure he had assembled after taking office. The outcome was the battle over government reorganization that was waged until 1939.[28]

The keynote of the effort was the phrase in Louis Brownlow's report proposing reorganization of the executive: "The president needs help." The larger goal of the various proposals was to broaden the reach of the president's executive authority and to increase the size of the staff. As Roosevelt told a member of Congress in June 1937, "The President's task has become impossible for me or any other man." But he did not seek to create the huge bureaucratic structures that have become characteristic of the modern White House. He believed that eight to ten assistants would suffice to relieve him of some of the routine burdens of his office and enable him to have more control over the actions of departments and agencies within his own government.[29]

The main aims of Roosevelt's initiative were to reduce the power of the civil service to slow down his programs, move the Bureau of the Budget from Treasury to the White House, and arrange for planning and regulatory agencies to be more responsible to the president. The ambitious plan encountered a cool reception from an increasingly conservative Congress in 1937 and 1938 as lawmakers sought to curb Roosevelt's power, not to extend it. After a protracted and losing struggle by the White House, a much more limited piece of legislation emerged and went through Congress without difficulty in 1939, though the authority it granted to Roosevelt was good for only two years.[30]

In the new scheme of things that Roosevelt announced, the Bureau of the Budget, the president's office, and the National Resources Planning Board were folded into the Executive Office of the President (EOP), which became a reality on 25 September 1939. Roosevelt enlarged the White House staff with the six additional assistants he was now authorized to employ. What had been informal arrangements since the beginning of the twentieth century were now institutionalized.[31]

Although the White House aides under Roosevelt were supposed to cultivate "a passion for anonymity," the New Deal saw the emergence of presidential advisers as Washington celebrities in their own right. That had not been the case in the days of George B. Cortelyou or even for Woodrow Wilson's friend, Colonel Edward M. House, who had always tried to preserve his privacy, lest his influence with the president be undermined. Such men as Harry Hopkins, Benjamin Cohen, and Thomas G. "Tommy the Cork" Corcoran attracted press attention for the inside influence and public controversy as well. Roosevelt never allowed any of his aides to become too famous for too long. Nonetheless, the process demonstrated how the White House and its operatives were becoming the focus of attention from press and public.[32]

In practice, the new Executive Office of the President did not really change Roosevelt's administrative style or lead to the enhanced efficiency that he sought. Even in the wartime crisis that soon loomed for the United States, the president relied on his combination of competing bureaucracies and personal skills rather than on rationalized procedures and clear lines of jurisdiction. With the war in Europe under way, Roosevelt paid less attention to the faltering New Deal programs and spent more time as commander in chief, where his right to concentrate on military issues was unquestioned.

More than any other circumstance the foreign policy crises that the nation confronted during the late 1930s from Germany and Japan focused attention on the president and his leadership. Faced with a threat to its national existence, the country looked to Roosevelt for firm direction and effective policies. In the process, the federal government took on a greater role in the lives of most Americans. What would have seemed dictatorial actions a generation earlier now seemed appropriate responses to a national challenge. Yet changes in presidential power implemented for a specific purpose during World War II tended to become permanent features of the American political landscape.

The dangers of German espionage, and well-founded suspicions about the impact of agents of the Soviet Union, led Roosevelt to put more power in the hands of J. Edgar Hoover and his Federal Bureau of Investigation. Although the threat to government secrets of both nations was real, the bureau cast a wide net that ensnared in its surveillance techniques Americans on the left and the right whose crime was political dissent from the government's policies. Since Roosevelt found this investigative apparatus useful and Hoover politically untouchable, he acquiesced in the rise of federal law enforcement as something of a political arm of the presidency. It was a decision with fateful long-range effects.[33]

Roosevelt himself did a bit of in-house manipulation of his own Oval Office visitors. He had a taping system installed to record his conversations and presumably to maintain a record of what was said to use against those who later denied what they had said to him or repudiated their remarks. Primitive by the standards of a later time, the recording system was begun in 1940 and then fell into disuse. The possibilities of political blackmail and timely embarrassment of his enemies no doubt occurred to the wily Roosevelt. The experiment was soon abandoned, not on moral grounds but because the primitive technology did not permit efficient recording. Other presidents would return to the practice with more sophisticated recording devices. An ominous precedent had been set that would both enrich the historical record and tempt future presidents into inappropriate and finally illegal behavior.[34]

The potential danger of presidential power in wartime was best illustrated during World War II in the internment of Japanese Americans in camps in the West. Done in the absence of a genuine military threat and responsive to the racial prejudices of white Americans on the Pacific Coast, the relocation of loyal Americans not accused of specific crimes reflected a wartime hysteria to which Roosevelt gave way and which he did little to dispel. Never fastidious about the law and procedural issues, he acted as a commander in chief rather than as an upholder of constitutional rights. That he might have been setting a dangerous precedent does not seem to have affected his decision making in this area in any serious manner.[35]

In the case of sabotage against the United States by Germans landing from submarines on Long Island and in Florida in June 1942, Roosevelt did not use the civilian courts but instead created a military commission to try them for their misdeeds. The proceedings were speedy, and their results predictable. Six of the eight men involved were convicted and executed within a few weeks.

The others, who had told the FBI about the plot, were given long prison sentences. Some evidence indicates that the secrecy and the military character of the tribunal were designed to prevent the public from learning that one of the saboteurs had tipped the FBI off to the presence of the men in the first place. Roosevelt's actions, done in time of war, later became a precedent for similar military tribunals in the terrorist crisis that President George W. Bush faced in 2001. Critics on the left and the right found Roosevelt's exercise of presidential power in wartime a dubious example of his leadership.[36]

As a wartime leader, Roosevelt acted as a strategist on the world stage. On the big issues — support for Great Britain in 1940 and 1941, aid to the Soviet Union, defeating Germany first before Japan, and the unconditional surrender policy — his instincts were right and his personal leadership powerful. The evil nature of the main adversaries, Nazi Germany and Imperial Japan, justified the times when Roosevelt cut legal corners in his policies or was not entirely candid with his fellow citizens. The need for secrecy in many key instances was obvious and prudent.[37]

Yet a culture of concealment and executive discretion, even in a good cause, could become self-perpetuating and uncontrolled. The clandestine steps that Roosevelt took in 1939 and 1940 to assist the French and British in obtaining war supplies, for example, would have been controversial and politically embarrassing had they become general knowledge. The undeclared naval war against Germany in 1941 was a welcome step for the embattled British, who needed the protection against submarines that the Americans provided. However, the Nazis knew what was going on as their submarines were attacked; the American people were the ones left in the dark. Roosevelt's precedent of unilateral military action without public disclosure would prove enticing for many of his successors. Their endeavors would lack both the moral clarity of what Roosevelt did against the Nazis and his ability to keep news reporting under control.

The very process by which Roosevelt led the nation from Munich to Pearl Harbor became a kind of primer for the modern presidents who followed him. If the enemy was the equivalent of Adolf Hitler and the Third Reich or could be made to appear in the same menacing light, then a president could turn to the techniques and even the rhetoric of Franklin D. Roosevelt for inspiration. That Roosevelt had faced an evil aggressor who was not confronted until it was nearly too late became the famous lesson of the Munich analogy. Once that precedent was invoked, the presidents from Lyndon Johnson in Vietnam to George H. W. Bush with Saddam Hussein in Iraq felt justified in emulating Roosevelt's practices and deceits.[38]

The demands of World War II also elevated the president in popular esteem, as Roosevelt flew around the globe to world conferences with other Allied leaders. Though the old limitations against presidential travel had long since vanished, he made these trips no longer as a time of vacation or state visits but as an integral aspect of presidential leadership. Improvements in air travel meant that a president could keep in touch with the business of government even though he was half a world away. The press coverage of these events also put the president on a different plane of popular standing from his counterparts in Congress or his potential rivals for the White House. Roosevelt discovered, as did his successors, that overseas travel usually boosted the chief executive's stock in public opinion polls.

The war also produced another expansion of the physical reach of the White House. In an effort to find a place near Washington where the president could obtain relaxation and diversion, the White House staff located a rustic former tourist camp in the Catoctin Mountains some seventy-five miles from the nation's capital. Roosevelt dubbed it "Shangri-La," the name of the fictional utopia that had been the lure of James Hilton's novel *Lost Horizon*. From 1942 on, Roosevelt spent a number of relaxing weekends at the hideaway, apart from the perennial pressures of the White House routine. Other presidents would come to rely on the camp for the same purposes, and gradually the facility grew into a working equivalent of the White House itself in the years that followed.[39]

Though all twentieth-century presidents had endeavored to keep some sort of track of how the voters felt about their performance in office, Roosevelt occupied the White House when the systematic surveying of popular attitudes became a fixture of American life. To provide even more up-to-date information, an administration could hire its own private pollsters. For Roosevelt, knowledge about the ebb and flow of public opinion concerning neutrality issues helped with the timing of presidential events and the way in which issues were framed. The presence of opposition to interventionist initiatives also provided a convenient rationale to disarm critics who chided the president for not being more aggressive in leading the American people to help the Allied cause. With the ability to measure public opinion in this more precise way came the temptation to manipulate the polls themselves to achieve a desired result. Roosevelt's White House did not venture much into this treacherous area. Other presidents would find the temptation impossible to resist.

Franklin D. Roosevelt also shaped the modern presidency in a manner he probably never intended. The two-term tradition, begun by George Washington and reaffirmed by the experience of Theodore Roosevelt in 1912, had not been written down, codified into law, or made part of the Constitution. There had been controversies about the matter when Ulysses S. Grant was mentioned as a possible presidential candidate in 1880 and with even more force when Theodore Roosevelt sought the Republican nomination in 1912. The failure of both men to win the White House for a third time stilled some of the unease and reaffirmed the no-third-term rule as an axiom of American politics.

Thus when Roosevelt either allowed himself to be drafted for a third term in 1940 or shaped the conditions that produced his nomination, there was no constraint other than custom to prevent him from doing so. Despite pervasive grumbles about the third term and Republican attempts to make it a major issue, the voters returned Roosevelt to office over Wendell Willkie. Four years later, with World War II still raging, a fourth term to finish the conflict also seemed natural, and the matter did not materially help the Republican challenger, Thomas E. Dewey. The uncertain state of Roosevelt's failing health was carefully kept hidden from the news media and the electorate. Once Roosevelt had passed from the scene, however, Republicans made sure that no future president could duplicate his feat. The Twenty-second Amendment, adopted by the Eightieth Congress, limited all subsequent presidents to two elected terms, whether consecutive or nonconsecutive in nature.[40]

The change in the amount of time a chief executive could serve in the office reshaped the rhythm of presidencies for both Republicans and Democrats in ways that the authors of the amendment probably did not anticipate. The first year of a new presidency became crucial for enacting a domestic program. By the second year, with congressional elections impending in the autumn, Congress was usually less willing to take sweeping actions, and the clout of the new president had diminished. The third and fourth years of the first term were conducted in the shadow of an impending reelection contest. Presidents told themselves that these difficulties would be surmounted once a second term (or four more years) had been secured from the voters. Yet when presidents such as Dwight D. Eisenhower, Richard Nixon, Ronald Reagan, and Bill Clinton were safely reelected, the knowledge in Washington that their tenure was limited constricted their ability to push programs forward. Second-term presidents did not become powerless by any means, but they were more and more seen in Washington as figures whose day was passing rather than as executives to be feared and respected. Attention turned to the next presidential election and the possible candidates for that contest. As a result, the second terms usually produced political difficulties (Eisenhower and Lyndon Johnson) or debilitating scandals (Nixon, Reagan, and Clinton) that forestalled much in the way of real accomplishment. The term-limit amendment prevented another Franklin D. Roosevelt, but it placed limits on the exercise of the modern presidency whose impact is still imperfectly understood.

By the time Roosevelt died on 12 April 1945, the presidency had been transformed. Though it had not yet become the huge bureaucracy that it later reached, the White House reflected the principle that in Washington power now flowed toward the Oval Office and away from Capitol Hill. Roosevelt had also reshaped the public expectations for presidential leadership. The occupant of the White House must see to it that economic prosperity was maintained and, if hard times threatened, it was the job of the president to forestall them. In peacetime the chief executive had to engage the problems of the president and set the agenda for the future.

As a successful war leader, Roosevelt took the presidency onto the world stage and ended the nation's isolation from foreign problems. The president now had to ensure that international threats did not imperil national security, both with a strong military response but also with sound economic policies and the means to safeguard against internal subversion. All these forces enlarged the size and role of the federal government and thus the authority of the president.

Roosevelt also influenced the development of the modern presidency in a more subtle way. Until his administration, most presidents had donated their personal papers to the Library of Congress or allowed them to be dispersed. Some, such as Chester Alan Arthur and, to a lesser degree, the family of Warren G. Harding, had destroyed those documents that seemed to be controversial. With the exception of Rutherford B. Hayes and his library in Fremont, Ohio, the chief executives had not had special institutions devoted to the study of their time in office. Given the large amount of Roosevelt's personal papers (which came to some twenty tons in all), some permanent institutional home seemed more appropriate than his original choice of the National Archives. During his first term, he developed plans for the Roosevelt Library in Hyde Park, New York, and he devoted a good deal of time in the White House to the future operation of the facility.

The Roosevelt Library opened for research in 1946 but really came into its own as a scholarly venture in the 1950s and 1960s. As that happened, Roosevelt's successors set up their own presidential libraries in what became a pattern for future chief executives. The prospect of ready availability of presidential papers within a reasonable time after their owners left the White House made these facilities an attractive venue for researchers. The need to plan for a presidential library became an integral part of an administration, as academic institutions and communities vied for the honor of having a library or museum on their campus or in their town. Until 1974 and the Watergate scandal, the question of ownership of and access to these presidential papers was a matter largely of interest only to librarians and researchers.[41]

Many of the modern assumptions about how presidents should behave and be judged still derive from the Roosevelt example. Journalists track the first hundred days of each new president, whether there is a crisis or not and without much historical sense of why the span of time has any true meaning. Programs are measured by the extent to which they resemble or depart from the New Deal and its legacy. First Ladies are evaluated as they relate to the accomplishments of Eleanor Roosevelt. Even though the presidency has evolved well beyond the practices of Franklin D. Roosevelt, he continues to be the standard against which his successors are judged.

5

The Presidency in the Cold War Era
Harry S. Truman and Dwight D. Eisenhower

Franklin D. Roosevelt is usually credited with establishing the modern presidency, yet the two chief executives who came after him, Harry S. Truman and Dwight D. Eisenhower, were even more significant for creating the institutional framework that buttressed the White House in the Cold War era. Moreover, in waging the struggle with the Soviet Union, both men instituted the methods and assumptions that sustained what became known as the imperial presidency. Though neither Truman nor Eisenhower had illusions of personal grandeur in office, they saw grow up around them a political culture that regarded the president as a leader of almost transcendent importance to the nation and the world.

Harry S. Truman was an improbable architect of an imperial presidency. The son of a Missouri farmer and a politician who held modest local offices in his state before his election to the U.S. Senate in 1934, the bespectacled Truman did not seem prepossessing at first glance. As his rivals on the domestic and international scene were to discover, however, he had a strong and well-developed sense of his rights and prerogatives as a leader. Though he came to the presidency in April 1945 unaware of many aspects of American foreign policy, most notably the existence of the atomic bomb, the new president proved to be a quick study.[1]

An omnivorous reader from youth, Truman fancied himself a student of history with a command of the facts of the American past. He saw himself as the heir of the Democratic tradition of Andrew Jackson and Woodrow Wilson, and he came naturally to a strong executive style that mirrored his boyhood models. His desk motto, "The Buck Stops Here," was an indelible part of his presidential image. In fact, like most presidents, he was adept at shifting responsibility and blame to others when necessary. The new president was a shrewd political operator with skills honed in the competitive world of Missouri Democratic politics and from observing the Kansas City political machine of his mentor, Tom Pendergast.[2]

One Roosevelt legacy that Truman did not extend was the experiment with a tape recording system in the White House. He learned of the existence of the device shortly after he became president and was not impressed. He did authorize a test of the system on 23 May 1945, when he had a press conference recorded. After listening to the tape of the reporters' questions and his answers, Truman decided not to make further recordings. Some presidential conversations were later picked up either accidentally or as part of tests by the stenographer who had charge of the process. Truman did make an effort to record his thoughts and actions for posterity in a diary and through letters to his wife, but he did not regard tape recordings of presidential conversations as either ethical or wise.[3]

On the subject of the atomic bomb, Truman's decision to drop two nuclear weapons on the Japanese in August 1945 became one of the most controversial aspects of his time in the White House. From that time on, and especially after the Soviet Union developed the bomb itself, the life of Truman and all other presidents had to take into account the procedures and possibilities of using the nuclear arsenal of the United States in a moment of international crisis. The presence of military aides carrying the necessary codes and instructions to launch airplanes and later missiles for such a confrontation became an inescapable fact of life around which the modern presidency had to be organized. Little research has been done comparatively on the impact of this condition on the way that presidents carry out their other duties and responsibilities.[4]

Because he had seen, both from Congress and during his vice presidency, the loose administrative style of Roosevelt, the sixty-one-year-old Truman intended to bring more order and discipline to his White House. He was especially interested in the process of creating budgets for the federal government, an offshoot of his experience with budgeting in Missouri and his conduct of the Senate committee on waste and fraud in the defense industry during World War II. He worked closely with the staff of the Bureau of the Budget to align spending in the federal government with presidential priorities. This approach made the task of managing the federal bureaucracy more coherent than it had been under Roosevelt.[5]

Truman endorsed the Republican initiative that led to the establishment of what became known as the Hoover Commission to reorganize the executive branch. The original impetus of the legislation was to cut back on the size of the federal government, but Truman's upset victory in the 1948 election caused the chair of the panel, former president Herbert Hoover, to return to the previous Republican emphasis on strengthening the efficiency of the executive branch of the government. While the actual recommendations of the commission (the first of two such bodies) between 1949 and 1953 were on the margins in terms of institutional change, the thrust of the panel's work was to strengthen and affirm presidential leadership of the executive branch.[6]

Truman also excelled in instilling morale and a sense of purpose in his immediate White House staff. He gained the strong loyalty of such men as Dean Acheson and George C. Marshall because of his willingness to stand behind their actions during moments of crisis and to defend their work in public. Truman also commanded a similar respect from those who worked for him directly in the White House. He kept his aides informed of the larger purposes of his administration and shared credit with them when policies succeeded. Not always a shrewd judge of character, he kept around him some men who were little more than cronies, such as his military aide, Harry Vaughan, to the detriment of his reputation. On the whole, Truman used the White House staff with nearly the same effectiveness that Franklin D. Roosevelt had displayed but without as much internal discord and with fewer public quarrels.[7]

With the arrival of the Trumans at the White House, the security around the presidency loosened a little during his first term, as Truman took daily walks with the Secret Service in the neighborhood. Moving the chief executive from place to place became more routine again. The attempt to assassinate the president in November 1950, carried out by Puerto Rican nationalists while the Trumans were living at Blair House, led to a renewed emphasis on the president's personal safety during the remainder of his tenure. The wall that was insulating modern presidents from the American people grew stronger during Truman's administration.[8]

The president and his wife had left the White House because the mansion had finally deteriorated to the point of near collapse by the late 1940s. With the president away, the building was taken down and then reconstructed with a new subbasement, modern air-conditioning, and a renovated interior. In the half century since the White House was reopened, after the Trumans returned on 27 March 1952, the mansion has become a symbol of the modern presidency, seen on television from day to day. During the Cold War and then extending into the war on terrorism, the White House has become more guarded and secure. The days when reporters and an average citizen could simply come to the front and ring the bell have gone, along with the notion of the president as an accessible first citizen.[9]

The Truman presidency was the first to confront the new medium of television. For much of Truman's nearly eight years in office, television was in transition from novelty to an instrument of true mass communication. Fewer than .5 percent of American homes had a television set in 1948; more than one-third of American households did by Truman's last full year in office. The first broadcasts of national political conventions came in 1948, with more extensive coverage by 1952. The hearings of Senator Estes Kefauver of Tennessee into organized crime in 1951 became a popular hit and a political liability for big-city Democrats with whom the Mob was linked. For his part, President Truman insisted "on full use of [television] in all his major speeches," but he disliked how the televised hearings produced what the White House in 1951 called "Roman holidays."[10]

The accomplishments of the Truman administration occurred despite the liabilities of the president as a handler of the newspapers, radio, and television. Truman was not a compelling speaker when he was reading from a prepared text. His off-the-cuff remarks could be more persuasive and engaging. His penchant for commenting without considering the impact of his remarks sometimes led to memorable gaffes and missteps. His epistolary assault on the *Washington Post* music critic, Paul Hume, for a negative review of his daughter Margaret's singing was a notable example.[11]

The Truman White House faced a skeptical press corps and major newspapers that opposed the president's policies by and large. These conditions made for an adversarial relationship with the media that dominated Truman's presidency. The unwillingness to engage in spin endeared Truman to later historians, but it was more of a handicap to the administration while he was in office.[12]

The White House continued some of the practices toward the press that had been in place for decades. The press secretaries did not cultivate the media in any systematic way and instead relied on disseminating press releases and conveying information without special attention to presenting Truman in a more favorable light. In the case of press conferences, however, the custom of holding these weekly sessions in the Oval Office gave way by 1950 to meetings in the old State Department building near the White House. The renovation of the White House was one reason for this shift, but the number of journalists seeking to ask questions had simply become too large to be accommodated under the old system. Instead of shouting questions from a room filled with reporters, the journalists had to identify themselves when posing an inquiry. These arrangements made the press conference more stylized and formal than had been the case in the past.[13]

The administration did not go the one step further and allow for the broadcasting or filming of the weekly press conference. By 1951 Truman had agreed to allow the sessions to be recorded and transcribed. Radio reporters were then permitted, with the concurrence of the White House, to use excerpts of what Truman had said in their broadcasts. Newsreel coverage of the conferences was not allowed. In that sense, the Truman years represented a transitional phase in how press conferences were emerging as media events in their own right. Truman's 324 formal meetings with the press, though well below Roosevelt's all-time record, would come to seem an ideal of regular consultation with the media in the years that followed. At his last meeting with journalists, Truman said, "This kind of news conference, where reporters can ask any question they can dream up — directly of the President of the United States — illustrates how strong and vital our democracy is."[14]

If Harry Truman's contributions to the rise of the modern presidency did not lie in the public relations phase of his job, neither was it in the area of congressional affairs, where he struggled throughout his nearly eight years in office. Part of the problem lay beyond his immediate control. By 1945, the liberalism of the New Deal years had waned, and the conservative temper of the country had reasserted itself. The most striking evidence was the election of a Republican Congress in 1946. Unaccustomed in Missouri to dealing with a strong GOP presence, and an intense partisan by nature, Truman had little patience with the conservative initiatives in domestic policy that Republican members proposed. He vetoed the Taft-Hartley Act on labor relations in 1947, and the measure was passed over his veto. In like manner, Republicans ignored such Truman initiatives as national health insurance, a federal housing program, federal support for education, and an increase in the minimum

Presidents had to interact with the press on a regular basis even on vacation. Here Harry Truman conducts a press conference at his vacation spot in Key West, Florida. (U.S. Navy photograph, courtesy of the Harry S. Truman Library.)

wage. Because Truman wanted to expand the New Deal at the very time that many Republicans wanted to dismantle it, and because neither had the votes to prevail, there was no escape from gridlock.[15]

On one issue, civil rights for African Americans, Truman asserted his leadership in a way that no previous president had done, and with lasting consequences. He had to overcome the paternalistic racism of his upbringing, the practical need to keep the southern Democrats within the party, the probability that any civil rights initiative would destroy his political fortunes, the historical pattern of dodge and delay, and his own conflicting emotions on the subject.

He acted, albeit with some hesitation and second thoughts, because he followed his best instinct about what was right and because he revered the office of the presidency. He was outraged in 1946 when African Americans, some of them veterans, were beaten and killed in the South, and he named a blue-ribbon Committee on Civil Rights to study the volatile issue. The committee's pathbreaking report provided the first real education for Americans about the evils of racism and suggested remedies.[16]

Truman knew that civil rights legislation would have no chance in Congress, but in a powerful special message he proposed it anyway, because he was convinced that his country had come to a turning point on race and that the president had to lead. Refusing to give in to Congress and with virtually no public support, he issued two executive orders in 1948 to establish equal opportunity in federal employment and the armed forces. He also was the first president to authorize the Justice Department to issue friend of the court briefs in civil rights cases, the first to address the National Association for the Advancement of Colored People, and the first to campaign in Harlem. By the time he left office, history had turned. The nation's military, the most conservative institution in the country, was fighting the Korean War with mostly integrated forces, and no president thereafter could ignore civil rights. In this example of personal leadership, Truman elevated the role of the modern presidency and his historical reputation as well.[17]

To deal with Congress, Truman relied on his existing White House staff for contacts with Capitol Hill and his own personal relations with former Senate colleagues. That proved successful in the case of Senator Arthur Vandenberg of Michigan, who contributed to the bipartisan foreign policy proposals of the early Cold War era. The president did not, however, create any institutional mechanisms within the White House for formalizing relations with lawmakers. The practical day-to-day work of interacting with Congress was done through the Office of the Special Counsel, most notably by Clark Clifford, and later by Charles Murphy, who established procedures to monitor the progress of legislation. In fact, the disparate elements of organized congressional liaison were in existence in the Truman White House but were not brought together in any coherent form between 1945 and 1953.[18]

The demands of the Cold War and related national security issues dominated the Truman years and accelerated the consolidation of power in foreign affairs that had started under Roosevelt. As the global rivalry with the Soviet Union became the preeminent fact of American foreign policy, the need to concentrate power in the chief executive seemed self-evident. Not everyone in Washington wanted Harry Truman to be the one to wield the power,

Harry Truman showed how modern presidents could exert moral leadership in the area of civil rights. He addressed the National Association for the Advancement of Colored People at the Lincoln Memorial on 29 June 1947. (Courtesy of the Library of Congress.)

but the urgency of having a strong president commanded wide assent. As a result, enhancing the role of the executive agencies seemed required.[19]

The Truman years thus saw the consolidation of the cabinet posts that oversaw the armed services into the Department of Defense in 1949. Although the Pentagon never achieved the administrative efficiencies that proponents of unification desired, the welding together of a defense establishment provided presidents with the military means to exercise their power on a worldwide scale. At the same time, making the services work in tandem or even persuading them to furnish presidents with all needed information proved a continuing challenge for Truman and those who followed him.[20]

The previous ad hoc arrangements about intelligence and espionage that had marked American policy until the outbreak of World War II also seemed antiquated in light of the Soviet threat. The National Security Act (1947) authorized the creation of the Central Intelligence Agency. That in turn meant that presidents gained the capacity to mount covert operations across the globe. Truman expanded the authority to launch such operations, and he set several in motion during his second term. The daily summaries that Truman began to receive from the CIA eventually evolved into the president's daily brief, a fixture by which the president was updated on the condition of world affairs at the outset of each day. The National Security Act also set up the National Security Council, which Truman envisioned as a way of appraising the military and diplomatic issues confronting the nation. Over time, the NSC would become a rival to the State Department itself in shaping foreign policy.[21]

These increased capabilities to plunge the nation into overseas commitments arising from covert action would prove to be mixed blessings for presidents, but in the Truman era they appeared to be suitable responses to the major threat that the Soviet Union posed for the United States. The emergence of a foreign policy challenge that did not culminate in an armed conflict but that also did not recede quickly meant that the nation had to establish continuity and consistency in foreign policy. In turn, the presidency was the only institution in the government that could pursue a course of action on a sustained and coherent basis.

The policy that evolved after 1947 was the containment of the Soviet Union, to prevent its further expansion into Central and Western Europe, as had occurred in Eastern Europe as the Red Army advanced in 1944 and 1945. The other assumption was that if Soviet ambitions could be restrained, in due course the internal strains within their society would cause that empire to break apart. Truman never doubted the magnitude of the challenge; and his leadership, with the Truman Doctrine in 1947, the Marshall Plan in 1948, and the organization of NATO in 1949, was so decisive and prescient as to set the pattern of the containment policy for the entire Cold War period.[22]

As the containment mind-set developed under Truman, the conviction arose that the White House had to be alert for all evidences of Soviet probing of the borders of its contained domain and prepared to respond to any threat that endangered American interests in the world. An example of this kind of thinking became National Security Council Paper NSC-68, delivered to the president in April 1950, which depicted a confrontation between the United States and the Soviet Union that called for Washington to expand the nation's military power to meet this impending threat. In the Truman presidency, the assumptions of containment became a required part of the intellectual equipment at the White House.[23]

These trends meant that the president was expected to have access to knowledge about a wide range of countries and their political status. To maintain such an informed command of the world required that the president possess machinery in the White House to process the information that poured in on a daily basis. The president and his staff acted as a kind of de facto command center for the Free World in the struggle with Communism. The old distinction between war and peace simply vanished, and the White House, if not the president himself, was expected to be in a continuing state of readiness to respond to any foreign policy predicament that might arise.

The result was a conviction in the Congress and the public at large that the executive needed a wide sphere of discretion to follow policies overseas without an excessive amount of oversight from Capitol Hill. Congress was depicted as an unwieldy institution that could neither establish a coherent policy nor execute it in an effective way. The president, on the other hand, could do so, and he should not be unduly burdened by how he chose to function as a world leader.

There arose a relatively new concept in American presidential relations, that of the bipartisan foreign policy. In the past, the struggle between Republicans and Democrats had not stopped "at the water's edge," as Woodrow Wilson could have reminded everyone. But in the early Cold War years it was asserted that criticizing the president in a partisan fashion while he was abroad, for example, was inappropriate. Whenever possible, the two parties should cooperate to enable the nation to speak with one voice on the world scene. As Senator Arthur Vandenberg (R-Mich.), perhaps the leading exponent of the concept, put it, "It means that we strive by consultation to lift foreign policy above partisan issue." Bipartisanship was more often an ideal than a fact, but both parties taxed the other with failing to observe its principles when it suited them to do so. Presidents also found it a congenial concept to embrace as a way of disarming opposition from the other party.[24]

As the Communist threat evolved, traditional constitutional procedures also came to seem outmoded or simply irrelevant to the existing state of affairs. When the Korean War broke out in June 1950 after the North Koreans invaded South Korea in an effort to unite the two countries under Communist rule, the introduction of American armed forces into the Korean peninsula to save the military situation placed the United States in a major ground war in Asia. A formal declaration of war was regarded as inappropriate, however, because of the threat that it might in turn lead to a wider conflict with China and the Soviet Union. The president referred to it as a "police action," a term that did not do justice to the extent of the American commitment. Congress did not at the time object to Truman's action, but a process had started that would render a formal declaration of war an almost superfluous relic of an earlier and simpler era in American history.[25]

Although the nation was not at war in a technical sense of the term, Truman and his successors employed the war powers of the office freely in conducting such conflicts overseas. Hundreds of thousands of troops were deployed in distant lands, lengthy casualty lists resulted, and lives of citizens were disrupted, often for purposes that the public dimly understood. The Korean conflict was particularly difficult to explain as the battle lines stabilized and no victory appeared imminent. As the Korean War dragged on into stalemate in 1952 and 1953, support for the Truman presidency eroded. Presidents could initiate foreign involvements in the Cold War era on their own authority, but translating such decisions into lasting popular support was not an easy matter in the absence of a quick, decisive victory for the United States. Whatever such lessons were learned from Korea, however, did not provide a cautionary note later in the 1950s, when the American role in Vietnam deepened. Modern presidents rarely had a well-developed sense of history.[26]

Faced with an ideological conflict against a former wartime ally in the Soviet Union, Americans looked for an explanation of the dismaying turn-about in foreign policy that had transformed victory in World War II into a struggle with Communism. One ready answer involved Soviet espionage and the threat of internal subversion. Thanks to decoded messages and intercepts from the Soviets, the government had a good idea of the extent to which some of the national secrets had been compromised. These successes in counter-intelligence could not be revealed without endangering the sources of the knowledge. The Truman administration could respond to or forestall Republican charges that it was soft on Communism only by putting into operation its own security procedures to ferret out alleged subversives. Harry Truman's efforts to counter Soviet spying and to defuse the charges of his Republican critics have been seen as major presidential contributions to the onset of the McCarthy era of the 1950s.[27]

These tactics did not discover many Communists or still the increasingly intense Republican criticism that the president had little appreciation of the internal threat the nation faced. The regulations and procedures for check-ing the government workers and officials for subversive tendencies added a counterespionage element to presidential performance. Often dependent on J. Edgar Hoover and the FBI, these security checks, such as wiretapping and in some cases burglary, outgrew their original purpose. Presidents received a new means to monitor their political enemies and when necessary to discomfit them. In the stridently partisan atmosphere of the Cold War era, it was easy for presidents to be tempted into the use of such weapons. From there it was only a short journey to employing these techniques to mold public opinion toward a desired end.

Incumbent presidents had always possessed an advantage over a challenger in an election, but the employment of this asset grew under Truman in the 1948 election against Thomas E. Dewey of New York. Throughout much of the year, commentators predicted an easy victory for the Republicans, based on Democratic divisions on the right and the left of the party as well as on the unity of the resurgent GOP. How would Truman overcome the threat from Henry Wallace on his left and the defection of parts of the traditionally Democratic South because of the president's civil rights initiatives? Truman turned these negatives into positives in his spirited whistle-stop campaign and adroit attacks on the alleged "Do-Nothing" Eightieth Congress. Though the president's victory owed something to Dewey's ineptitude as a campaigner, it also attested to the ability of a modern president to frame the national agenda in his favor.[28]

Once his election was secured, however, Truman bumped up against the political limits that would define the presidency for the rest of the century. The Congress had a working majority of Republican and Democratic conservatives whose opposition to Truman's social legislation reinforced the inherent tendencies of the political system toward inaction. As a result, Truman's Fair Deal initiatives stalled on Capitol Hill in 1949 and 1950, and the outbreak of the Korean War ended chances of any serious domestic program being passed.

During the last two years of his presidency, Truman's political standing deteriorated in the wake of such events as the firing of General Douglas MacArthur in April 1951, Republican attacks over the Communist issue, and the televised hearings on organized crime by Tennessee senator Estes Kefauver, which revealed links between Democratic big-city machines and some mobsters. Truman's attempt to seize the nation's steel mills by an executive order in 1952 was held by the U.S. Supreme Court to be unconstitutional because it asserted a power as commander in chief during the Korean conflict that went too far.[29]

By the time that Truman announced in late March 1952 that he would not seek another term, he had little prospect of renomination or reelection anyway. He left office in January 1953 with very low poll numbers and the aura of a failed presidency about him. Like Woodrow Wilson in 1921, a rehabilitation of Truman seemed an improbable prospect in January 1953.

Harry Truman made his last contribution to the modern presidency with the rebound in his reputation that began in the 1960s and accelerated during the 1970s. As scholars reconsidered him as a politician and an international leader, the manner in which he had run the White House and managed foreign policy seemed to have more positive aspects than had been recognized at the time of his departure from Washington. The president appeared to have the knack for making the government work as he wished and for coming to the right conclusion about foreign policy issues. His decisions about the Cold War had created the framework within which future presidents operated, and he seemed a good model to follow. The opening of Truman's papers at his presidential library in Independence, Missouri, attracted scholars who revived the former president's standing.[30]

In recent decades, Truman's reputation as president has once again receded because of his identification with the Cold War and some of the repressive aspects of the McCarthy era's anticommunist spirit. What he did to institutionalize the modern presidency has thus received more criticism than praise. Nonetheless, Harry Truman had taken the chief executive beyond the personalized style of Franklin D. Roosevelt, and he also laid the foundation for the more bureaucratic methods of Dwight D. Eisenhower.[31]

An analysis of Eisenhower's eight years as president in terms of the institutional history of the office usually hinges on the way his administrative approach to his responsibilities is judged. Harry Truman predicted that his successor's training in the military would ill suit him for the demands of being president. "Poor Ike," as Truman put it, would issue orders as he had done as a general and then find that nothing had been done within the federal bureaucracy. Modern scholars, on the other hand, portray Eisenhower as a hidden-hand executive who moved with skill to persuade others to do what he wanted without leaving many traces of his instructions or influence. The latter interpretation has been a major element in the Eisenhower revisionism that has lifted the president's reputation during the past two decades.[32]

The key to understanding Eisenhower as a maker of the modern presidency lies in his experiences as a leader of a wartime coalition and in his personal reaction to the two chief executives with whom he served. Eisenhower became convinced that successful leaders share the credit with their subordinates and submerge their own ego in the process. Confident of his own intellectual abilities, he did not need to be told how smart he was. At the same time, he appreciated how clear lines of authority, in his capable hands, could facilitate decision making by the president. He had seen the administrative chaos, as he perceived it, under Roosevelt, and he was not impressed with what seemed to him Truman's backroom manner. Thus, Eisenhower came to the White House in 1953 with "certain ideas about the system, or lack of system under which it operated."[33]

Circumstances eased the changes that Eisenhower wanted to make. He brought to the presidency the immense prestige that he had gained as the general who had won the war in Europe and led the Allies to victory over Nazi

Germany. Although he inherited a stalemated conflict in Korea, he did not encounter the economic crisis that had faced Roosevelt in 1933 or the wartime decisions that had confronted Truman in April 1945. The Cold War had settled into the pattern it would follow for nearly four decades, a challenge that Eisenhower's management skills could adjust to readily.

As the first Republican president in twenty years, Eisenhower, at least initially, was spared the intense sniping from his own party that had plagued Harry Truman during his second term. Eisenhower had a freedom of action in foreign policy that enabled him to pursue policies that Republicans would have denounced as treasonous under a Democrat. As advocates of his election had argued, he could negotiate an end to the Korean conflict on terms that Truman could have had a year earlier without the denunciations that the Democrat would have encountered. Yet by the close of his administration, Republican criticism of Eisenhower, led by Senator Barry Goldwater, intensified as the president was accused of being too willing to accept the persistence of the New Deal.[34]

In one area of foreign policy, however, the new president faced a significant challenge to his leadership. After twenty years of Democratic rule, some Republicans, especially those of a more conservative bent, were eager to cut back on the presidential authority that had burgeoned under Roosevelt and Truman. One manifestation of that spirit was the Bricker amendment, designed to write into the Constitution explicit limits on the power of treaties and executive agreements to affect the nation's internal affairs. The measure was first introduced by Senator John W. Bricker of Ohio in 1951. Described by his Republican critics as "an honest Harding" (both William Allen White and Alice Roosevelt Longworth get credit for this phrase), Bricker had been Thomas E. Dewey's running mate in 1944, and he was deeply convinced of the dangers of treaty provision to national sovereignty. His amendment had gathered impressive support in the Senate by mid-1953.[35]

Eisenhower and his aides knew that the amendment would impose constraints on the ability of the president to carry on foreign policy and to make meaningful treaties. The White House negotiated with Bricker to soften the impact of the amendment, and they also collaborated with other senators to shape effective alternatives. In February 1954 the Senate turned down the Bricker amendment and other attempts to achieve the same result. Behind the scenes Eisenhower used his skill to deflect blame for the rejection of the amendment toward others in his administration while attaining the result he wanted. A serious threat to presidential autonomy had been avoided.[36]

As part of his executive style, Eisenhower used a recording system in the White House to keep track of his decisions and as a means of verifying what individuals had said to him. The president employed a Dictabelt, placed in the Oval Office between 1953 and 1959, to record some one hundred meetings; a small number of the belts have survived. Eisenhower had begun the reliance on dictaphones during the war years, and he naturally extended the procedure in his White House service. According to documents in the Eisenhower Library, some memos and transcripts based on these recordings were prepared, but the extent to which Eisenhower himself depended on these materials is not clear. The need that presidents felt to have an accurate record of what people had said in their presence was becoming more urgent as the technology of making such recordings became more sophisticated.[37]

Once in office, Eisenhower set up a staffing arrangement that sought to relieve the president of minor burdens, allowing him to concentrate on major issues. Having more than once been a chief of staff in the army, he believed that the president needed a deputy who could oversee the functional activities of a wide range of aides who in turn had specific responsibilities for individual areas of the presidency. In that setting, Eisenhower could operate as the overall director of the administration, be its face to the public, and yet avoid being overwhelmed by the flow of paper and the trivial daily issues that arose in the course of any presidency.[38]

The man that Eisenhower selected to be his chief of staff in the White House was a former governor of New Hampshire, Sherman Adams. Adams became famous in the 1950s as the tireless, hard-driving White House leader who functioned as a de facto assistant president. An icy New England demeanor added to his legend in Washington. Indeed, Adams did what Eisenhower wanted him to do, was not the president's sole source of information, and had less influence over major decisions than the Washington press corps realized.[39]

Beyond Adams, Eisenhower constituted a White House staff that was organized around specific functions and tasks. While presidential aides sometimes moved from one issue to another as occasions demanded, for the most part they stayed within their own areas of responsibility. This approach became characteristic of the Republican presidents who followed Eisenhower. The Democratic chief executives, on the other hand, tended to rely, as

Roosevelt and Truman had, on generalists who could shift from subject to subject, especially in moments of crisis.[40]

Within this new system, Eisenhower proved to be more of an innovator in the operation of the presidency than his contemporary critics perceived. In the area of press relations, the president and his press secretary, James Hagerty, dispensed with the remnants of the older ways of handling conferences with journalists. Reporters were furnished with recordings and film of the president handling questions. When shown on television and in movie newsreels, these performances proved effective, despite derogatory comments about the president's syntax from some reporters. Privately, Eisenhower said to Hagerty that "press conferences are really a waste of time. All these reporters are interested in is some cheap political fight."[41]

From the poll evidence of Eisenhower's continuing popularity, the public experienced no difficulties in understanding what the president meant to say to the newsmen he addressed. Eisenhower did not go the logical next step and allow for live televising of the press conferences. Hagerty recognized the important change that Eisenhower had made. As he noted in his diary, "This manner of the President being on television is almost the same thing as the start of Roosevelt's fireside chats on radio."[42]

One consequence of making these sessions more formal occasions was a reduction in the number held. Since more political capital was riding on each presidential appearance, the press conferences became more difficult to stage and therefore more demanding of White House staff time. The possibility of holding weekly press conferences receded as frequency lost out to convenience.

James Hagerty turned into something of a celebrity in his own right during the administration. His background in journalism made him popular with his former colleagues, who appreciated the extent to which he sought to open up press conferences to all media. As time passed and Eisenhower's confidence in his press secretary became clear, Hagerty's role as a spokesman for the administration expanded. His twice-daily briefings became media events in their own right. Hagerty's openness was less evident in his handling of Eisenhower's illnesses, when he made sure that the press had ample measures of trivia but provided little in the way of real information about the state of the president's health.[43]

Like Franklin D. Roosevelt, Eisenhower tracked public opinion through extensive use of polling. Employing private firms and materials supplied by

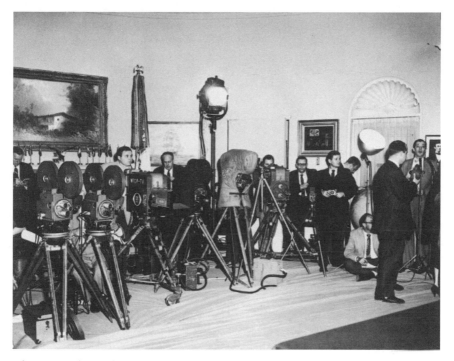

The new medium of television enabled presidents to reach the public more readily, but cameras in the 1950s were bulky and cumbersome, as this shot of preparations for a presidential announcement by Dwight D. Eisenhower in the White House reveals. (Courtesy of the Dwight D. Eisenhower Library.)

the Republican National Committee, the White House kept watch on the president's popularity. So sophisticated did the operation become that the advertising agency Batten, Barton, Durstine, and Osborn (BBDO) conducted regular tracking polls weekly in the early years of Eisenhower's first term. Their numbers also helped to shape the president's advertising strategy for the 1956 reelection race. By the 1950s, polling had become an integral part of the conduct of the presidency under chief executives of both parties.[44]

Faced with a Congress that for much of his tenure was in Democratic hands, Eisenhower sought to bring order to that aspect of the presidency as well. In 1953 he established the Office of Congressional Relations (OCR) and put in charge of the operation General Wilton B. Persons, who had experience from his army days working with Capitol Hill during World War II. The office processed the requests for patronage that came from Republicans eager to have federal offices for their constituents after twenty years of Democratic dominance. The OCR also tracked the major items of the Eisenhower legislative program. The office used the services of such skilled operators as Bryce Harlow to ensure that Eisenhower's relations with lawmakers were as productive as possible. As a result of its good performance in the 1950s, the OCR became a fixture in subsequent administrations.[45]

Eisenhower also sought to make his cabinet a more functioning part of the administration. He held regular weekly meetings of the department secretaries and told them that their advice was valued. The cabinet secretary created discussion papers for these gatherings, and these documents formed the basis for the debates that ensued. Few of Eisenhower's successors followed his example or had his patience with listening to cabinet officers talk about their responsibilities, and the cabinet shrank in importance as part of the presidency during the second half of the twentieth century.[46]

A more enduring innovation of the Eisenhower era was the establishment of what came to be the post of national security adviser. The position was originally known as the presidential assistant for national security affairs. Although the National Security Council had been set up during the Truman years, the president had kept the post of the executive secretary of the NSC restricted to managing the paper flow of the panel and overseeing its staff. Eisenhower, on the other hand, wanted the aide who supervised the workings of the NSC to have more power in the council's deliberations. During his administration the size of the NSC staff expanded to nearly thirty members, but that was still small compared to its later growth.[47]

The three men who served as national security advisers under Eisenhower did not become household names or gain the notoriety of a McGeorge Bundy under Kennedy or a Henry Kissinger under Richard M. Nixon. That was not Eisenhower's style. He regarded the national security adviser as an honest broker presenting alternatives on major foreign policy issues to the president. The White House considered the NSC as an aid to the administration and did not let the panel become a rival force to John Foster Dulles at the Department of State. Nonetheless, in less disciplined hands than those of Eisenhower, such a possibility soon became a reality.

With these varied aspects of the presidency at his disposal, Eisenhower did not employ them to maximize the public's perception of him as an activist,

Dwight Eisenhower began the modern institutional procedures of presidential-congressional relations. This portrait, taken 30 March 1955 on the White House steps, shows, front row, left to right, Carl Albert, John McCormack, Sam Rayburn, Eisenhower, Joseph Martin, and Clarence Cannon, with John Foster Dulles behind Cannon. (Rayburn Papers, CN 11412, courtesy of the Center for American History, University of Texas at Austin.)

involved president. Nor did he wield them to serve his own political ends. Instead, he operated behind the scenes in many instances to produce the results he sought, without public fanfare. His proclivity for the hidden-hand approach to his duties has become famous, since Fred I. Greenstein first devised the term during the early 1980s. His handling of Senator Joseph R. McCarthy is often cited as the most striking example of Eisenhower's use of this method.[48]

During the controversy with McCarthy in 1954, Eisenhower resisted efforts by a congressional committee probing the Wisconsin senator to subpoena members of the president's staff about conversations and actions regarding McCarthy. The president invoked executive privilege as the rationale for refusing the request, and he did so in sweeping terms. He maintained that it would imperil the candor that the chief executive needed from his aides in conducting the people's business. The president's move rested on shaky constitutional grounds, but it commanded respect because of Eisenhower's prestige and the public sense that he had nothing to hide. Other presidents in the future would find that using executive privilege when their honesty was questioned soon was regarded as evidence of a desire to withhold damaging information from the public or law enforcement. Executive privilege became for presidents the political equivalent of using the Fifth Amendment.[49]

Eisenhower had a unique set of personal circumstances that no other modern president would possess. His triumph in World War II accorded him a legitimacy that cut across party lines. Although Democrats could and did disagree with his policies, it was implausible to suggest that his leadership skills were lacking. Thus, Eisenhower did not feel it necessary to employ the White House apparatus to pump up his own status in the office. He could select the issues with which he chose to be involved without the criticism that he was weak and indecisive, at least in his first term.

Like so many of his modern successors in the presidency, Eisenhower found that his first four years were more successful than his second term. He was the first president to experience the debilitating impact of the Twenty-second Amendment on the office. During his first term, he ended the fighting in Korea, launched the interstate highway system, and reduced the influence of Senator Joseph R. McCarthy within the Republican party and the U.S. Senate. In actions ominous for the future, the Eisenhower administration expanded the American commitment in Southeast Asia after the collapse of the French in Indochina. But as with any presidency, there was more to be done in a second term that presumably would be more productive than had been the first. Eisenhower would learn that the opposite was usually the outcome.

Eisenhower had good reasons to consider stepping down after a single term. In September 1955, he suffered a massive heart attack that hospitalized him for more than a month. A man in his mid-sixties with a history of coronary problems might have taken the attack as a sign to slow down, but pressure quickly mounted for him to serve another term. On the one hand, the White House disclosed more information about Eisenhower's condition than had been done in the case of Woodrow Wilson or Franklin D.

Roosevelt when they were ill during their presidencies. But on the other, the president and his press secretary made sure that the news the public received worked to buttress support for a run at a second term rather than raising questions about Eisenhower's health. Subsequent administrations, following the Eisenhower example, discovered that it was possible to release information about a president's health in ways that kept the press happy without disclosing all the facts about the true conditions of the chief executive's medical status.[50]

The 1956 presidential campaign against Adlai Stevenson was victorious, and the Eisenhower-Nixon ticket received another four years in office. During the second four years, however, the president found the national political environment less friendly. His unwillingness to endorse the Supreme Court's decision involving the desegregation of schools helped lead to the Little Rock crisis of 1957. The economy soured toward the end of the decade. Meanwhile, the Democrats retained control of both houses of Congress, despite Eisenhower's win in 1956, and the opposition made sweeping gains in the 1958 congressional races. As the political focus shifted to the 1960 presidential contest, where Eisenhower could not be a candidate, the momentum of the administration stalled. The president was playing defense against Democratic initiatives with the veto power and his remaining political influence.

Outside of public view in the clandestine world of American foreign policy, the Eisenhower White House extended the reach of the presidency with its sponsorship of covert actions in foreign countries to prevent what the administration deemed anti-American or procommunist governments from taking power. These initiatives were largely successful while Eisenhower was in office, but the precedents they created proved troublesome for those who came after him.

In Iran in 1953 and in Guatemala a year later, the United States orchestrated coups to topple governments presumed to be leaning toward the Soviet side or that were antagonistic to American interests. During the rest of the Eisenhower presidency, the Central Intelligence Agency set in motion other covert schemes to destabilize Third World nations. When Fidel Castro came to power in Cuba in 1959 and moved rapidly to align himself with the Soviet Union, the administration launched planning for a raid of anti-Castro rebels. The theory was that their landing in Cuba would trigger a popular uprising against the new government. Although the initiative had not been approved by the time Eisenhower left office in January 1961, it represented a powerful commitment that John F. Kennedy pursued to a foreign policy disaster.[51]

Eisenhower did not dwell much on the potential risk to American diplomacy of covert actions, and the ones he approved resulted in temporary successes for the United States. The idea that the president should have the power to circumvent constitutional channels to meet the Communist threat was one that commended itself to informed politicians of both parties at the height of the Cold War. Little attention was given to the inherent risks of interfering in other countries and the potential long-term adverse consequences to the United States, even if such ventures seemed to work.

To implement these schemes, the presidency needed the means to stage and carry out these intelligence plots. As a result, the size of such organizations as the CIA and the National Security Agency (NSA) expanded during the 1950s. Though their existence gave Eisenhower and other presidents the weapons to execute covert initiatives, they also created massive bureaucracies with a vested interest in such policies. Needing something to do to justify their budgets and personnel, the spy establishment could exert subtle and crass pressures on presidents to pursue clandestine actions. There was something inherently fascinating about the world of espionage that made it hard for presidents to resist its allure, even one as well informed and thoughtful as Dwight Eisenhower.

The shadow world that resulted was insulated from effective scrutiny. Whether an operation worked or not, the response was always the same. To discuss the performance of the CIA or the NSA or even the FBI would risk compromising their effectiveness. The upshot was that no effective outside appraisal of the outcome of clandestine operations occurred during the Eisenhower administration. Instead, their work became an integral part of the modern presidency. Not until the 1970s would the results of intelligence operations be examined and some constraints established.

In the domestic sphere, Eisenhower accepted the permanency of the New Deal, much to the dismay of conservative Republicans. The president shared their intense distaste for much of what Franklin D. Roosevelt had begun, but he recognized that demolishing the welfare state would have meant political disaster for the Grand Old Party. Eisenhower did not encourage new initiatives, except in response to Democratic pressure from Capitol Hill. As a result, the domestic policy side of the White House saw few changes during the 1950s. In the area of civil rights, the failures of the Eisenhower administration left the issue to his Democratic successors to resolve. The president's success in winning southern electoral votes in his two elections presaged the southern strategy of Richard M. Nixon and foreshadowed the erosion in the Republican appeal to black voters.[52]

Perhaps the most important contribution that Eisenhower made to the growth of the modern presidency was an intangible one. By his emphasis on continuity in domestic affairs and his capacity to avoid foreign policy debacles, he established that the gains made in presidential power during his administration were a permanent aspect of the American political environment. Had the modern presidency been seen as a Democratic innovation only, there might have been other Republican attempts to restrain executive power. Eisenhower saw to it that deference to presidential authority was as bipartisan as any aspect of the nation's governance could be.

Ironically for Eisenhower, the election of 1960 focused on the issue of whether his leadership for the past eight years had been effective enough. While John F. Kennedy did not attack the popular chief executive directly, his campaign promise to get the United States "moving again" implied that the incumbent had been too passive in meeting the needs of society. The Democratic emphasis on an alleged missile gap between the United States and the Soviet Union was a major issue in the campaign indictment of Eisenhower's record. Promises to provide a more involved and purposeful presidency ran through the Democratic appeal. In pursuing civil rights, for example, the platform pledged "the strong, active, persuasive, and inventive leadership of the President of the United States." The party also said that it would "organize the policymaking machinery of the Executive branch to provide vigor and leadership in establishing our national goals and achieving them."[53]

Much of this was campaign rhetoric, but it also embodied the conviction of many Democrats that Eisenhower, despite the important changes he had made in how the presidency functioned, had not been modern enough to meet the challenges at home and abroad. Leadership in the White House had to be seen in operation to work with maximum effectiveness in deterring the enemies of the United States and in engaging the nation's domestic difficulties. As Henry Kissinger said to Arthur M. Schlesinger during late summer, "We need someone who will take a big jump — not just improve on existing trends but produce a new frame of mind, a new national atmosphere."[54] Whether action alone would be enough remained to be determined, as the power of the modern presidency passed from Eisenhower to John F. Kennedy on 20 January 1961.

6

The Souring of the Modern Presidency
John F. Kennedy and Lyndon B. Johnson

After two decades of uninterrupted growth in the power of the modern presidency, the 1960s saw the first signs of popular questioning about the increasing authority of the American executive. The skepticism did not begin during the opening three years of that decade, when John F. Kennedy was in the White House. The way in which Kennedy approached the office, however, laid the foundation for the problems that Lyndon B. Johnson encountered in foreign policy. Both men conducted their administrations in a manner that rejected the institutional precedents set under Dwight D. Eisenhower. The results did not suggest that notable improvements in presidential leadership had occurred.

John F. Kennedy became president in January 1961 with one of the thinnest policy backgrounds of any chief executive in the twentieth century. After three terms in the House of Representatives, from 1947 to 1953, Kennedy won a Senate seat in 1952 and gained a landslide reelection six years later. Never much interested in legislation, the Massachusetts senator spent his first term in uncertain health and in his second immediately began a presidential run. His involvement in labor reform legislation in 1959 represented his one serious commitment to Capitol Hill. Perhaps because he was not tied to a legislative record, Kennedy proved to be an excellent presidential candidate, whose rhetoric aroused powerful expectations about how he would get the nation "moving again." The exact means of achieving such goals, however, were left undefined when his presidency got under way, following his narrow victory over Richard M. Nixon in the 1960 election.[1]

Kennedy had been thinking about the nature of presidential leadership since his student days at Harvard, and his writings when in Congress, even though largely drafted by others, had returned to the same theme. Yet he had not formulated a clear sense of how he would conduct the day-to-day business of the White House except that he would not emulate his predecessor. The advice that he received about organizing the White House played down Eisenhower's arrangements and looked to a return to the practices and techniques of Franklin D. Roosevelt. Kennedy and his men believed that the staffing arrangements under Eisenhower had been too formal and too structured. The result had been that the president, in their opinion, had been insulated from new ideas and fresh thinking. Under the new president, the staff would be more loose and less tied to the bureaucratic routine so that the White House could be a more energetic and innovative place for the 1960s.

This approach represented a return to the Democratic style of the presidency, where generalists ranged into different areas and dealt with issues and problems as they arose. While it put a premium on spontaneity and quick thinking, it also allowed less time for the framing of opposing alternatives on policy matters. The president himself did not like being tied to formal procedures, and that ethos permeated his administration. In practice, the fabled freshness and élan of the Kennedy era turned out to have serious weaknesses when it came to practical implementation.[2]

Despite some initial stumbles, Kennedy showed a deft touch in handling the public relations aspect of the presidency. At the suggestion of his press secretary, Pierre Salinger, the president took the next step with press conferences and began holding them live for a national television audience. The byplay between president and journalists was fascinating, and Kennedy enjoyed the experience of give-and-take. The first such conference was held on 25 January 1961 in the State Department auditorium. There had been some grumbles from newsmen about the change when it was first announced after the elections. James Reston, the influential columnist of the New York Times, dubbed it "the goofiest idea since the hula hoop." But the departure was such a natural extension of what had been done under Eisenhower that it caught on at once. After all, the president had reached an audience estimated at 60 million people.[3]

The Kennedy press conferences emerged as one of the popular media events of the early 1960s. The president prepared for them in a systematic manner, since any gaffe would be magnified for the television audience. These intensive rehearsals served the purpose of informing Kennedy about pending issues, which, with his quick mind, he absorbed rapidly. Since the event had not yet evolved into a media spectacular, a fair degree of actual news was elicited from the president as well. The telecasts did help to transform the reporters from faceless scribes into media celebrities in their own right. That process, in turn, would intensify the examination of the workings of the presidency as a means of generating ratings for television itself.

As time passed, however, some people in network television thought that Kennedy relied too heavily on the press conference format and should be doing more in other areas. "The rough consensus" was that "the President has not made as good use of TV as others," as Jack Gould, the *New York Times* television critic, reported to his superiors in April 1963. Reporters would have preferred more interviews with Kennedy to explore issues in depth, but that would have raised questions of cost for the networks and equal time constraints as far as the Republicans were concerned.[4]

At a time when the presidency was still an object of deference, the media helped Kennedy take the celebrity aspects of his position to new levels of international superstar status. His apparent youthful energy (which did not take into account his weak back and reliance on painkillers) and the glamour of his young and beautiful wife Jacqueline contributed to the public impression that vitality and exuberance had reappeared in the White House for the first time since Theodore Roosevelt had occupied the office at the turn of the century. "The palpable love affair between the White House and a jade called Culture shows signs of reaching an impassioned peak this year," gushed two writers in the *New York Times* in January 1962. On a more mundane level, Hollywood helped the cause with an implausible film about the president's combat experiences as a PT-boat commander in the South Pacific. The movie was a commercial failure.[5]

The president and his wife contrived to create an atmosphere of elegance and sophistication that captivated the nation. The president was depicted as

---

Following page: John F. Kennedy was a celebrity from the moment he sought the presidency. An enthusiastic crowd presses the candidate as he campaigns in Charlotte, North Carolina, in October 1960, and Kennedy's face expresses some of the dismay that went with the process. (Photograph by Bruce Roberts, from the Roberts Collection, CN 11468, Center for American History, University of Texas at Austin.)

Notwithstanding his physical ailments, John F. Kennedy conveyed an impression of youthful vigor and energy that helped make him a presidential superstar. (Courtesy of the Library of Congress.)

a sponsor of the arts and culture even though his reading tastes were conventional and his knowledge of music and art rudimentary at best. His fascination with the James Bond spy novels of Ian Fleming was made to appear more penetrating than President Eisenhower's fondness for westerns. Skillful speechwriting and the aura of his wife's love for early-nineteenth-century French decor helped push the notion that the age of Theodore and Edith Roosevelt had been recaptured. In so doing John and Jacqueline Kennedy established expectations for cultural leadership in the White House that their successors would find difficult to equal.[6]

Artifice and a healthy dose of deceit had always been part of the presidency. Under Kennedy, media management and outright deception reflected some troubling aspects of the modern chief executive. The president's casual view of his marriage vows, as well as his voracious sexual appetites, were known to many reporters and gossiped about in well-informed circles during the early 1960s. The press observed the code of silence that still shrouded the personal lives of politicians (and protected their own dalliances) and did not delve into the president's many extramarital affairs or his involvements with women on the fringes of organized crime.[7]

Such a conspiracy of silence succeeded because the exploration of presidential lapses was still out of bounds for respectable press inquiry. During the Kennedy years there began to be some efforts among right-wing Republicans to bring the president's sins to light, and these scandalmongering books did attract an audience. For the most part, however, the Kennedy White House used the goodwill of the press to keep Kennedy's misdeeds in the shadows. Kennedy was a master at giving favored reporters such as Benjamin Bradlee of *Newsweek* the illusion of friendship and just enough access to satisfy their desire to be on the inside of events without making the journalists real players. When reporters did not succumb to presidential blandishments or contradicted the official line on a subject such as Vietnam, the president was quite willing to employ the more blatant forms of pressure with publishers and advertisers to bring the scribes back into line.[8]

Yet good relations with the press and media manipulation, though important to Kennedy, could take the new president only so far. Because he had made so much of his Democratic activism during the presidential campaign, he faced immediate comparisons with Franklin D. Roosevelt and the One Hundred Days of 1933. Indeed, the expectations of such a fruitful period arose even before Kennedy was elected. The situation of the two presidents could not have been more different in the objective circumstances that they confronted. In 1961, with the nation at peace and relatively prosperous, there was no national economic crisis or tangible sense of national urgency for Kennedy, despite his efforts to strike such a note in his inaugural address. Part of the point of Kennedy's strident language on that occasion was to arouse public opinion for the challenges the new president meant to pose. His election margin over Richard M. Nixon had been so narrow and his working majority in Congress so tenuous that ambitious national legislative programs were also out of the question. If Kennedy was to be a strong president and gain a second term in 1964, he would have to do so by presidential initiatives in foreign policy rather than as an architect of laws and programs.[9]

The levers of power in the White House established under Roosevelt, Truman, and Eisenhower were there for Kennedy to grasp in 1961, but the machinery of the modern presidency did not come with instructions for its

wise use in all situations. The new president did not admire the formal institutions of government; indeed, he viewed them all with suspicion. The Department of State, for example, was to his mind a necessary but somewhat
fossilized bureaucracy. Therefore he planned to run foreign policy from the
White House and have the secretary of state, Dean Rusk, play only a subordinate role in overall policy making in foreign affairs. His national security
adviser, McGeorge Bundy, operated a little State Department from the White
House. The resulting informality suited Kennedy's distaste for procedures that
cramped his initiatives and required him to listen to people he found dull.
The working theory was that organizational looseness would facilitate honest debate within the administration and thus make for better decision making, but that did not occur under Kennedy.[10]

In casual settings where the group dynamic emphasized quick thinking
and crisp, articulate answers, the measured response or the thoughtful answer often became the casualty of the Kennedy zest for rapid-fire responses.
Toughness was also prized, and a willingness to negotiate or to reject the
hard position was less welcome. This was odd since Kennedy himself so
often came to a more nuanced and less strident stance than many of his
more assertive advisers. But in the cut and thrust of the debate, dissenting
opinions on foreign policy did not receive as much attention as they sometimes deserved.

The first example of this trend was in the Bay of Pigs episode during spring
1961, when Kennedy dealt with the planning for an invasion of Cuba based
on preparations started under Eisenhower. The informal and ad hoc way in
which the decision was made meant that questioning voices about the venture were not heard in an effective manner. The result of not examining carefully the underlying presumptions of the scheme was a foreign policy fiasco
that disrupted the momentum of the new administration at the outset and
wounded the credibility and prestige of the United States.[11]

Following the Cuban debacle, Kennedy did not establish mechanisms to
improve the manner in which advice came to him and was then evaluated.
Instead, he placed more reliance on his brother, Attorney General Robert F.
Kennedy, and on his speechwriter, Theodore Sorensen, to screen potential
decisions for possible dangers. This technique survived the Cuban Missile
Crisis of fall 1962 when an Executive Committee (ExCom) of White House
insiders dealt with the threat of a nuclear confrontation after the Soviet Union

deployed missiles in Cuba. The success in avoiding a catastrophe seemed to validate Kennedy's methods as president.[12]

In the case of Vietnam, however, the administration never implemented procedures that would have allowed for a careful assessment of the risks inherent in the mounting American involvement in Southeast Asia. With no one in the White House clearly in charge of the problem, Kennedy and his team accepted the premise that the Communist insurgency in South Vietnam must and could be defeated. Optimistic statements led the American people to believe that the conflict was being won.[13]

There was no means in the administration to frame the alternatives in Vietnam so that the potential costs of further intervention could be evaluated. When the situation deteriorated during fall 1963, Kennedy and his advisers immersed themselves in the plotting to topple the president of South Vietnam, Ngo Dinh Diem, without thinking through the ramifications that eventually included Diem's assassination.[14]

The death of Diem serves as a final example of the fascination during the Kennedy years with sinister gimmicks and trickery as tools of presidential action. The Bay of Pigs left the president with a strong animus against Fidel Castro and the conviction that any means was justified to bring down the Cuban ruler. That view led in turn to a bizarre series of plots to kill Castro. Although the defenders of the president have asserted that these schemes went forward without his knowledge, it is clear that John and Robert Kennedy created a climate in the White House where such covert ventures received implicit sanction at the highest levels. The administration was fortunate that these ill-advised plots did not become public knowledge until more than a decade after Kennedy's death. The idea that strong presidents could work outside the law to accomplish their foreign policy goals was a creed with dangerous implications.[15]

The president also brought technology and secrecy into the Oval Office with the installation of the most elaborate presidential tape-recording arrangement up to that time. Created to monitor what visitors said to Kennedy and to furnish him with materials for his memoirs, the recording machinery was state of the art for 1962. Its existence was closely guarded from all but a few of his advisers, and the resulting tapes do illuminate many of the important events of Kennedy's presidency, especially the Cuban Missile Crisis. The ethics of taping individuals without their knowledge did not trouble President

Kennedy, whose view of morality tended to be flexible in any circumstances. The Kennedys also had no qualms about widespread wiretapping of his friends and enemies to plug leaks and to gather damaging evidence for use against suspected individuals.[16]

During the Kennedy presidency, the system of record keeping that had maintained the papers of each president since the Taft administration finally broke down under the weight of the paper that came to the White House each year. To replace the numerical filing system, archivists in the Executive Mansion turned to a categorical arrangement under broad subject headings, with subdivisions for executive and general documents. A confidential file system was kept for more sensitive records, along with detailed chronicles of the president's calendar and daily movements. In addition, a White House name file tracked the individual letters and memoranda of people who interacted with the presidency. As these documents proliferated and as presidential libraries came into use, the records of the presidency provided a fascinating cross-section of American opinion on the nation's highest office. The modern presidency was in that sense one of the most historically accessible institutions in the nation, with a precise documentation of the behavior and thoughts of its occupants.

The Kennedy administration also used the services of a pollster, Lou Harris, whose firm often worked for Democratic clients. The president followed these surveys closely since the narrowness of his 1960 victory was always in his mind. Harris did not come into the White House as an official member of the staff so that a distance could be maintained between the president and the molding of public opinion. The continuous mode of campaigning that reached its peak under Richard Nixon was already in formation under Kennedy.[17]

As part of its crusade against organized crime, the Kennedy administration sent one of their trusted aides, Carmine Bellino, to the Internal Revenue Service as early as January 1961 to look into returns of persons whom the White House suspected of mob ties. Later, as conservative opposition to the White House surged, the Kennedys used the IRS to undermine support for the right-wing movement and to cast doubt on these conservatives' credibility as critics of the Democratic president. Though these tactics did not go as far as those that occurred under Richard Nixon, the pressures of the Kennedy administration on the tax-collecting agency illustrated that modern presidents of all political stripes could abuse executive authority when it suited them.[18]

Kennedy's domestic priorities were less ambitious than his foreign policy pursuits. In part, the lack of a working majority in the House of Representatives limited his options. The new administration had to expend much of its political capital in 1961 simply to reshape the House Rules Committee so that legislation it favored might receive floor action. Kennedy retained the Office of Congressional Relations that Eisenhower had started. Lawrence "Larry" O'Brien, who had run Kennedy's presidential campaign, headed the operation. O'Brien and his staff became quite adept at handling the day-to-day work on Capitol Hill, and in a more favorable political environment the office would have been an efficient adjunct for the White House. The administration could not change the negative political arithmetic in Congress, however, and Kennedy's legislative program largely stalled between 1961 and 1963. A tax cut and a civil rights bill were in the pipeline by the time of his death, but they faced an uncertain future during a presidential election year.[19]

Despite the mixed record of his administration, Kennedy somehow represented the modern presidency at the height of its power and influence. The circumstances of his death and the legends that surrounded his life were indispensable to the president's favorable posthumous reputation. Decades after his murder he ranked in public opinion polls as one of the nation's greatest presidents. His standing with his fellow citizens seemed impervious to the steady erosion of his esteem among historians and political scientists during the 1980s and 1990s. More revelations fed the popular fascination about his life without detracting from the high regard in which average Americans held Kennedy and his wife.[20]

The Kennedys' biggest contribution to the modern presidency was glamour and celebrity. Not since Theodore Roosevelt had a chief executive garnered such elements of matinee-idol adoration as Jack Kennedy. Although some of this status derived from Kennedy's appealing personal qualities, it rested to a far larger degree on the elements of public relations and hype that had marked his career since he entered politics in 1946. There was always a sense of exaggeration in all of his prepresidential accomplishments. His first book, *Why England Slept* (1940), became a best-seller because his father bought up copies by the thousands. The wartime heroism Kennedy displayed in the South Pacific was elevated to mythical proportions with the timely assistance of a laudatory *Reader's Digest* article that became a staple of his early political campaigns. His Pulitzer Prize–winning book *Profiles in Courage* was a largely ghostwritten project, and the award itself came through the intervention of a newspaperman, Arthur Krock of the *New York Times,* who was close to Kennedy's father.[21]

None of these contrivances was different from the behavior of other presidential hopefuls in individual cases of their own, but Kennedy permitted these promotional devices to occur on his behalf with little sense of shame or embarrassment. He cultivated a wry detachment from all his father did, but he was quite willing to profit from the political rewards of these manipulations. In many respects, John F. Kennedy was not so much made the president, in Theodore H. White's phrase, as marketed as one. With Kennedy, the culture of celebrity, which had been an element on the fringes of the White House for most of the century, became a central element in how the president was to be portrayed.

Since stardom had raised Jack Kennedy to the White House, it was natural to continue these successful practices once he had taken the oath of office. From the new president's fragile medical condition to his sexual adventurism, these aspects of his life and character were carefully kept under wraps and out of the public gaze. Instead, Kennedy and his wife contrived occasions where their youth and vitality conveyed an aura of sophistication and good taste. With the impact of network television at its postwar height, a telegenic president and First Lady gave the nation its first true presidential glamour couple.

Because of the brevity of his term and the political stalemate that he faced, Kennedy did not have to ask the American people for any of the real sacrifices he had alluded to in his inaugural address. With prosperity returning and the boom of the 1960s getting under way, there was a rising tide that lifted his administration. Only toward the end of 1963 did the president address such issues as civil rights, where political capital would have to be expended and the authority of his office exercised. For the most part, Kennedy's time in office, even with the Cuban Missile Crisis and the developing problem in Vietnam, was a period when the modern presidency seemed to have mastered the demands of foreign and domestic affairs.

The assassination of President Kennedy in Dallas on 22 November 1963 marked a significant transformation in the history of the office that went well beyond the traumatic transfer of power to Vice President Lyndon B. Johnson. The shock of Kennedy's death revealed the fragility of the institution and the social continuity it provided to the nation. The inability of the Warren Commission, despite the plausibility of its conclusions, to persuade the country of the motive behind the president's death and the identity of his assassin fueled conspiracy theories that persisted four decades after the event. Meanwhile, the pain of the Vietnam War and Johnson's style as president would accelerate the process of doubting the value of modern presidents as powerful leaders of the nation.

The legend of John F. Kennedy as a president who would have avoided the Vietnam quagmire and forestalled the domestic upheavals of the 1960s, had he lived to win and serve a second term, proved a compelling tale. That it probably masked a more sober alternative of involvement in Southeast Asia and revelations of Kennedy's personal lapses did not detract from its force as a social mythology. For both of Kennedy's immediate successors, Lyndon B. Johnson and Richard M. Nixon, the ghost of John F. Kennedy cast a shadow over their records and the development of the modern presidency.

With the administration of Lyndon B. Johnson, the steady accretion of presidential power that had commenced at the turn of the century reached a turning point. As the Johnson administration became more enmeshed in Vietnam while simultaneously seeking social reform through the Great Society at home, voices on both ends of the political spectrum advanced critiques of presidential authority. What had seemed on the whole a healthy process of providing presidents with the means to meet the challenges of the postwar world was reappraised, and those means were seen as elements in an imperial presidency that overreached its constitutional and moral limits.

Such a result seemed unlikely in the immediate aftermath of Kennedy's death, when Lyndon Johnson grasped the power of the presidency with seemingly sure hands. The fifty-five-year-old Texan calmed a traumatized nation and emphasized that his administration would continue to follow Kennedy's policies. Indeed, it appeared that the former Senate majority leader might prove more adept than Kennedy had been in persuading Congress to adopt a tax cut bill and to pass legislation on civil rights. As an avowed heir of Franklin D. Roosevelt, Johnson was poised to enact the agenda of the post–New Deal that had been stalemated in Congress for a generation.[22]

Johnson himself came to the presidency rich in Washington experience and a lifetime of observing the occupants of the White House from Herbert Hoover on. He had overseen the National Youth Administration in Texas for a year and a half in the mid-1930s, but his recent experience had been in running his Senate staff. On Capitol Hill, he was notorious as a whimsical task-master, vituperative and bullying one moment and contrite and conciliatory the next. Managing the presidency and a White House staff of more than four hundred members would be a challenge for a driven man who relished such demands. Johnson was also anxious to establish himself as a great president, perhaps even outdoing his beloved Franklin D. Roosevelt.[23]

His first instinct was to stress the links between himself and Kennedy, even though his three years as vice president had been painful ones for the proud Johnson. "I think Kennedy thought I was autocratic, bossy, self-centered," Johnson recalled in 1969. The new president kept in place Kennedy's cabinet but gradually replaced the White House staff with people he believed he could trust. Throughout his presidency, he craved orderly decision making and smooth, efficient processing of presidential choices. He spent a great deal of his time in pursuit of that elusive goal. At various times, Bill Moyers, Robert Kintner, and Marvin Watson operated as a kind of de facto White House chief of staff, but in reality Johnson served in that post himself for most of his presidency.[24]

Johnson's management style combined tension, coercion, and blandishments. Rarely reflective himself, he discouraged careful deliberations about alternatives and emphasized initiative and self-starting among his advisers. He often emulated Franklin D. Roosevelt in setting two or three aides to deal with the same issue, in what one of the staffers called a "bear pit technique." In that sense, Johnson, like Kennedy, followed the Democratic method of using rival generalists rather than relying on Eisenhower's system of aides with well-defined areas of responsibility.[25]

The new president, however, was incapable of creating procedures and then letting the staff operate on their own. A lifetime of micromanaging the actions of his aides and the details of legislation disposed Johnson to believe that he knew more and could do better than most of the people who worked for him. He was probably correct that he could do their jobs better, but he could not simultaneously do all those tasks more successfully than all of his staffers could. The impulse to pick up the telephone and cut through the red tape was one he rarely resisted. Often his intervention led to impressive results. On other occasions, it simply stirred up confusion and muddied the waters. Even someone with Johnson's prodigious energies could not master every detail of how his government functioned on a daily basis.[26]

One illustration of Johnson's obsession with the workings of his administration and his desire to control information was the use of the taping system
in the White House to an even greater degree than Eisenhower and Kennedy
had used it. Sensitive to his place in history, Johnson had been having aides
make shorthand accounts of his telephone conversations since the early 1950s.
Once he became president, he expanded the dictaphone recording system in
the White House to include his bedroom, Camp David, and the LBJ Ranch
in Texas. He insisted that immediate transcripts be made, and he often employed the record of a previous conversation when talking to a person he
wished to influence.[27]

The results of the tape are riveting. They provide a record of Lyndon Johnson
in action, cajoling, bullying, and persuading. For historians they are a trea-
sure trove of data about the volcanic president at work. Although some people
in Washington sensed that Johnson must be making a record of his conversations at the time, the existence of the taping system was not generally known
during his presidency. He did disclose its operation to Richard Nixon in
November 1968. Nixon resolved to have it removed and did not intend at the
outset of his administration to use such a system for himself. Johnson's taping venture attested to the extent to which some modern presidents wielded
all the tools of technology to exert control over their working environment
and the political system.[28]

In contrast to Johnson's intense and often disorganized approach to managing his staff was his wife's orderly and innovative style as First Lady. Lady
Bird Johnson brought in Elizabeth "Liz" Carpenter as staff director and press
secretary. This appointment became the first step toward a genuine staffing
structure for a president's wife. Subsequent additions to the First Lady's operation included aides to interact with Congress, to link with outside pressure
groups, and to manage the media as a means of furthering the goals of her campaign to improve the environment. The emergence of a small bureaucracy,
paralleling that of the president, to sustain the work of the First Lady was an
important institutional contribution of the Johnson White House.[29]

Johnson was concerned with his own popularity as it affected his ability
to lead, so he installed a pollster inside the White House to monitor the surveys that came in from Lou Harris and Johnson's favorite, Oliver Quayle.
When the polls were favorable, the president flaunted them. After the Vietnam War produced discouraging numbers, the White House put out infor-

mation questioning the accuracy of the polls themselves. One aide drafted ghostwritten letters for others to write, raising issues about how the surveys were taken. More than any other president before him, Johnson wove polling into the daily operation of the presidency.[30]

Like Kennedy, Johnson also turned to the Internal Revenue Service to monitor and to discomfit political enemies. The number of White House requests for checks on tax returns went up significantly during Johnson's presidency. Dissenters from the war in Vietnam had their returns targeted. The radical magazine *Ramparts* came under scrutiny when it exposed links between the Central Intelligence Agency and the National Student Association. Yet Johnson's use of the IRS seems to have been more spasmodic than systematic in its approach. The precedent he set would impress Richard Nixon.[31]

Lyndon Johnson had risen to the presidency through the tangled world of Texas Democratic politics, and he brought great strengths and corresponding weaknesses to the Oval Office. On the positive side, he had amassed an unrivaled knowledge of how Washington operated. Though never bookish or a great reader, he had assembled through experience and the process of passing legislation for two decades a formidable grasp of the workings of Congress, bureaucratic agencies, and Washington politics. Probably no modern president better understood the legislative process and how to manipulate it. One-on-one, Johnson had impressive powers of persuasion, as his recently released taped telephone conversations make clear.

But with his strengths came accompanying weaknesses. Having mastered the one-party setting of Texas, Johnson never really understood the national Democrats and, more important, their Republican opponents. He thus believed that partisan differences were somewhat illusory and could readily be compromised in search of a bipartisan consensus. He did not devote much time to the internal structure of his party, and he shifted the fund-raising emphasis to wealthy donors beholden to the president for access and favors. In the process, the grass roots of the Democrats withered. He did not regard partisan politics as an ongoing process in the way that the Kennedy White House had done.[32]

An even greater personal failing was Johnson's lifelong tendency for exaggeration and deceit, even when those two qualities were not required to achieve a cherished result. A poor public speaker, he did even less well on

Few presidents have followed television coverage with more attention than Lyndon Johnson. He had three sets in the Oval Office so he could monitor the networks. In the end, few presidents have been more inept than Johnson in dealing with the television medium. (Photograph by Yoichi Okamoto, courtesy of the Lyndon B. Johnson Library.)

television. Combined with his distrust of reporters and the news media in general, these drawbacks made it uncomfortable for him to deal either with criticism or sustained political difficulties. Johnson had the potential to be a great president, but the downside of his personality left open the possibility of even more enduring failures as well.

His relationship with the media was one area where Johnson was never at ease as president. He had grown up with the compliant, amateurish reporters of the major Texas newspapers, who did the bidding of their conservative publishers. In his years in the House and especially as majority leader of the Senate, he had cultivated Capitol Hill scribes such as William S. White, who sang his praises and rarely posed hard questions. Although Johnson had extensive and lucrative radio and television holdings in Texas, he never grasped how video was reshaping the way politicians had to present themselves to the public. He remained resolutely old-fashioned in the way he gave speeches and approached the television camera.[33]

After the practiced grace of Jack Kennedy on television, Johnson seemed like a throwback to a preradio age. He was too gauche for the new medium and seemed awkward and out of touch. Never happy with criticism of his performances, he resisted efforts by aides to present him in less structured settings where he could be spontaneous and more appealing. Instead of adapting to conditions that he could not change, he continued to appear stiff and remote on television. As a result, his effectiveness as a communicator diminished just when his presidency most needed such talents.

In his other dealings with the press, Johnson mingled contempt and deceit that multiplied his troubles over the life of his administration. Believing that every reporter had a price, whether it was inside access or ego gratification, Johnson initially approached Washington journalists after 1963 as though they were courtesans or lackeys. He told his press secretary George Reedy in April 1964 that reporters were "not the masters of the White House. They're just the servants and we give them what we want to give them." It did not take long for the working press to discern how the new president really felt about their work.[34]

When reporters were critical, despite presidential blandishments, Johnson soured on the press corps in general. Thereafter, he delighted in inflicting petty slights, such as unscheduled trips on weekends or other surprise announcements that disrupted the personal lives of the journalists. When news of potential presidential appointments leaked out, as it usually did in Washington, the president would select other candidates just to show the press his independence. These tactics did not change the behavior of the media; they made Lyndon Johnson look foolish and small.[35]

Johnson's larger problem with the Fourth Estate was his lifelong habit of dissembling. In Texas that had not been a journalistic issue because reporters did not say much about it. Even in the Senate, Johnson's tendency to play fast and loose with the truth had not hurt him. On the national stage, however, where every presidential utterance was scrutinized, reporters noticed and wrote how Johnson had deceived them about the size of his first budget in 1964 and other matters. The phrase that became current was Johnson's "credibility gap," a takeoff on the missile gap of a few years earlier. It was still inappropriate to dub the president an outright liar, but Johnson would soon make that possible.[36]

In operating the White House, Johnson kept in place the Office of Congressional Relations under Larry O'Brien, and it worked with even greater efficiency than during the Kennedy years. During the first two years of his presidency, before the political climate darkened in the wake of Vietnam and the race issue, Johnson enjoyed a string of legislative triumphs that enacted Kennedy's program and then pushed forward to pass the major elements of his own Great Society agenda. The laws poured out in what seemed an unstoppable flow — education, conservation, solutions to urban problems, and health care — as Johnson drove himself to realize his dream of exceeding Roosevelt and the New Deal.[37]

But by fall 1965 the receptivity of lawmakers to the president's legislative entreaties faded. The worsening situation in Southeast Asia and the impact of the racial unrest in the major cities diminished enthusiasm for his priorities. The Democrats elected to the House in his landslide win over Barry Goldwater saw their reelection prospects for 1966 darken. Though Johnson was still able to get some measures through in 1967 and 1968, the legislative magic of 1964 and 1965 had vanished. His skill with Congress proved to be transient and beyond repair by procedural changes within the White House.[38]

Part of Johnson's problems with Congress arose because of his willingness to engage a major social issue that Eisenhower had dodged and that Kennedy had dealt with seriously only in 1963. As a southerner, Johnson knew that critics were waiting to see what he would do about civil rights. The new president, despite his defenses of segregation laws in the past in Congress and his crude language in private, had a greater sense of the inequities that African Americans confronted than any other modern president. Even at the risk of spending political capital or placing in danger the traditional Democratic hold on the South, Johnson intended that broad civil rights legislation would be one of the legacies of his administration.[39]

Although he never forgot political calculations in his handling of the civil rights issue and sometimes fell short of his best impulses, Johnson put the moral authority of the White House behind black aspirations as no president before or since had done. The legislation of his era — the Civil Rights Act of 1964, the Voting Rights Act of 1965, the Civil Rights Act of 1968 — attested to his commitment. So too did his appointment of blacks to the cabinet and other agencies as well as the nomination of Thurgood Marshall to the Supreme Court. Dedication to social justice has not been one of the hallmarks of the modern presidency, but that quality sets Lyndon Johnson apart from other chief executives after 1952.

The central issue of Johnson's performance in the White House, however, was the Vietnam War. On that conflict, Johnson rested the fate of his presidency and his historical reputation. Yet from the outset of his involvement with the problem, the president refused to face the true dimensions of the American presence in Southeast Asia. It was a dilemma to be managed and deferred so that his political position would not be threatened. He dodged the bullet through much of 1964 and then found himself enmeshed in the issue as his second term began in early 1965.[40]

The war did not interrupt Johnson's progress toward election in his own right in November 1964. Faced with the challenge from the embodiment of the new conservative spirit within the Republican party, Senator Barry M. Goldwater of Arizona, Johnson was able to assemble the resources available to an incumbent president to defeat his outmatched rival in a landslide. In the way he handled the war during the contest, Johnson laid the groundwork for troubles to come.[41]

In the Tonkin Gulf incident of August 1964, Johnson parlayed an ambiguous military encounter with North Vietnamese naval forces into an attack on the United States that convinced Congress to grant him virtually unlimited powers to repulse aggression in Southeast Asia. But the president and the military could not prevent all the facts of these muddled engagements from coming out some years later. When they did so, the revelations inflicted serious wounds on Johnson's political integrity and undercut his rationale for the war itself.

Ardent in his desire to achieve a blowout victory over Goldwater, Johnson raised the rhetorical stakes by promising neither an escalation nor a pullout from South Vietnam, once he was elected in his own right. As he put it on the campaign trail, stopping Southeast Asia from becoming Communist did not necessarily involve ordering "American boys 9 or 10,000 miles away from home to do what Asian boys ought to be doing for themselves." Johnson qualified his remarks with comments about not pulling out of the region, either, and he no doubt assumed that the campaign language would serve its temporary purpose and then be filed away as a dead issue. After all, as one young man of draft age at that time recalled, "Republican presidential candidate Barry Goldwater would send us to Vietnam, not Johnson."[42]

Television with its half hour of nightly news raised these promises above the level of previous campaign oratory and transformed them into solemn pledges to be broken at a president's peril. Johnson knew that contingency plans were going forward to intensify the war in Vietnam, but he could not tell that to the voters, lest he be seen as an advocate of war in the way his campaign operatives were depicting Goldwater. But the capacity of presidents to say one thing in public and do another in private was diminishing in ways that Johnson did not comprehend. The president relied on the mystique of his office and the people's faith in their leaders, but after Kennedy's death that too had begun to slip away.

So when Johnson began to bomb North Vietnam and introduce greater numbers of ground troops into South Vietnam in 1965, he delivered a telling blow to the political system of the United States itself and to the presidency in particular. Disguise it as he might with references to the commitments of earlier presidents to Southeast Asia, he confronted the American people with the spectacle of a president who had said one thing and then done another. The more he attempted to justify his course in televised speeches, the more inauthentic he came to appear.

Johnson was in a tough predicament. He believed with good reason that if he withdrew from South Vietnam the Republicans would raise the charge that he and his party were soft on Communism. That is why he had said at the outset of his presidency that he did not want South Vietnam "to go the way China went." At the same time, he knew that a war in Asia would frustrate his plans for domestic reform. He was also aware, as he told friends in 1964 and 1965, that he did not see how a war in Southeast Asia could be won. "A man can fight if he can see daylight down the road somewhere," he said to Senator Richard Russell on 6 March 1965. "But there ain't no daylight in Vietnam. There's not a bit." Yet he did not feel secure enough to share his doubts with the American people. In a fateful set of decisions, the president hoped to be able to apply just enough military force to produce a negotiated settlement without becoming enmeshed in a quagmire in South Vietnam.[43]

These aims and the political finesse that would be required to accomplish them were beyond Johnson's prodigious talents as president. His background in Texas politics had not prepared him to communicate with the national electorate. Moreover, he suffered in comparison to John F. Kennedy as a performer, but Johnson's problems were more pervasive than that drawback. In Texas, he had been able to get away with a mixture of pork barrel politics, disguised appeals to racial prejudice, and a modicum of anticommunism. He had never been required to defend his positions from reasoned attacks, from either the right or the left. For all the talk of the persuasive power of "the Johnson treatment," he had not so much convinced as bullied the people whose votes he needed.

But presidential coercion no longer worked in the 1960s. Johnson had to offer a rational argument for involvement in Vietnam. In so doing, he marshaled the weapons of the modern presidency through position papers, timely leaks, and a series of speeches. Once these rituals had been carried out, then it was up to the American people to support "their president." As Johnson often said, the nation has only one president at a time.

But for the first time in the history of the twentieth-century presidency, the assurances from the White House had to compete with images of the faraway war on television, where the fighting was not going as well as the Pentagon and the White House claimed. The administration was not used to a state of affairs that called into question the words of its spokesmen. In World War II and Korea, the reporters had supported the war effort, and the White House had accepted the presence of the press as a fact of life. Future presidencies would be less accommodating toward the media.

As the war in Vietnam became more bloody and stalemated, Johnson's domestic political base frayed under the pressure of dissent from the left among Democrats and increasing unhappiness among white voters on the right with the perceived consequences of the civil rights revolution. The urban riots of the mid-1960s and the long hot summers that they brought in their wake convinced many Americans that the Johnson White House had carried its War on Poverty and social programs too far. Republican arguments against big government proved politically powerful as the GOP made substantial gains in the 1966 congressional elections.

The last two years of Johnson's administration saw the power and the prestige of the presidency dwindle under a repeated series of shocks. The White House escalated the war in Vietnam through 1967, and the military was making plans to use even more troops the following year. As domestic dissent over these policies mounted, Johnson found himself more and more a prisoner in the Executive Mansion, much as Woodrow Wilson had been nearly fifty years earlier during his illness. The ability of the president to move about the country in safety was much reduced. Only military bases offered secure venues for his appearances. The reach of the modern presidency remained long in terms of affecting the lives of Americans, but for the occupant of the White House the capacity to persuade his fellow citizens to follow unpopular policies had shrunk into a kind of presidential impotence.

By early 1968, the Tet Offensive against American and South Vietnamese forces convinced most Americans that the war in Asia could not be won on terms the nation could accept. Johnson's renomination by the Democratic party faced growing challenges from Senators Eugene McCarthy of Minnesota and Robert Kennedy of New York. With his political support collapsing and uncertain about his own health over another four years in office, Johnson announced in a nationwide television address on 31 March 1968 that he would not be a candidate for his party's nomination.[44]

The decision proved a fateful one in the evolution of the modern presidency. Harry S. Truman sixteen years earlier had been an unlikely candidate for what would have been almost a third full term when he announced his retirement in March 1952. Johnson, on the other hand, had been in the presidency a little more than four years and was widely presumed to have been seeking reelection when 1968 opened. His announcement meant that the inherent advantages of incumbency were not enough to protect a president from the effects of failed policies and pervasive popular discontent with him personally. Winning the presidency was thus a mixed achievement for a politician. It might secure the winner a place in history, but it could also provide a ticket to oblivion, even with all the imperial trappings of the office.

Lyndon Johnson's administration had thus shattered the mystique of the imperial presidency and made the position less imposing and more vulnerable. The mistakes he had made, other presidents had made before him. But Johnson's attempt to wage war abroad and to pursue social reform at home at the same time put a premium on a deft mastery of national politics that the Texan simply did not possess. In the process he wounded the institution of the presidency for more than a generation. Once skepticism about the legitimacy of the modern presidency was introduced into the American political system, it proved impossible to restore the credibility that had once attached to the office.

Johnson's successor, Richard M. Nixon, inherited the problems that his predecessor could not solve. Like Dwight D. Eisenhower in 1953, Nixon had a chance to be a Republican peacemaker who ended war and restored a semblance of domestic peace. Instead, he approached the presidency as an extension of a partisan campaign, and the crimes of his administration deepened the wounds of the modern presidency in the 1960s.

7

The Rise of the Continuous Campaign
Richard Nixon

During the congressional election campaign of 1966, Richard M. Nixon criticized the policy of President Lyndon B. Johnson toward the Vietnam War. "He is the first president in American history who has failed to unite his own party in time of war," said Nixon in one of the frequent speeches he was making for Republican candidates nationally. When Johnson went to Manila to meet with the president of South Vietnam and other Allied leaders in late October, Nixon charged that the meeting was simply a political ploy to aid the faltering Democratic party.[1]

In a White House news conference after his return from Asia, an angry Johnson responded that Nixon was "a chronic campaigner" who was prone "to find fault with his country and with his government during a period of October every two years." Nixon turned Johnson's cutting remark to his political advantage in the days before the election. The episode was one of the elements in the victories that brought the Republican party forty-seven new House seats and a gain of three seats in the Senate.[2]

As a political exchange, this battle was a clear triumph for Nixon. Johnson later conceded that his statement had been "dumb." Yet the president had, in his fatigue and anger, hit upon a fundamental point about Nixon that would shape the latter's approach to the White House when he arrived there in January 1969. More than any other chief executive before him, Nixon embraced the concept of the permanent political campaign as president. He geared up institutions within the White House to sustain such an effort. "The staff doesn't understand that we are in a continuous campaign," Nixon told his chief of staff, H. R. Haldeman, on 25 March 1971. His example was followed by his immediate Republican successors as well as by Bill Clinton.[3]

Previous presidents, including Lyndon Johnson and Franklin D. Roosevelt, certainly had interwoven governance with politics in their administrations. But there had not been, even in the most partisan cases, such a direct nexus between the style of a presidential campaign — fund-raising, jockeying for partisan advantage, and efforts to frustrate the opposition — and the way the White House functioned, as proved true during Nixon's five and a half years in office. Even if the principle was often violated, the notion existed that a president should govern in a style that subordinated partisan considerations to the national interest. Between inauguration and the start of a reelection campaign, for example, stretched several years in which the president should not always be thinking of how a second term could be won.

Under Nixon, this concept, timeworn and obsolete as it had become, vanished. The campaign never stopped, and the presidency itself emerged as an extension of that effort. Added to the mix was Nixon's conviction that such an approach was necessary in a political universe that was hostile to him and all his goals. Facing enemies who he believed would stop at nothing, Nixon was convinced that all measures were justified to retain political supremacy. In his view, Kennedy and Johnson had used illegal methods against him in the 1960 and 1968 campaigns, and their friends would use them again to oppose his presidency if they had the opportunity. He therefore resolved to use the same weapons, once he held power. The result was a presidency that moved inexorably toward illegality from its earliest days.

Thus, Richard Nixon had a dual impact on the evolution of the modern presidency. His involvement in the Watergate scandal cover-up and the other crimes of his presidency brought about his resignation in August 1974 and produced serious restrictions on the power and autonomy of future chief executives. The measures that he had instituted in the way of implementing the permanent campaign that did not involve illegal activity remained an important if troubling legacy of his years in office.

Richard Nixon was one of the most puzzling and enigmatic personalities ever to occupy the presidency. He could be brilliant in his analysis of foreign policy questions, and he had an encyclopedic grasp of American politics. Whether he meant to or not (and that is still a subject of much dispute), his administration pushed through environmental legislation and expanded spending on social programs. Nixon has in fact been dubbed "the last liberal president." His defenders credit him with opening a new relationship with the People's Republic of China and with pursuing policies toward the Soviet Union that eased tensions between the two superpowers. Despite the disgrace of Watergate, Nixon, in this view, was a president of substantial achievements brought down by political enemies and personal excesses.[4]

To his detractors, Nixon's crime-ridden presidency was the fulfillment of a career driven by paranoia and a dark view of his political adversaries, along with hefty doses of racism and anti-Semitism. From his first entry into politics, Nixon had practiced political hardball and a win-at-any-cost mentality. The presidency simply gave him greater scope to pursue his divisive policies and to deal with his personal demons. Watergate was thus the logical culmination of his personality defects.

There is no doubt that Nixon was a strange and tormented individual. His family background in California was one of insecurity and a lack of genuine affection. One of his aides, Bryce Harlow, believed that Nixon "as a young person was hurt very deeply by somebody . . . a sweetheart, a parent, a dear friend, someone he deeply trusted. Hurt so badly he never got over it and never trusted anybody again." Nixon grew up introverted and shy but wanted very much to be accepted and included in male activities. He played football at Whittier College despite a lack of physical coordination that relegated him to the scrub team.[5]

Following law school at Duke and a stint in the navy during World War II, Nixon returned to Southern California, ran as a Republican for Congress in the 1946 election, and won. From the start of his public career, he proved adept at debating his opponents and using the issue of anticommunism to advance his fortunes. He had little regard for the voters he represented. "You've got to be a little evil to understand those people out there," he once remarked. Nixon won a Senate race in 1950 and two years later went on the Republican ticket as Dwight D. Eisenhower's running mate. Eight years as vice president enriched his knowledge of American politics but did not bring him close to real power. He lost a close presidential contest in 1960 to John F. Kennedy and a gubernatorial race in California two years later, but people who predicted his political demise were premature. He won the Republican nomination in 1968 and defeated Hubert Humphrey and George C. Wallace in the fall election.[6]

Nixon wanted to be a great president in foreign affairs to outdo Eisenhower and Kennedy, two men whom he very much envied. He told a reporter in 1967 that the nation "could run itself domestically without a President. All you need is a competent Cabinet to run the country at home. You need a President for foreign policy." That may explain his detachment from economic and domestic policy issues except as they related to his reelection chances or how history might view his presidency. As he said about matters relating to the international economy and the value of the dollar, "I don't give a shit about the lira."[7]

To help the federal government run by itself on domestic issues, Nixon took up the Republican reorganizational impulse that extended back to William Howard Taft. Most of what Nixon did bore little resemblance to the promises he made during the 1968 campaign. On the stump he indicated that he would strengthen the role of the cabinet and control the size of the executive branch. Once in office, the president found, as he had done during the Eisenhower years, that listening to cabinet members was boring. The size of the White House staff also expanded under Nixon to over five hundred members.[8]

With his own attention fixed on foreign policy concerns, Nixon hoped that he could devise new arrangements that would enable trusted White House aides to oversee the departments and regulatory agencies. That would counteract the effect of Democrats in the bureaucracy who would otherwise frustrate Nixonian initiatives. The domestic priorities of the administration would be advanced without draining the president's time and energies. Working through the businessman Roy Ash, formerly of Litton Industries, and a council appointed to reorganize the government, the Nixon White House spent many hours on reorganization and the pursuit of what the president dubbed the New Federalism.[9]

For an executive who sought tidiness and efficiency in his White House, Nixon had a penchant for quick fixes as an administrator and a fascination with decisive, crisp aides who seemed to have new ideas. He responded to such men as Daniel Patrick Moynihan and John Connally, with their sweeping answers and innate self-confidence. The result was a good deal of administrative confusion on the domestic side of the White House, from which also emerged programs and policies that contradicted Nixon's reputation as a conservative. These areas of achievement included the environment, affirmative action, Native American affairs, and the ambitious but unsuccessful drive for welfare reform.[10]

The most important administrative legacy that Nixon provided to the modern presidency was the Office of Management and Budget (OMB), established in 1973 as a replacement for the Bureau of the Budget. Since the OMB had the capacity to pass on all budgets within the executive branch before they were relayed to Congress, it gave the White House the kind of authority over the budgetary process that had been contemplated since Taft first proposed the idea. In the process, the role of the director of the OMB became one of the most powerful positions in Washington.[11]

The changes that Nixon proposed in the workings of the presidency had merit, as the willingness of his successors to use the same techniques has shown. But reasonable ideas became mixed together with the excesses of the administration to defeat some of the president's more grandiose notions. By the second term, Nixon envisioned a system of "politician managers" scattered throughout the federal government to execute administration policies and to overawe dissident federal employees. The peremptory demand for the resignations of cabinet officers and other officials after the 1972 election was part of this initiative. By 1973, however, the capacity of Nixon and his men to reshape the government eroded under the blows of Watergate.[12]

Although he had a valid point in his wariness of the permanent bureaucracy in Washington, Nixon also underrated the willingness of government employees to make the system work on behalf of any president. As sure of his own views as any president ever was, he did not have much patience with divergent opinions. Claiming that Democrats in the government would stymie his initiatives provided good cover for an inherent unwillingness to engage in the give-and-take that democratic governance demands. The presidency was not an instrument of persuasion for Richard Nixon. It was a means of command and control, and in domestic policy such an imperious style had only a small chance of success.

In foreign policy, Nixon saw himself as the lonely statesman above the partisan fray, crafting diplomatic triumphs like an American Charles de Gaulle or Winston Churchill. He and Henry Kissinger could reshape the world through adroit use of the "madman theory" of foreign policy. By being unpredictable and seemingly out of control at times, Nixon hoped to persuade the Soviet Union, China, and North Vietnam to bend to his will.[13]

The petty details of the president's role in diplomacy bored him, especially such rituals as meeting personally new ambassadors accredited to the United States. For a president notoriously inept at small talk, these ceremonies were a potential hazard, and Nixon sought ways to avoid them or to dispense with them entirely. Believing that he already knew what he needed to understand world affairs, the president saw nothing to be gained from interacting with emissaries whom he would probably never encounter again.[14]

Since Nixon did not much like formal governmental institutions anyway, he had little patience with the traditional role of the Department of State in foreign affairs. Diplomats and foreign service officers, with their procedures and inconvenient questions about other countries, simply stood in the way of implementing a president's grand design. He thought it far better to conduct foreign policy through the president and his national security adviser from the White House, where secrets could be kept and surprises prepared. An instinctive loner, Nixon did not want to confront departmental barriers to his wishes. Like his hero Woodrow Wilson, the new president saw consultation as obstruction and commentary on his foreign policies as disloyalty, even within his own government.[15]

Nixon's overall approach to the presidency flowed from the nature of his personality as a politician. Where most men and women entered public life because they enjoyed being around people and pressing the flesh, Nixon preferred to spend time in solitary contemplation of the task before him. Moody and impetuous, he wanted a White House that took into account his preference for isolation and that insulated him from outside distractions. One of these potential diversions, for example, was his wife and her concerns as First Lady. Among the oddest aspects of Nixon's presidency are the impersonal memoranda that he sent to Pat Nixon about White House arrangements and functions.[16]

Nixon's personal requirements necessitated a strong chief of staff who could manage the daily business and keep people away whom the president did not wish to see. For Nixon, that key aide became H. R. "Bob" Haldeman, who acted as the president's "son of a bitch." To make his job work, Haldeman exercised a dominant influence over Nixon's schedule, which papers the president saw, and which people gained access to the Oval Office. Not since Sherman Adams a decade earlier had there been a White House chief of staff with the control over access that Haldeman possessed. Along with another Nixon aide, John Ehrlichman, Haldeman emerged as a kind of minicelebrity in Washington in the early years of the Nixon presidency. His fame was of a negative kind, but he served Nixon as the lightning rod that the insecure president demanded. Haldeman's diary is filled with his recognition that he was there to listen to Nixon's monologues at all hours of the day and night.[17]

Though Nixon wanted the White House staff to be large enough to carry out a variety of political and policy tasks, the real decision-making insiders of the administration receded to personal levels not seen since the turn of the century. Haldeman managed the daily work of the five hundred to six hundred people in the White House complex; Kissinger dealt with foreign policy. One or two other aides such as Ehrlichman were in on the key decisions about politics and domestic affairs. For the rest of the staff, Nixon was a remote figure whose temperament and intentions had to be divined like those of some imperial potentate.

With limited emotional and physical stamina, Richard Nixon needed to have his time carefully supervised to prevent him from becoming fatigued. At those moments, alcohol would impair his judgment. Yet he was obsessive about being perceived as a hard worker, and he gave out the impression that he subsisted and governed on very little sleep. To have time for the naps he needed and to work effectively, he sought seclusion in a small private office in the Old Executive Office Building where, surrounded by his yellow writing pads, he could work or catch up on his sleep. These devices, Nixon believed, saved his valuable energies for the important decisions only the president could make. There he scribbled private memoranda to himself about his need to be more focused and to engage in rituals of self-improvement as he pursued a place in history.[18]

The problem with this strategy was that Nixon obsessed about small and irrelevant details. Although he liked to be depicted as a global statesman, interested only in the large sweep of world affairs, he micromanaged his presidency as much as Lyndon Johnson had. To track press coverage, for example, he insisted that a daily summary of newspaper and magazine commentary be prepared for his perusal every morning. This document was far more elaborate than the press commentary that George B. Cortelyou had begun at the turn of the century. Nixon's aides annotated many of the articles and ensured that the president's attention would be drawn to offending commentary. Poring over it, Nixon made notes beside items that interested him and then instructed his staff to take appropriate action to follow up on his jottings. Peremptory orders would go out to punish this or that reporter or to respond to some unfavorable news story.[19]

No president could have kept track of all such directions in the daily rush of activity, and the staff either deferred a response or took no further steps

Richard Nixon preferred to work alone, and so he sought refuge in the Lincoln Sitting Room in 1971 when he was working on a speech. (Courtesy of Richard Nixon Library.)

when Nixon was embarking on a course that seemed odd or politically dangerous. More important, the process allowed Nixon to think he was hard at work when he was only spinning his intellectual wheels. It also fed the notion that he was the target of a media bias against his administration. In the hands of his aides, that assumption became a self-fulfilling prophecy that diverted important energies from the president and the men around him.[20]

The extent of Nixon's involvement with the trivia of his duties was daunting. The precise wording of presidential thank-you notes, White House invitations, food selections for menus, the music played at receptions, all these called forth a Nixonian memo from "RN" for the attention of his retainers. For a man who so often lamented that he did not have time to think about the big issues, Nixon allowed himself to be drawn into minutiae again and again. In April 1970 he "chewed" Haldeman "out worse than ever has as P" over the issue of whether the CBS program *Sixty Minutes* should devote twenty minutes or an hour to a tour of the White House with his daughter Tricia. How much of Nixon's emotional and physical resources as president were frittered away in this mindless self-indulgence remains to be determined, but it was clearly substantial.[21]

If the president lacked the self-discipline to assign himself rational priorities for his own duties, then he could use the machinery of the modern presidency to establish a productive routine for himself. But since Nixon was intent on presenting an image to the world of a confident, self-assured executive in the model of a Harry Truman or a Jack Kennedy, it was necessary that the public at large not know of the president's insecurities or emotional needs. The result was the dedication of much staff time to presidential image making on a scale that even Nixon's predecessors had not attained. Once institutionalized, this process became self-perpetuating in subsequent administrations.

It was not enough that President Nixon be judged by his deeds in office in the fashion of William Howard Taft or Harry Truman. From the earliest days of his presidency, the press and public received a barrage of information about how hard Nixon was working, how cool he was in moments of crisis, and how nonpolitical and objective his decisions were. Frequently, Nixon compared himself in private with other presidents, always to his advantage, and then sought to have his subordinates get the word out to the press about his superiority. Though the presidency had always had a self-referential quality for its occupants, most of those who preceded Nixon had been largely content

Richard Nixon had almost no aptitude for sports and little physical coordination, but he played golf. Here he sinks a putt as his celebrity companion, the comedian Jackie Gleason, looks on in surprise. (Photograph by Dirck Halstead, the Dirck Halstead Collection, Center for American History, University of Texas at Austin.)

to let their deeds shape their public image. In Nixon's case the need to depict himself as a strong, confident chief executive was a major element in his reliance on White House institutions to promote his positive self-image and to build domestic support for his policies.

To accomplish these results, the traditional role of the White House press secretary as a link with the reporters who covered the president was clearly inadequate. Nixon neither liked nor trusted the press, and their needs had a low claim on his time and energy. "I was bored by the charade of trying to romance the media," Nixon later wrote. He installed Ron Ziegler as his press secretary because Ziegler's modest abilities and lack of public stature meshed with Nixon's desire to diminish the direct impact of the print and electronic media. "Nixon was able to program Ziegler. He was absolutely programmable," concluded the White House aide Charles Colson. It did not take long for the press corps to determine that the youthful and un-informed Ziegler had no real access to serious White House information. Once a figurehead was in place, the president then took further steps to render the White House reporters an inconsequential element in covering his presidency.[22]

At first the new administration wanted to relocate the White House press corps to the Old Executive Office Building across the street. When that idea aroused a tepid response from journalists, who saw themselves being moved away from the center of power, the Nixon people covered over the swimming pool that had been in the White House since Franklin D. Roosevelt's day and created a new press headquarters that has remained in use ever since. With a podium for the press secretary and other officials, and the reporters placed as an audience, the press briefings became mini press conferences of their own each day.[23]

The upgrading of press facilities was cosmetic. The effort of the Nixon years was to downgrade independent press coverage and to relegate the Washington reporters and the electronic media to the margins. Nixon's infrequent night-time press conferences were changed from the afternoons, as under Kennedy, so that these events occurred in prime time on the East Coast. That made it harder for morning newspapers with tight deadlines in the East to have much coverage and analysis of what the president had said. The number of actual presidential news conferences fell to 39 during Nixon's time in office, down from Lyndon Johnson's 132 during a similar period in the White House. The multitude of such conferences held during the Coolidge, Roosevelt, and Truman presidencies came to seem utopian. Nixon accelerated the descent of the press conference as a presidential institution from the heights it had attained during the period from Roosevelt through Eisenhower.[24]

Nixon delighted in making statements about what he had done first as president, even if some of these comments were based on faulty historical arguments. In 1970, using third-person, as he often did, he wrote that "RN is the first president who came into the Presidency with the opposition of all these major communication powers." This statement would have puzzled Franklin D. Roosevelt, who faced more press hostility from the owners of the large Republican newspapers than Nixon ever did, but it clearly exemplified Nixon's near paranoia about his relations with the mainstream media. "Do you think, for Christ sakes, that the *New York Times* is worried about all the legal niceties?" he asked in June 1971 as the controversy over the Pentagon Papers developed. "Those sons of bitches are killing me."[25]

The solution in the new president's mind was to install White House institutions that would allow his administration to circumvent the press. To that end, an Office of Communications was established with the longtime Nixon friend Herbert Klein as its first director. Its public purpose was, as Klein told the press, "to eliminate any possibility of a credibility gap for this administration." Nixon himself promised an emphasis on "the need for free access to information in all departments of the government, to the extent that it does not endanger national security." These reassuring statements proved to be largely window dressing for an administration intent on reducing the flow of information to the media.[26]

The actual purpose of the Communications Office was to create a kind of quasi-journalistic operation that would put out favorable information on the Nixon administration in the guise of news. Klein and his staff prepared news releases, facilitated access for reporters outside of Washington, and provided speakers to defend Nixon's policies. It functioned, as Nixon intended it to do, very much like a continuing political campaign. Even Klein later remarked that in the Nixon White House "an amazingly excessive amount of time was spent worrying about plans to conjure up better and more favorable coverage."[27]

Although the Office of Communications represented in theory an effort to broaden ties between the White House and its various constituencies, it soon became a means of generating popular opinion itself. Nixon believed that the Democrats and especially John Kennedy had benefited from "a constant representation in letters to the editor columns and a very proper influence on the television commentators." Though the direct evidence for such influence may have existed only in Nixon's mind, he concluded that it would be wise to create such sentiment from the White House on a sustained basis. He constantly urged his aides to devise ways to plant stories and favorable letters in newspapers that the administration deemed unfriendly. He told Haldeman in November 1969 before a major address on Vietnam, "if only do one thing get 100 vicious dirty calls to the *New York Times* and *Washington Post* about their editorials (even though no idea what they'll be)."[28]

The techniques employed included a letter-writing operation directed by the Republican National Committee that produced up to sixty letters weekly to major media outlets. An aide estimated that each letter cost about one hundred dollars to produce, a bargain when one of the missives appeared in the *Washington Post* or the *New York Times*. The White House also used phone banks to stimulate calls to newspapers and radio stations, asking for fairer coverage of Nixon and his policies. Aides set up shadow committees that endorsed Nixon's initiatives in foreign and domestic policy. These panels then sent out mass mailings asking for support of the president. For Nixon, who believed that his goals were supported by a great "silent majority," it made sense for the presidency to evoke and even to produce the sentiments he wished that majority to adopt.[29]

These activities imparted a sense of accomplishment to the men and women who worked for Nixon. They believed that they were creating favorable attitudes toward the president. They also demonstrated that the modern presidency had become less about dealing with real national problems and more about presenting favorable impressions of the presidency and its occupant. Engaging issues, however, lacked the emotional wallop that went with defeating a political enemy or re-creating the ethos of a campaign. Many times the practitioners of presidential make-believe under Nixon and his successors convinced themselves that they had been engaged in the public's business when all they had done was to take part in executive ballyhoo.

The campaign-style thinking that these activities reflected blended with the melodramatic point of view of the president and his men to move the Nixon White House in less legal directions. If the president was opposed by unscrupulous "bad guys" and "evil" enemies, as Haldeman noted in his diary, then it was important to preempt any assaults that these adversaries might launch. Properly outraged at the excesses of the Kennedy and Johnson administrations when they were directed against him, Nixon did not conclude that such tactics were beneath the dignity of a president and wisely to be avoided. Instead, he decided that it was both appropriate and prudent for his administration to strike first through the use of government agencies such as the Internal Revenue Service and by taking other, even less savory measures. Believing that the "IRS is full of Jews," Nixon urged his men to launch probes of "the big Jewish contributors of the Democrats," or, as he put it, "Could we please investigate some of the cocksuckers?"[30]

Another element moving Nixon's presidency toward illegality was the obsession with secrecy that permeated the White House. To carry out his diplomatic initiatives toward Vietnam and later China, Nixon believed, as did

Henry Kissinger, that absolute confidentiality was essential. Their valid point, however, lost some of its persuasive power when it became evident that their lust for secrecy was directed not so much at keeping enemies such as North Vietnam and China in the dark as it was at preventing the American people from being informed about what was being done in their name. The impulse for widespread wiretapping, for example, derived from press disclosures about bombing in Cambodia in 1969, which was no news to its targets, but it was not common knowledge in the United States. Embarrassment to the administration rather than a concern for national security launched a campaign to root out leakers that became a recurring obsession of the Nixon White House.[31]

Like most of his twentieth-century presidential counterparts who faced the problem of leaks to the press, Nixon displayed outrage when they occurred. Although Nixon had said that "LBJ and other presidents have overreacted, and he won't" when confronted with leaking, precisely the opposite response occurred. The concern with leaks affected how the administration responded to the disclosures of the Pentagon Papers in the *New York Times* and the *Washington Post* during summer 1971. To placate the outrage of Nixon and Kissinger over the disclosure of these secrets of the Johnson administration and Vietnam, the president approved the formation of what evolved into the White House Plumbers unit. The task of this cadre of inept counterespionage types was to punish those people in and out of government who had the temerity to leak classified documents. The Justice Department was seen as too legalistic and constrained by the rule of law to handle such matters. Since no administration has been immune from leaks of one sort or another, the determination that Nixon and his men evidenced to cut down on all such unauthorized disclosures was bound to prove self-defeating.[32]

Several forces came together to facilitate decisions in the Nixon White House to engage in what Haldeman called "hardball politics." Like most politicians, Nixon and his associates expected to be throwing the hardballs, not standing at home plate receiving them. So by mid-July 1969, Nixon was telling aides of his desire to "set up and activate 'dirty tricks'" operations from the White House. The money for such endeavors came from leftover campaign funds from the 1968 presidential race. With ready access to then unregulated and unreported cash, it seemed easy and effective to set seasoned operatives in motion against likely political opponents. Convinced that the presidency was above legal restraints, Nixon did not expect that these illicit endeavors would ever see the light of day. At the same time, he did not take any discernible steps to ensure that trained and experienced people were used for a risky venture. He accepted the assurances of his advisers that the White House could rely on men such as sometime spy and spy novelist E. Howard Hunt.[33]

From his own experience, Nixon proved creative at finding things for his men to do in the dark shadows of American politics. Using the Internal Revenue Service to harass partisan enemies, which his predecessors had also done, was too tempting a tactic to resist. Compiling a list of enemies for future reprisals came naturally as well. With a future presidential election in mind, identifying possible opponents and undermining their chances were logical steps for the Nixon White House to pursue. The president should not just be the leader of his own political party; he should employ the weapons of the presidency to determine the choice of the Democrats in 1972.[34]

That these steps had to be taken in secret attested to their novelty as direct actions of the presidency. Even more staff time had to be allocated to these White House activities. In turn, the need for secrecy bred the desire for ever more political intelligence and inside dope about potential opponents. Most such information about the fractious Democrats and their chronic arguments could easily be gleaned from a careful reading of daily newspapers, but that was either too mundane an approach for presidential aides or not enough to satisfy Nixon's conspiratorial lust for reassurance that he was always one step ahead of his unscrupulous enemies.[35]

The late 1960s and early 1970s were a time of social turmoil as the passions that the Vietnam War had stirred produced repeated protests and sporadic acts of violence. Like the Johnson administration before it, the Nixon White House was convinced that the antiwar left had ties to the Communist world. In January 1969, Nixon told Kissinger: "I want to hear a CIA analysis in depth of worldwide common factors of youth disturbances." When the CIA and the FBI could not identify such ties, these conclusions did not comfort Nixon and his associates. In their minds, the absence of evidence attested to the inefficiency and incompetence of these investigative agencies. The president's men would simply have to find the facts on their own.[36]

The next step in the chain of logic then was to create within the executive branch more coordination in the gathering and processing of "internal domestic intelligence." Though there were legitimate issues about how well the

FBI and even the CIA operated in this field, the underlying problem was that they were not telling Nixon what he wanted to know. Therefore, Nixon set in motion efforts to establish his own sources for intelligence gathering through a White House aide, Tom Huston. The zealous Huston embarked on a plan that would have had a serious impact on the civil liberties of American citizens while simultaneously diminishing the role of the FBI. Naturally, such an initiative encountered opposition from the aging J. Edgar Hoover, which in turn generated more time and effort in the Nixon White House to resolve the bureaucratic impasse.[37]

Previous presidents had often criticized the performance of the chief executives who had come before them, but Nixon proved innovative in his use of government records to blacken the reputations of his predecessors. And if the records did not show what Nixon's operatives wanted them to demonstrate, then some plausible fabrications were in order. With the assistance of such unscrupulous operatives as Charles Colson and E. Howard Hunt, Nixon proposed to concoct phony historical documents to implicate John F. Kennedy in such mistakes or misdeeds as the Bay of Pigs in 1961 or the murder of South Vietnamese leader Ngo Dinh Diem in 1963. To have the agents of the president engage in fakery on such a potentially grand scale was another of Nixon's unique contributions to the evolution of presidential power.[38]

These wacky schemes did not produce the results that Nixon desired, and his efforts to stem leaks through the FBI and CIA also proved futile. When the White House Plumbers broke into the office of Daniel Ellsberg's psychiatrist, the caper yielded no usable information and was carried off in a notably inept manner. The key point in the history of the presidency was the establishment of a covert operation in the White House itself. In essence, Nixon believed that the presidency was not a part of the government required to interact with other agencies. It should function instead as a government in itself, in which illegal activities were acceptable because they were being carried out in the name of and with the knowledge of the president.[39]

With the barrier against illegal activity broken and the 1972 presidential election approaching, the development of surreptitious means to disrupt the political opposition was no great stretch for the men in the Nixon White House. Convinced that the president was indispensable to world peace because of his initiative with Communist China and the apparent winding down of the Vietnam War, Nixon and his colleagues were persuaded that electing a Democrat would be a national calamity. No one asked if Nixon's achievements would be enhanced if he simply stood on the historical legacy of his term and retired. For Nixon himself, with his addiction to power, another elected term would move him past Kennedy, Johnson, and Truman and into a league with his mentor Eisenhower.

Since the national interest demanded a Nixon triumph, any chance of a Democratic success must be extinguished. Confronting the opposition only with the tough weapons of American politics left open the slim possibility of an upset in the fall. The electorate could not be allowed even the chance of a fatal error in judgment when the presidency was at stake. The incumbent must see to it that democracy produced the correct result, even if extralegal measures were employed. So by early 1972, the White House and the attorney general, John Mitchell, opened discussions about how to disrupt the Democratic National Convention and undermine the leading anti-Nixon candidates. Only questions of practicality and the risk of possible disclosure figured in the discussion of these schemes. Otherwise, using the presidency as a means of covert action seemed entirely appropriate.[40]

By the time these clandestine ventures were in progress, Richard Nixon had long since put aside his initial opposition to Lyndon Johnson's practice of taping conversations in the White House. In 1971 an even more elaborate voice-activated system of recording conversations in the Oval Office was in place. Nixon's purpose in authorizing these tapes was to provide an accurate record for himself that he could use in writing his memoirs after the presidency. Voice activation had to be employed because he was so inept in dealing with even the simplest machinery that he could not be relied on to press a button to start the tape rolling. Sometimes he remembered that the system was in operation and guided the conversations accordingly. In other instances, he forgot the recorders' presence and indulged in the profane, often anti-Semitic, language that characterized the private Nixon.[41]

So convinced was Nixon that he would never be caught and that presidents could move beyond legality with impunity that he did not consider the tapes any kind of threat to his continuation in office, even while he initiated the cover-up of the Watergate scandal that led to his potential downfall. The possibility that the tapes might ever be the focus of legal action such as a subpoena from an independent counsel seemed outside the scope of political reality. Nixon had internalized the assumptions of the modern presidency to such an extent that he never contemplated the diminution of executive authority in the future.

Yet by 1971 and 1972, a reaction against the imperial aspects of presidential power had begun to appear, and it intensified during the two years that followed. The scholarly literature produced such works as Arthur Schlesinger Jr.'s *The Imperial Presidency* (1973), in which a defender of the use of executive authority under Franklin D. Roosevelt, Harry S. Truman, and John F. Kennedy had second thoughts after the performance of Lyndon Johnson and Richard Nixon. Congress sought to restrict what Nixon and other presidents could do in foreign policy through the War Powers Act (1973), which was passed over Nixon's veto. For the moment, the temper of the nation was turning against the excesses of the modern presidency as the dimensions of Nixon's assertion of executive primacy became clear.[42]

Although the Watergate scandal broke open with the arrest of the burglars in the Democratic headquarters located in that building in June 1972, the White House was able to contain it throughout Nixon's successful race for reelection against the divided Democrats and their candidate, George S. McGovern. The power of incumbency and the ineptitude of the Democrats produced a landslide victory for Nixon and Spiro Agnew. In the aftermath of the result, Nixon hoped to consolidate his power over the executive branch and exert enhanced influence with the press. As Haldeman recorded in his diary, Nixon had said, "Most second terms have been disastrous and . . . someone should write this, because [Nixon's] determined that his won't be." With the end of direct American involvement in Vietnam in early 1973, Nixon could believe that, except for Watergate, a period of presidential accomplishment lay ahead and there was no reason for him not to push on with his agenda as forcefully as he had done in the first term.[43]

But the Watergate scandal did break during the first half of 1973, and Nixon's presidency never recovered. As the revelations of the cover-up and the White House horrors unfolded in 1973 and 1974, the disclosures led to a number of important institutional changes in presidential practices that circumscribed the actions of future presidents. One key development arose from the problem of an administration that was accused of corruption or criminality and was endeavoring to investigate its own misdeeds. The need for an independent prosecutor to conduct an inquiry apart from the Department of Justice meant that the president and White House aides came under a kind of legal scrutiny that had rarely happened in the past. In turn, the necessity for present and former White House officials to engage legal counsel raised the potential price of serving a president in ways that proved to have unintended and often unpleasant consequences for the people involved. Criminal investigations of White House aides, once almost unthinkable, became routine as the Democrats and Republicans exploited this new weapon for partisan purposes after 1974. By the 1980s and 1990s, the process had become virtually a cottage industry in Washington and a continuing source of distractions for presidential administrations of both parties.[44]

Related to this problem was the issue of Nixon's presidential papers and the White House tapes. These documents and records had been regarded as the personal property of the chief executive, to be disposed of as he wished. By the 1970s the expectation was that a Nixon presidential library would join the others that had been or were being constructed. Lyndon Johnson had taken a large income tax deduction for donating his presidential papers to the United States, and Nixon followed suit with his vice-presidential papers. That latter gift became an issue as impeachment probers examined his personal finances and questioned the appraised value of the papers. The larger concern was whether future presidents should derive a large financial windfall from documents generated during the performance of their official duties on behalf of the American people.[45]

Nixon's White House tapes complicated the problem. They were needed first for the various prosecutions of Nixon aides, but in time they would move into the realm of historical documents. To whom did these recordings belong, the former president or the people of the United States? Congress turned to the problem of the ownership of presidential papers in legislation that passed four years after Nixon's resignation. The Presidential Records Act of 1978 declared that such documents of future presidents were the property of the United States and established procedures for making them available in a timely manner after the president left office. Far from settling the matter, the legislation created new problems of deciding when presidential papers should be opened and under what circumstances.[46]

Congress attempted to exert control over the Nixon tapes in the Presidential Recordings and Materials Preservation Act of 1974, which mandated disclosure of the information in the tapes "at the earliest reasonable date." The

Nixon tapes then became the subject of protracted litigation as the lawyers for the former president and his family endeavored to regain control of the recordings and transcripts. These proceedings continued until the mid-1990s, when an agreement was reached to release a larger portion of the presidential recordings. Almost three decades after the departure of Nixon from the White House, large portions of the tapes have not been transcribed, and the historical assessment of Nixon's performance in the White House has suffered, as a result.[47]

Richard Nixon added another innovation to the institution of the modern presidency during the two decades between his departure from the White House in disgrace in August 1974 and his death from a stroke on 22 April 1994. Previous chief executives such as Theodore Roosevelt, Herbert Hoover, Harry Truman, Dwight D. Eisenhower, and Lyndon B. Johnson had written memoirs (or had used ghostwriters) to explain their actions as president and to try to influence history. None had felt the need to rehabilitate a damaged personal and political reputation as Nixon did.

Once Nixon had regained his health in 1975, he embarked on a career as an author to renew his credentials as an expert on world affairs. Books of reminiscences and policy advice poured out in a steady stream and attained a wide audience. The former president went on television at home and abroad to explain Watergate and to emphasize his foreign policy achievements. He traveled to meet with world leaders and saw a private presidential library erected at Yorba Linda, California. As memories of his scandals faded, Nixon's persistence with this last campaign paid off. The public forgot his crimes and errors and treated him as the elder statesman he wished to be. With enough energy, money, and time, it seemed that even the most scorned president could retrieve some of his historical status. By late 2001, Bill Clinton was making noises about repairing his historical image in the Nixonian manner.[48]

The larger impact of Richard Nixon's presidency was the confirmation that being a strong executive did not necessarily equate with political virtue. Power was a morally neutral quality in modern presidents, and the belief that presidents needed to be unfettered to do good things meant, as Lyndon Johnson and Nixon had shown, that they could do bad things as well. In reaction to these revelations, the political system endeavored to constrain future presidents from being another Nixon. That understandable goal led in some instances to political cures that proved as troublesome as the evils they were meant to prevent. The proliferation of independent counsels became a notable example of this trend.

One of the clichés of the Watergate era was that the system worked in exposing Nixon's misdeeds and forcing his resignation. So bizarre and outlandish were the excesses of Watergate and Nixon's presidency that they came to seem unique to the character of Nixon himself. The extent to which these problems grew from the evolution of the modern presidency received some attention. But with the Cold War still going on in a world filled with nuclear weapons, the modern presidency seemed a necessary resource at a dangerous time. The nation looked to Richard Nixon's successor, Gerald R. Ford, to restore national confidence and to rehabilitate the presidency as an instrument of political leadership. That was a difficult task, as Ford's brief tenure in the White House would show. Nor would Ford's replacement, Jimmy Carter, prove adept at meeting the demands of the office. The modern presidency faced more troubled times during the decade of the 1970s.

8

The Modern Presidency under Siege

Gerald Ford and Jimmy Carter

In the evolution of the modern presidency, the administrations of Gerald R. Ford and Jimmy Carter seem a six-year pause between the dark passages of Richard Nixon and the conservative tumult of Ronald Reagan. Because of the circumstances in which they found themselves and their own limitations as leaders, Ford and Carter slipped into the damning category of one-term failed presidencies. Their years in the White House have been regarded as virtual primers in how not to be effective modern presidents.

Ford and Carter were held back because they did not govern in the mode that had emerged during the 1960s of conducting a permanent campaign and playing down the importance of substantive policy decisions in office. In the case of Gerald Ford, who was thrust into the office after Nixon's resignation in August 1974, he devoted the remainder of 1974 and most of 1975 to foreign and domestic problems, with only modest attention to renomination and election a year later. By the time he turned his attention to the quest for the GOP nomination in 1976, he faced a serious threat from Ronald Reagan on his right.

Jimmy Carter came to the White House in 1977 with the sensibility of a man who saw a bright line between politics and governance. He did not just discourage the injection of politics into presidential decisions; he abhorred it as a governing approach. When he too realized that he would have to fight for the Democratic nomination against Edward Kennedy in 1980 and then face the candidacy of Ronald Reagan on the Republican side, his political position had deteriorated to such a degree that his administration closed after a single term. In the end, what made Ford and Carter failed presidents was their inability to meet the basic standard for success as a modern chief executive — the capacity to win and serve more than a single term. In that respect, both men were seen as lacking in the strength and ruthlessness to succeed as presidents.

Both Ford and Carter had to deal with the residual effects of the Johnson-Nixon years on the presidency itself. Though Americans would soon return to their admiration for the strong chief executive, for the rest of the 1970s they indicated that they wanted to see restraint in the use of presidential power and modesty in the way the office was conducted. Congress asserted itself to limit presidential authority and in the process gained a major voice in what the White House could and could not do. Whoever followed Nixon into the presidency would have faced the consequences of the overreaching that had occurred between 1963 and 1974.

Gerald Ford did not have time to put his own stamp on the White House, and his brief tenure reflected Nixonian policies without his predecessor's conspiratorial spirit or indulgence in criminality. Ford's approach grew from his experience as an electoral politician and a legislator who had labored in the House Republican minority for most of his twenty-five years in Congress. Though he was a tough, partisan Republican, he did not regard Democrats as agents of evil to the extent that Nixon had done. Ford deemed the presidency as a place where things should be done rather than as an arena for posturing and self-indulgence. While he retained the organizational structure of a strong White House chief of staff, he dismantled the machinery that had sustained Nixon's permanent campaign. He also abandoned his predecessor's efforts to reshape the structure of the federal government.[1]

The relief that the nation felt at the departure of Nixon and the end of what Ford called "our long national nightmare" over Watergate gave the new president a thirty-day honeymoon. The press-driven euphoria vanished when in early September Ford pardoned Nixon for his Watergate crimes. Unless the country wanted to subject the former president to the rigors of a criminal trial, the decision made sense. The problem was with the timing and the appearance that a deal had been possible between Ford and Nixon. In a sense, the Ford presidency never recovered from the impact of the Nixon pardon.[2]

That was too bad, because the Ford administration cast a shadow forward into the three Republican presidencies that took place between 1981 and 2002.

Many of the key officials in the Ford White House and the president's election campaign in 1976 were significant figures in the administrations of Ronald Reagan, George Herbert Walker Bush, and George W. Bush. Though Ford did not succeed in mastering the demands of the modern presidency himself, his tenure in the White House provided instructive examples to major participants in the Republican party about how the mistakes of the Nixon-Ford era could be avoided in the future.

Gerald Ford came to the White House in August 1974 from a long career in the House of Representatives, where he first served in 1949. His tenure as a lawmaker exceeded even that of Lyndon Johnson's. Since his goal was to be Speaker of the House in what was then the unlikely event of a Republican majority, Ford did not have to develop administrative skills in running his own House office. The legislative process and the routine of constituent services allowed for a good deal of looseness in the operation of his daily business. The affable and relaxed lawmaker did not impose a firm hand on his busy staff, even as a House leader.[3]

When Nixon selected Ford as the vice president to replace the disgraced Spiro Agnew in fall 1973, the new incumbent of the nation's second highest office had little time or need to think about administrative issues. He was an extension to the existing White House operation, and Ford emerged as a well-traveled defender of the beleaguered Nixon presidency. That posture became untenable in summer 1974, when Nixon's political situation collapsed. Revelations from the White House tapes about the president's key role in the Watergate cover-up forced Nixon's resignation. Suddenly, Ford faced the real likelihood that he could become president in a situation that did not resemble any that a vice president had ever confronted. Ford's transition was a matter of hours and days. Unlike those vice presidents who had come to office after a chief executive died or was assassinated, Ford watched his predecessor leave the White House and fly to California in temporary disgrace.[4]

The public relations phase of the Ford presidency began well, with his statement to the nation on taking office. Without condemning Nixon in any way, Ford suggested that he would restore honesty and integrity to the modern presidency. His normality and easygoing demeanor, not to mention the apparently ordinary quality of his family, emphasized the contrast with the often dark and brooding Nixon. Ford thus made his most important contribution to the presidential institution simply by making the shift from one chief executive to another seem regular and legitimate. There was no sense that an inappropriate transfer of power had taken place. The Constitution had survived a severe test, but the continuity of government had not been broken. Whatever else he did as president, Gerald Ford would receive historical credit for guiding the nation calmly through a major political crisis.[5]

That his first month in office proved to be the high point of his presidency attested to the strengths and weaknesses Ford brought to his new job. First, he faced the general perception in Washington that he was not a very intelligent man. This was unfair to Ford, a graduate of the University of Michigan and the Yale Law School, but the new president did not have the glib, articulate style that Washington often took as evidence of an intellect. The standing jokes about Ford, disseminated by Lyndon Johnson, were that the Michigan Republican had played football without a helmet and also lacked the ability to walk and chew gum at the same time. Johnson's derisive remarks may even have been cruder in some versions. Though never a deep thinker, Ford was more than the sum of these clichés about his brainpower.[6]

On the other hand, Ford had qualities of personal charm, honesty, and lack of pretense that had eluded Lyndon Johnson and Richard Nixon. In the House, Ford had made friends on both sides of the political aisle and created a reservoir of personal trust that had made his appointment as vice president move with such smoothness through the Congress. The Ford family also seemed a political asset, especially the new First Lady, Betty Ford. Her candor about her breast cancer in autumn 1974 won wide praise for alerting women to the dangers of the disease. She and the new president were in denial about her persistent problems with chemical dependency and alcoholism, however. These issues were not discussed in an honest way until after the Fords had left the White House.[7]

While the press corps gushed about the Fords in August 1974, the president faced a new situation about media coverage of his personal style as his administration evolved. As the television networks expanded late-night programming on weekends in search of younger viewers, barriers of restraint and taste in dealing with presidents loosened. A program such as Saturday Night Live, begun in October 1975, depended for its ratings on topical humor that could establish a running gag for regular watchers. The young comedian Chevy Chase found a rich vein for satire when Ford had several well-publicized slips as he descended the steps of Air Force One. Endlessly shown, these scenes of a clumsy presi-

By Gerald Ford's presidency, technology permitted news conferences to be held on the visually attractive White House lawn, and presidential handlers moved the chief executive into these bucolic settings. Ford speaks to the press corps on this occasion. (Photograph by David Kennerly, the David Kennerly Collection, courtesy of Mr. Kennerly and the Center for American History, University of Texas at Austin.

dent became a fixture in the popular culture. For the press, presidential trivia served as a way of dealing with the person in the White House that eliminated the need for substantive analysis, which often produced bored viewers and lower ratings. Ford's erratic golf game that sometimes endangered spectators reinforced these stereotypes.[8]

Even had Gerald Ford been a gifted administrator, he would have faced a set of trying circumstances with the White House staff that he inherited. Nixon had gone to California, but his people were still ensconced throughout the executive branch. Some Nixon associates such as Henry Kissinger, who served as secretary of state and head of the National Security Council, had to be retained as a matter of public confidence. By 1974 Kissinger was seen as the key architect of American foreign policy, embodying continuity with the achievements of the Nixon years toward China and the Soviet Union. As Kissinger noted in his memoirs, "Ford was more intimately involved in the execution of policy than Nixon ever was," but during his first year the new president relied on his secretary of state for guidance as he learned the ropes of foreign policy. When Kissinger emerged as a lightning rod for the Republican right wing over the policy of détente with the Soviet Union, his role in the Ford White House diminished. In that way there was, as Richard Cheney noted, "at least the appearance, and I think partly the reality, too, that the president was less the captive of a single adviser."[9]

During the last months of 1974 and into 1975, Ford eased out such Nixon holdovers as General Alexander Haig and installed men and women with whom he felt more comfortable. He experimented with a more decentralized decision-making process during his first months in office, the "spokes in a wheel" arrangement that gave his major advisers equal access to him. The system led to more confusion than clarity in presidential decision making. In time, Ford concluded that he needed a chief of staff on the Eisenhower model with the power to enforce discipline. He turned to Donald Rumsfeld, who had worked in the Nixon White House before becoming ambassador to the North Atlantic Treaty Organization (NATO). Haig became supreme commander of NATO in December, and Rumsfeld joined the Ford team.[10]

Rumsfeld, or "Rummy" as he was known, displayed the aggressive administrative qualities that would become famous during his stint as Secretary of Defense during the administration of George W. Bush. He trimmed back the size of the staff and insisted on more discipline among the loosely organized Ford team. Henry Kissinger called him "the skilled full-time politician-bureaucrat in whom ambition, ability and substance fuse seamlessly." Rumsfeld had little patience with the spokes of the wheel concept. "In that system, with the spokes coming in, the president is in the center, and the chief of staff is the grease. All the grease does is get overheated and have to be replaced." When Rumsfeld moved on to the Defense Department, Richard Cheney succeeded him and proved equally adept at running the White House. For all its problems, the Ford administration came to be a proving ground for those men who would be senior officials in the Republican presidencies that followed. Their experience in the Ford years reinforced the general Republican devotion to the Eisenhower-Nixon model of the strong White House chief of staff, albeit without the obvious arrogance and political ineptitude of the Haldeman style.[11]

Once he was in office, Ford faced the issue of naming a vice president, a new function for a chief executive in light of the Twenty-fifth Amendment.

Ascending to the presidency with very little notice, Gerald Ford works in the nearly empty Oval Office in the early days of his administration. (Photograph by David Kennerly, the David Kennerly Collection, courtesy of Mr. Kennerly and the Center for American History, University of Texas at Austin.)

Ford's selection of Nelson A. Rockefeller, the former governor of New York and bane of Republican conservatives, did not become the success that Ford had contemplated. The choice confirmed doubts about Ford's presidency from the right wing of his party. In the residue of political suspicion that followed Watergate, Congress put Rockefeller through a rigorous set of hearings that took two months to complete before his designation was confirmed. There were still some problems with the presidential and vice-presidential transitions that the Twenty-fifth Amendment had not resolved. These issues did not reappear after the Rockefeller episode, but they represented a potential danger for future modern presidents.[12]

Gerald Ford's good start as president ended a month after it began with his pardon of Richard Nixon on 8 September 1974. During those thirty days from 9 August on, it seemed for a moment as if the nation might once again have a trustworthy chief executive on whose public word citizens might rely, whatever their partisan differences. That tentative return of confidence in the presidency dissipated with Ford's Sunday morning announcement of his clemency for Nixon.

On the merits of the issue, Ford had a better political case than appeared at the time. A criminal trial for a former president, or even his testimony as a witness in cases against his former aides, would have had a damaging impact on the institution itself. Moreover, Nixon was in poor health with phlebitis after Watergate, and any criminal proceedings against him would have been delayed. Thus the problem of his legal jeopardy would have been prolonged for an indefinite future. That prospect would have meant a continuing public relations problem for the new administration. Ford decided that the pardon for Nixon represented his best option.[13]

The way in which the pardon was announced, however, backfired on the president. After the Ford family attended church on Sunday morning, the president declared on national television that he had granted Nixon "a full, free and absolute pardon" for whatever offenses he might have committed during his presidency. The administration coupled the pardon with an amnesty program for individuals who had evaded the draft for Vietnam. To the people of the United States, the announcement smacked of a deal between two Washington insiders and a return to politics as usual. Since Nixon did not have to make even a tacit admission of guilt, the pardon itself seemed one-sided. President Ford made an unusual and unprecedented gesture when he testified as a sitting president before a House committee looking into the pardon episode. These conciliatory moves never erased the impression that he had moved precipitously in pardoning his predecessor.[14]

To a degree, Ford had relied on the inherent prestige of the modern presidency to sustain his pardon of Nixon. A relative novice in national politics, despite his many years in the House, he did not appreciate the need to build a public case for his decision or the dangers to his new administration if his action did not please the public. With intensive television coverage already gaining strength, he found that defining moments for presidents could come early and leave an enduring impression.

Troubles mounted for the fledgling Ford presidency during the remaining months of 1974 and into 1975. The Republicans suffered damaging losses in the House of Representatives in the 1974 elections, as a severe recession and voter anger over Watergate took a political toll. The ineptitude of the response of the Ford White House to the economic situation compounded the damage to the president. Such ineffectual gestures as the WIN campaign, complete with buttons, to "Whip Inflation Now" indicated a gimmicky side to Ford's approach that further eroded the president's credibility.

With the aid of some seasoned operatives from the Republican ranks and his own sense of growing into the job, Ford did better in 1975 but could not escape the perception that he was a caretaker president following a failed administration. The fall of South Vietnam during spring 1975 and congressional revelations about excesses of the CIA under previous presidents meant that Ford became the target for suspicions and recriminations regarding the dark side of the modern presidency. Though he was the least imperial chief executive since Harry Truman, he grappled with the fallout of the sins of his immediate predecessors.[15]

For a time it seemed as if Americans actually wanted a return to the first citizen model of the presidency, in the mold of the nineteenth century. Self-deprecation, a disclaimer of ambition, and a reduction in ceremonial splendor were the order of the day in the mid-1970s. Presidential candidates in both parties stressed their distance from the ways of Washington and their disdain for its customs, a posture that became almost mandatory for presidential candidates in the decades that followed. Ford made some minor gestures in this direction. Bands played the Michigan fight song rather than "Hail to the Chief" at his rallies and speeches. As a professional politician and longtime resident of the nation's capital, he could not plausibly run against the city or its institution as well as his challengers did.[16]

A moderate conservative without a hard ideological edge, Ford found himself between a Democratic Congress determined to scale back presidential power and a Republican party moving rightward toward Ronald Reagan and the conservatism that flowered during the 1980s. With Congress, Ford used the veto power to block initiatives that interfered with presidential authority or prerogatives. He battled with Capitol Hill on issues such as oversight of foreign policy and gave little ground to his former colleagues on these subjects.

The challenge that Ford faced within his own party in 1975 and 1976 grew from the love affair with Ronald Reagan that took hold in the GOP after the departure of Spiro T. Agnew and Richard Nixon. The right wing of the party chafed at Henry Kissinger and the policy of détente with the Soviet Union that the administration pursued. A sense that the United States was losing the military and economic race with the Soviet Union permeated this element of the party. They believed that Ford was not doing enough to rebuild American power. Though they liked him personally, they saw his wife as culturally permissive, wrong on the subject of the Equal Rights Amendment, and deaf to the moral dimensions of abortion. Reagan said as the campaign heated up that Ford "has shown neither the vision nor the leadership necessary to halt and reverse the diplomatic and military decline of the United States."[17]

The conventional wisdom in 1976 was that an incumbent president could still be sure of his party's nomination, even one who had come to the White House as an appointed vice president. However, Ford's perceived sins in foreign and domestic affairs led Ronald Reagan and his partisans to contest the Republican nomination in 1976. Neither the president nor his challenger liked or respected the other. The race that ensued was divisive for Ford's chances to win the presidency in his own right. It seemed that he would dispose of Reagan easily in the early going, but the former California governor rebounded in the spring to close the gap. The duel went down to the Kansas City convention before Ford narrowly prevailed. The existing assumptions about incumbency had been reinforced, just barely.[18]

Yet so crippled had Ford's candidacy been in the fight with Reagan that he faced an uphill task in the election struggle with Jimmy Carter. A strong, cohesive Republican campaign nearly put Ford over the top in November 1976, but Carter, with pervasive support from the South among blacks and southern Evangelicals, won out in a squeaker election. In January 1977 the Ford presidency passed into history. Although Gerald Ford made few substantive contributions to the evolution of the modern presidency, he did maintain the legitimacy of the office in the wake of Nixon's resignation and the Watergate scandal. Unable to stop the flow of power toward Congress, he slowed the process and asserted the case for executive prerogatives. A second Ford term would probably have seen a more disciplined administration than that of Jimmy Carter, and Ford's growth in office would most likely have continued.

With the arrival in Washington of James Earl "Jimmy" Carter Jr. in January 1977, the period of revolt against the modern presidency crested and then soon receded. Carter's presidential candidacy captured the temporary popular desire for a limited chief executive and rode it to the White House. As the nation's problems accumulated, however, the desire for strong leadership soon reappeared. As an avowedly nonpartisan, managerial president, Carter proved incapable of rising to the challenges of his term. Running for the

Democratic nomination in 1976 essentially exhausted his store of ideas as a politician. In office, he worked hard and achieved some creditable results, but he left the presidency quite weakened after his single term.[19]

For Jimmy Carter to run for president in the first place was an act of political daring. When the idea first occurred to the candidate and his staff in 1972, the nationally unknown Carter was governor of Georgia. He had been elected after a stint as a state senator. Limited to a single four-year term in the Georgia statehouse, Carter faced the end of his statewide career in 1974. Surveying the dilapidated state of the Democrats after the Nixon landslide in 1972, he decided that a centrist southerner might have a chance to win the nomination in the next four years. He was not impressed with his potential competition in the party and thought that his candidacy might prosper. Almost no one outside his small circle of advisers gave the notion any credence. Yet Carter had correctly sensed that traditional assumptions about how presidential nominations were won no longer applied.[20]

While Carter had been a naval officer and the manager of a peanut warehouse in Plains, Georgia, his brief run in politics had not revealed any serious thought about the nature of the presidency or much executive capacity on his part. In his national campaign, the gubernatorial record in Georgia, including such technical devices as zero-based budgeting, was held up as an admirable accomplishment. So too was his enlightened record on civil rights. The record of governing Georgia, however, indicated that he had liabilities as an executive in working with the legislature, dealing with the press, and making timely decisions. None of these experiences provided much grounding for the demands that he faced when he became president. Nor is there much evidence that Carter, amid the rigors of his campaign, devoted much thought to what he wanted to do as president on either the domestic or foreign side. A man of abundant self-confidence in his own abilities, he simply thought that he could pull off the presidency as he had done with other personal and political challenges in the past.[21]

Jimmy Carter's quest for the White House and service as president went through three distinct phases. From late 1974 through the Democratic National Convention in July 1976, he and his aides waged a skillful primary campaign that capitalized on the divisions within the Democratic ranks to secure a strong grip on the nomination. Beginning the general election campaign with a wide lead over Gerald Ford, Carter ran a lackluster race that, combined with some untimely mistakes by his rival, including one in their final debate, enabled the Georgian to slide into the presidency. Then came Carter's four years in office, which developed into a running disaster for the president and his party.

In the first and happiest phase of Carter's rise to national prominence, he developed the anti-Washington outsider themes that resonated with an electorate tired of government excesses after Vietnam and Watergate. Carter promised a government "as good as" the American people and avowed that he "would never lie" to the voters while in the White House. The flattery of the first statement and the implausibility of the second seemed to persuade enough Democrats that Carter might be a winner. His fresh face and appealing manner, combined with the fissures in his party, enabled him to emerge as the front-runner in the early stages of the nomination contest. Carter's proclaimed status as a born-again Christian gave him a strong appeal to Evangelical Christians, especially in the South. Not a normally Democratic voting bloc, the Evangelicals responded to his pietistic language and his social conservatism, relative to the other candidates.[22]

From the outset, however, there were warning signs that Carter's packaged appeal might not travel well. Reporters noted that the candidate tailored his speeches differently to white and black audiences. Moreover, he could not always provide specifics about his policy proposals, especially their costs. His positions on hot-button issues such as abortion were artfully vague. His personality, while ingratiating at the start, had harder edges that came out when he was challenged or attacked. None of his rivals, however, was able to dent his public image. He won pluralities in primary after primary and in the process rolled up delegates toward the nomination. For the moment, Carter was winning, and he thus became the hot political flavor of the first half of 1976.[23]

Once he had peaked at the Democratic National Convention, however, Carter and his record came under the cold-eyed scrutiny of the seasoned Republican campaigners who rallied around Gerald Ford. Carter was ill-prepared for the rigors of a national campaign, as his misstep in the interview with *Playboy* magazine indicated. Discussing "lust in his heart" with some coarse language for the raunchy magazine clashed with the impression Carter was sending to the voters and revealed his inexperience with the demands of the national limelight. The more the voters got to know him, the less they liked him, and his lead in the polls melted away as the election approached. In an election that featured two weak campaigners, Carter proved to be a little less inept than Gerald Ford.[24]

Since he had won the White House, Carter failed to recognize that the presidency had been impaired by the events of the preceding decade. Restoring the authority of the office would require more than crowd-pleasing gestures and a sincere attitude. Yet he approached the responsibilities as if the presidency was as powerful as it had ever been. He needed only to carry out the rituals of the job, and the prestige of the presidency would automatically do the rest. As so much of his administration reflected, Carter's innate sense of the presidency had a formalistic, textbook quality to it that was ill suited for an institution in flux after the traumas from 1965 to 1974.

Having attained his improbable political goal, Carter acquired or let show a high degree of arrogance in the transition process and during the early months of his presidency. Believing that he had defeated a corrupt and ineffective Democratic establishment ensconced in Washington, Carter and his "Georgia Mafia" saw little reason to defer to congressional sensibilities or the style of doing business in the nation's capital. Since the administration would have to work with the Democratic leadership on Capitol Hill to get anything done, such an attitude bordered on the bizarre. But the new president apparently believed that, like Woodrow Wilson, he could rouse the hinterlands against Congress whenever he wished to get his programs implemented.[25]

Carter came to Washington from a one-party state where Republicans had not yet emerged as serious rivals to the Democrats on the local level. He had little experience with national Democrats and even less with the Grand Old Party. He thus believed that the presidency could operate on a nonpartisan basis, with political considerations put aside. He would simply show politicians what the right thing to do was, and the logic of his argument would persuade doubters. As his vice president, Walter Mondale, put it, "Carter thought politics was sinful. The worst thing you could say to Carter if you wanted to do something was that it was politically the best thing to do." In many respects, Carter's approach to governance looked back to the business progressivism that had characterized southern politics in the 1920s and still had deep roots in the region.[26]

Such an approach to Washington would have been difficult to carry off for a man of charm and charisma in the presidency of the 1970s. For some-

Presidential informality reached its height when Jimmy Carter, wearing a sweater, delivered a speech to the nation from the White House. (Courtesy of the Jimmy Carter Library.)

one with Carter's aloof stance it was impossible. Yet the Carter White House compounded the problem with gratuitous slights to such key personages as House Speaker Thomas P. "Tip" O'Neill and other legislative heavyweights. Having been elected largely through his own efforts, Carter saw little need for anyone's help, and if the offended parties got angry, so be it. His aide, Hamilton Jordan, delighted in not returning phone calls from Democratic senators as a way of showing the power and clout of the White House. Carter's relations with Congress started off badly and never really improved over the course of his presidency.[27]

Not having run a large organization and mindful of the need to avoid Nixon's precedents, Carter sought a White House organization that emphasized openness and access to the president. In a return to the spokes of the wheel system, Carter said, "I never have wanted to have a major chief of staff between me and the people who worked for me." Instituting the organizational structure that evoked Franklin D. Roosevelt and John F. Kennedy, Carter envisioned a system where only the president would know the larger picture, and he would make the ultimate decision. In practice that meant that issues large and small flowed toward the Oval Office. The most celebrated case was the degree of Carter's personal involvement over who was allowed to use the White House tennis courts.[28]

Although the president did not name a White House chief of staff until 1978, many of the actual duties of the post were the responsibility of Hamilton Jordan, who had been with Carter since the Georgia governorship. Jordan was a bright man but lacked managerial skills and Washington connections. He served Carter well as a sounding board and political counselor. He was, however, overmatched in his White House role. Rather than cultivating the Washington media and Congress, he ignored and alienated them. This, coupled with his marital problems and some erratic personal behavior at social events, made him into a symbol of what seemed wrong with the Carter presidency.[29]

Carter began his administration determined to show that he would not be identified with the imperial aspects of his office. On Inauguration Day, he, his wife, and his children walked from the Capitol to the White House. It was his most popular gesture along these lines. Other such acts included not having "Hail to the Chief" played wherever he appeared and the sale of the presidential yacht *Sequoia*. Carrying his clothes bag off Air Force One was another presidential habit. Generally, the public applauded, but these policies did not sit well either with the press corps or with Washington insiders who liked to bask in the vicarious glow from the White House and its occupant.

Compounding Carter's image problem was a more aggressive media that did not like the president or his wife and treated him with ill-disguised contempt. The Watergate mentality fed the journalistic desire to expose scandal and a sense among reporters that they should participate in making news, not just cover events. The financial dealings of Carter's friend and appointee, Bert Lance, provided fodder for such disclosures in 1977. Journalists were emerging as distinct celebrities in their own right. Some members of the Fourth Estate saw themselves as more than equal to the politicians they scrutinized. Carter and his press secretary Jody Powell did not fully grasp the changes in how the media worked and were not inclined anyway to adapt to these new realities. The result was running tension between the press and the White House throughout Carter's presidency.[30]

As president, Carter suffered from a lack of charisma and star quality. Not since John Kennedy had a chief executive displayed such attributes, but in the late 1970s, as cable television began to penetrate American homes and pop culture pervaded society, it was no longer enough for a president simply to do the job. The celebrity process focused attention on the private lives of the president and his family with an intensity that had not been so persistent in earlier decades. The eccentricities of the Carter family, including his raffish brother Billy and his Evangelical sister Ruth Stapleton, became grist for the tabloid mills and eroded the credibility of Carter himself.

As a chief executive, Carter did make substantive changes in two areas that led to shifts in how the presidency operated. Despite periodic promises to upgrade the vice presidency in the postwar years, the office had remained a subordinate part of most administrations, as Richard Nixon and Lyndon Johnson could have confirmed. Carter elevated the role that Walter Mondale played into one of real weight. The vice president had an office in the West Wing, and a member of Mondale's staff had a place on the president's staff as well. Mondale met regularly with the president, and the two men forged a good working partnership. Having grown up in the coalition politics of Minnesota, Mondale found Carter's reluctance to practice bridge building to

Democrats baffling. "Carter's got the coldest political nose of any politician I ever met," he said in later years. Nonetheless, the two men transformed the functions of the vice presidency in ways that Ronald Reagan, Bill Clinton, and George W. Bush later emulated.[31]

As far as Rosalynn Carter and the place of the First Lady was concerned, the presidential couple simply carried forward the personal and political partnership that they had begun with Jimmy Carter's entry into public life. To the surprise and dismay of the media, Mrs. Carter made a diplomatic tour of Latin America for the administration. She saw to the establishment of a presidential commission on mental health, one of her favorite causes. Moreover, she campaigned for Democratic congressional candidates as her husband's surrogate in 1978 and on behalf of his renomination in 1980. When she attended cabinet meetings to be informed about administration policy, a flap ensued about the alleged intrusion of the "Steel Magnolia" into a male preserve. Enhancing the role of the president's wife proved one of the institutional legacies of the Carter White House.[32]

Another lasting change that Jimmy Carter made in the operation of the modern presidency came in 1978 with his use of Camp David as a negotiating center for meetings between Egypt and Israel. The presidential retreat offered clear advantages for conducting prolonged discussions in isolation and privacy. Dwight D. Eisenhower had met there with Nikita Khrushchev in the 1950s, but formal negotiations had not taken place. The success that Carter achieved with the Camp David Accords alerted subsequent presidents such as Bill Clinton to the policy possibilities of the retreat.[33]

The key to presidential success did not lie with these changes in White House procedures, however well intentioned they may have been. Carter had come to the presidency promising much in the way of programs and enhanced efficiency at performing his duties over the records of Nixon and Ford. It soon became apparent that on-the-job training would not be enough to compensate for Carter's lack of political skill in Washington, his inability to deal with Congress and his party, and his growing lack of rapport with the American public. The modern presidency required qualities of self-confidence, personal charm, and intellectual discipline that eluded him after 1976.

The result was a presidency that staggered from crisis to crisis amid a worsening economy and a deterioration in the nation's position in the world.

Inflation, unemployment, and rising taxes fueled popular resentment against Carter and led Republicans to embrace the tax-cutting policies that have marked them since the late 1970s. In world affairs, despite Carter's triumph with the Camp David Accords, the stature of the United States seemed in jeopardy before the apparent resurgence of the Soviet Union. That country's invasion of Afghanistan in 1979, the Iranian Revolution that same year, and the turmoil in Central America made it seem that the United States had entered a period of international decline. These setbacks provided ample ammunition to Carter's Republican critics. As Donald Rumsfeld said at the Republican National Convention in 1980, "We see peace threatened, our defenses weakened, the military balance tipped, the Soviet Union and its agents from Cuba and Vietnam expand, exploit, invade, and repress."[34]

Two events in 1979 defined the unraveling of the Carter presidency. During the summer, as rising energy prices drove inflation up, the president announced that he would address the nation on the problem. Then the speech was put off as Carter and his top aides repaired to Camp David for eleven days of meetings and introspection. The president then delivered a televised address on 15 July 1979 that warned the nation of a "crisis of confidence." He spoke of "the erosion of confidence in the future" and noted a "crisis of the American spirit." Although the word *malaise* did not appear in the text, the speech soon had the word attached to it because of remarks at a press briefing by one of Carter's speechwriters. The failure to coordinate the message and its follow-up cost Carter heavily in the public mind. The initial reaction to this call for action on energy was positive, but the president undercut his own theme with his next public step.[35]

Two days after the speech, Carter demanded the resignations of his cabinet and dropped four members, three of them for their ostensible lack of loyalty to him. The purge did not achieve the results Carter had sought. Firing Joseph Califano, the secretary of health, education and welfare, and Brock Adams, the secretary of transportation, both respected liberals, made Carter seem political and petty. The president then gave Hamilton Jordan the job of White House chief of staff and thus went back on his campaign promise that he would not have a chief of staff on the Nixon model but would designate a man with few friends in Washington. The episode conveyed the impression of an administration adrift as the economy and world situation worsened.

The extensive media coverage of the whole process underlined how the capacity to follow breaking events on a twenty-four-hour basis was shifting the ground rules for modern presidents.[36]

That change became even more obvious when militants in Iran stormed the American embassy in Tehran and took more than sixty Americans hostage on 4 November 1979. Some were later released, but fifty-two stayed in captivity for more than a year. The episode represented the failure of U.S. foreign policy, with the fall of the regime of the shah of Iran earlier in the year and the appearance of the fundamentalist Islamic state under Ayatollah Khomeini. The hostage taking became an ongoing media event, one that proved embarrassing and frustrating to American public opinion. When Walter Cronkite of the CBS *Evening News* closed each nightly broadcast with the number of days the hostages had been held in captivity, his words repeated the humiliation that Americans felt and directed attention back to the ineptitude of Carter and his administration. The relentless pressure of the news cycle ate away at the president's already faltering credibility.[37]

The decline in Carter's standing sparked another political challenge to a presidential nomination in 1980 in the person of Senator Edward M. Kennedy of Massachusetts. Through the use of a "Rose Garden strategy" that emphasized Carter's official duties and campaign appearances on his behalf by the First Lady and other surrogates, the president repulsed the efforts of Kennedy, who proved to be less than a stellar candidate on his own merits. But Carter was winning the renomination of his own party, and his efforts to position himself for the general election proved less rewarding. He authorized a military raid to free the Iranian hostages, but that venture ended in a disaster on 25 April 1980. The helicopters in the mission experienced equipment failures and crashes that killed eight American servicemen. The ill-starred episode stirred new doubts about Carter's competence as a national leader, particularly when he termed what had happened "an incomplete success."[38]

Notwithstanding the accumulating political burdens of Carter's record, the president and his team believed that they could still repulse the attacks of the Republicans and their presidential candidate, the former governor of California Ronald Reagan. The advantages of incumbency seemed to be on Carter's side, along with the perception that Reagan would prove ill suited to the demands of a national presidential campaign.[39]

These assumptions turned out to be incorrect, and Carter's presidency ended in a landslide rout that propelled Reagan to the White House and his party into control of the U.S. Senate in November 1980. The race was actually close until the final presidential debate and the closing days of the campaign, when the wavering voters broke for Reagan in decisive numbers. His question in the last debate about whether Americans felt better off than they had four years earlier crystallized the mind of the electorate. Though the modern presidency gave its occupant marked advantages over a challenger, it was not an infallible insurance policy against policy and political failures of the kind that Jimmy Carter experienced in the White House between 1977 and 1981.[40]

Being the president had never represented an easy political task, but the demands for the position seemed to be intensifying as the 1970s ended. Richard Nixon, Gerald Ford, and Jimmy Carter had been, in their very different ways, talented and hard-working politicians who had devoted abundant energy to the rigors of the presidency. Yet each had come up short in a key aspect of the job. The modern presidency had an uncanny capacity to reveal precisely the character flaw that presidential campaigns, in the case of Nixon and Carter, were designed to mask. Nixon could not stay within the law, and Carter could not translate piety and commitment into effective leadership.

Although his presidency had not succeeded, Jimmy Carter used his years after the White House to refurbish his historical reputation through good works at home and abroad. Unlike Nixon's quest for vindication, Carter's exertions grew from his religious faith and his desire to achieve social betterment. Through the Carter Center and the Carter Presidential Library in Atlanta, the Carters sponsored conferences, wrote numerous books, and pursued causes that ranged from Habitat for Humanity to mental health. The former president also became a kind of freelance roving diplomat, as his efforts to supervise elections in underdeveloped nations and his pathbreaking trip to Fidel Castro's Cuba in 2002 demonstrated. The respect that the postpresidential Jimmy Carter earned from his fellow citizens in these endeavors enhanced his standing, as memories of his failed administration receded in the minds of Americans too young to have remembered his problems in the White House. The Nobel Peace Prize, which he received in the fall of 2002, seemed fitting recognition of the success of his postpresidency.

After a decade and a half of a troubled and scandal-ridden presidency, there was a real concern in 1980 whether the nation's highest office could be made to work at all. The British writer Godfrey Hodgson said in that year, "My own hunch is that the presidency will never again be at the center of the national consciousness in quite the way it was between 1933 and 1973."[41] The election of Ronald Reagan seemed to settle the question in the early years of his presidency, but the further evolution of the administration revealed that success in the White House in the late twentieth century extended trends toward the entertainment and celebrity aspects of the office in significant ways. An actor president was in large measure the logical result of an institution that had become as much about show business as about governance.

9

The Modern Presidency in a Republican Era
Ronald Reagan and George H. W. Bush

After fifteen years of false starts and unsuccessful presidents, the modern presidency revived as an institution in the 1980s when Ronald Reagan won two terms and served them in full, the first chief executive to do so since Dwight D. Eisenhower. By 1989 talk of failed presidencies and a crisis of confidence about the office had faded away. When Reagan transferred power to George Herbert Walker Bush in January 1989, the consensus was that the presidency had returned to its proper place at the head of the American government.

The four years of George H. W. Bush that followed Reagan revealed, however, the fragility of the modern presidency for its occupants. Though Bush achieved victory in the Gulf War in 1991 and his popularity ratings soared, his failures with the economy and his apparent lack of vision cost him reelection in 1992. The vagaries of public opinion and political circumstances remained beyond the control of the president and his aides.

The historical legacy of Ronald Reagan's eight years is a heated battleground for conservatives and liberals who endeavor to address the president's domestic and international impact. Though some scholars have made use of the records of the Reagan White House, restrictions on the release of the archival treasures of the presidency mean that normal historical assessments of Reagan are still in a preliminary stage. Moreover, the president was not a man who put down on paper his innermost thoughts. Some friends and biographers wonder about the extent to which Reagan had an introspective life at all. A woman who knew the president told the speechwriter Peggy

Noonan that Reagan "lived life on the surface where the small waves are, not deep down where the heavy currents tug." In any case, Reagan is likely to rank with Franklin D. Roosevelt and Lyndon Johnson as the most inscrutable of the modern presidents. At least one biographer, Edmund Morris, had to create a fictional character of his own to explain to himself the Reagan enigma.[1]

The mystery of Reagan's character as a leader and the nature of his presidency run through the memoirs of the people closest to him in the White House. Secretary of State Alexander Haig and his ghostwriter likened the Reagan White House to "a ghost ship; you heard the creak of the rigging and the groan of the timbers and sometimes even glimpsed the crew on deck. But which of the crew had the helm? Was it [Edwin] Meese, was it [James] Baker, was it someone else? It was impossible to know for sure." Another more friendly Reagan adviser, Martin Anderson, said that Reagan "made decisions like an ancient king or Turkish pasha, passively letting his subjects serve him, selecting only those morsels of public policy that were especially tasty." Then, there was Colin Powell, who said, "The President's passive management style placed a tremendous burden on us. Until we got used to it, we felt uneasy implementing recommendations without a clear decision."[2]

The key to Reagan's opaque personality lies in his Hollywood experience, not simply as an actor but as a star in that society. More than any other president before him, Reagan came to the White House trained in the methods of show business and celebrity. Born in 1911 in Illinois, he worked as a popular radio announcer in Iowa until 1937, when he moved to California to become a movie actor. A natural screen presence and a talent for pleasant, nondemanding roles advanced his career over the next four years at Warner Brothers. He took naturally to the rhythms of moviemaking. He knew his lines each day, was not temperamental, and accepted direction as part of a common effort to improve the final product. He enjoyed being a center of attention but recognized that he should not let people think that the adulation he received had gone to his head.[3]

World War II and military service in California interrupted the momentum of his career. In the 1940s he made more pictures, some of them successful, but remained below the top tier of cinematic stars. By the late 1940s, he left his Democratic heritage and moved toward Republicans and conservatism. During the next decade, he worked on and off in television for General Electric, where he gained valuable training in speaking to audiences as a visiting personality. He also refined his conservative views on foreign and domestic issues into an all-purpose oration that friends called "the Speech."[4]

Reagan made his first large public impact when he presented a nationally televised version of the Speech for Barry Goldwater's flagging presidential campaign in 1964. "A Time for Choosing," delivered with Reagan's practiced skill, gave him a luster among Republican conservatives that endured for thirty years. From that point, Reagan won the California governorship in 1966, challenged Gerald Ford for the Republican nomination in 1976, and defeated Jimmy Carter to win the White House in 1980.[5]

Many commentators have noted Reagan's acting background as a key to his presidential performance, a contention that has some validity. As he told David Brinkley while preparing to end his term in late 1988, "There have been times in this office when I've wondered how you could do the job if you hadn't been an actor." Reagan was right that the office demanded a dramatic element, as the two Roosevelts and John F. Kennedy had well understood. But it was not enough to be an accomplished thespian, though that certainly helped. What Reagan brought from his Hollywood days to the White House was the experience of being a star and the sensibility that came with that status in the movie industry.[6]

Hollywood insiders and observers can point out, as Joan Didion has recently done, that Reagan was never a true star in the sense of his contemporaries Errol Flynn, James Stewart, and Henry Fonda. In terms of box office clout in the late 1930s and 1940s that is surely true. But Reagan had played the lead in numerous films, he had been the subject of lavish fan magazine attention, and he had been treated like a star, albeit a secondary one, for most of his working life in the picture business. With that condition came certain perquisites that were easily assumed when he became the greatest star in American politics in 1980.[7]

Hollywood stars had an entourage to see to their personal and professional needs. They moved through life with an arranged schedule of public appearances, time on the set, and private rest. Only with such a support system could their work get done and their base of popularity be sustained. Such a routine came naturally to Reagan, whose energy flagged as the day went on and who needed periodic rests to operate at his best level. A political campaign had aspects that resembled moviemaking in that the star/candidate alternated between long stretches of being "off," when his apparatus prepared the next event, to rallies and appearances where he was "on," until his political directors yelled what amounted to "Cut" before another scene was readied.

The secret for stars is getting what they want and need from the people around them to ensure a high standard of their own performance. Ronald Reagan and his wife had a well-developed sense of what the new president required in the way of institutional arrangements to do his best in public and private settings. Although Reagan wanted and needed clear direction in terms of his daily schedules, purpose of meetings, and public expectations, he did not want to be in the hands of a single powerful chief of staff in the White House during the first term. The Reagans had experience with that idea in the person of the political operative John Sears, who had initially run the presidential campaign in 1980. Sears had to be fired when his imperious manner alienated other members of the Reagan entourage.[8]

While not prodding his aides to come up with a team-oriented approach to running the White House, Reagan did not object when the men around him evolved the troika system, with James A. Baker as chief of staff, Edwin Meese as counselor to the president in charge of policy issues, and Michael Deaver as the overseer of the White House media operation. Although the arrangement moved away from the strong chief of staff model of governance, it was not a Republican spokes of the wheel system, either. Baker, Meese, and Deaver acted as coproducers of the Reagan presidency during the first term. Especially during the first two years of the administration and in the 1984 presidential election, they put him on the public stage in settings that maximized his performing talents.[9]

Reagan introduced a number of practices that became standard for his successors. Brief radio addresses had been one way that Reagan kept in touch with his conservative base after he left the California governorship in 1974. These short broadcasts suited well his ability to get a policy issue explained in clear, simple terms. In the White House it was natural to continue the practice every Saturday morning. The number of people who heard "the president's weekly radio address," as it soon became known, was less important than the press coverage that the event engendered. Soon the Democrats had their weekly response, too, as did the Republicans when Bill Clinton became president. By instituting this regular radio session, Reagan both shortened the fireside chat and made it an indelible part of the nation's political landscape.[10]

The State of the Union address gained new show business aspects under Reagan. No longer just a televised rendering of a president communicating with Congress, Reagan's addresses introduced heroes, prominent Americans, and human examples of policy needs among the guests sitting in the visitors' gallery. Aware of the network penchant for reaction shots, the Reagan team produced State of the Union messages with as much care as an Academy Awards show. Two decades after Reagan, even state governors were emulating his techniques in their televised State of the State addresses. How lawmakers were seen reacting to what the president said became a staple of talk shows in the days after the speech. American political discourse was permanently Reaganized in many such subtle ways.[11]

The concept of organizing the president's day around the news cycle and network television coverage realized its full political potential during the Reagan presidency. The new president was accustomed to working from a daily shooting schedule anyway, and he found it reassuring to have an agenda of the next day's events ready for him before he went to bed. Then he ticked off the events as he completed each one. Hitting his marks and saying his lines with practiced professionalism, he moved seamlessly through these routines with the skill of the star who knows that the fate of the production depends on his competence and reliability.

To place the president in the best light in the most systematic manner possible, Reagan's White House managers thought through every aspect of how his presidency should be presented to the American people. The role of the print media was to be diminished even more directly than the Nixon presidency had sought to do. A key premise of the Reagan team was that the modern presidency was more about the visual images that viewers saw each day than the substance of what the president said or what was said about him by reporters or his political opponents. As the White House aide Richard Darman told the CBS correspondent Lesley Stahl after she ran a story about the Handicapped Olympics that was critical of the president's policies toward the handicapped and disabled, "Nobody heard what you said." Instead, he boasted to her, "They just saw the five minutes of beautiful pictures of Ronald Reagan. They saw the balloons, they saw the flags, they saw the red, white and blue. Haven't you people figured out yet that the picture always overrides what you say?"[12]

The advent of Reagan on the national scene also occurred when changes in the role of the media worked to the president's advantage. Mindful of a

Presidential campaigns rarely used modes of transportation other than planes by the 1980s, except to create pleasing images and a sense of political nostalgia. Here Ronald Reagan campaigns from the back of a train in an effort to link the popular modern president with the age of the whistle-stop. (Photograph by Dirck Halstead, the Dirck Halstead Collection, Center for American History, University of Texas at Austin.)

succession of failed administrations and popular perceptions of a liberal media bias, the major news organizations gave Reagan easier coverage than his predecessors had received. The president's ingratiating manner and evident popularity provided part of the explanation, but shifts in the nature of the media were at work as well. As prominent journalists became well-paid personalities in their own right, their sympathy for conservative political positions grew. The evolving attitude toward politics emphasized entertainment over substance, and Reagan's presidency provided compelling drama that boosted the ratings as well. The mutually interdependent relationship between the media and the White House worked to Reagan's advantage in his first term.[13]

All the media skills of the Reagan White House would have been of little avail had the president's policies not scored well with the electorate. Reagan came into office as the country's basic conservatism regained its dominance over the political scene. In years past, Republicans had offered a stern blend of fiscal responsibility and programmatic austerity in their conservatism — balanced budgets and cuts in Social Security and other New Deal programs. During the 1970s, their focus shifted to tax cuts, heightened defense spending, and an avoidance of "root canal economics." Conservatism lost its hard edge and sought to become more palatable to voters. Its main advocates also proved adept at making their case in the media, despite their frequent complaints of a left-wing bias in major newspapers and on networks.[14]

Reagan thus offered a less painful, more soothing style of governance. The president preached from his bully pulpit that it was possible in a single term to reduce taxes, increase defense spending by a significant percentage, and balance the budget in his first term. During the primaries, George H. W. Bush had called this formula "voodoo economics." As vice president, Bush and other Republicans embraced the Reagan vision as a way of reducing social spending, returning money to taxpayers, especially wealthy ones, and meeting the threat from what was believed to be a resurgent Soviet Union. Unlike John F. Kennedy, Reagan did not speak of paying any price or bearing any burden in his cause. The government was the problem, Reagan said, and when its dead hand on taxes and spending was removed, then the nation could get about being strong and free again.[15]

In the first two years of the Reagan presidency, his message resonated well with Washington, in and out of Congress. With a Republican Senate and a

Democratic House on Capitol Hill, Reagan used the political momentum of his landslide victory and the wave of national sympathy after the attempt on his life to achieve passage of his tax cut program. The willingness of the Democrats to press for their own advantages in the bill made the resulting measure as much the product of special interests as wise public policy. As Richard Darman later wrote, "In what was consciously advertised as a fundamental test of the Reagan presidency, there was little room or time for cautious qualification." The key point was that the new president had realized one of his campaign priorities within months of taking office, an event that had not happened since Lyndon Johnson's Great Society initiatives in 1965.[16]

A second key dramatic event in Reagan's revival of the authority of the presidency was his handling of the August 1981 unauthorized strike by the Professional Air Traffic Controllers Organization (PATCO). The confrontation between the president and what appeared to be an arrogant and greedy labor organization was made to order for Reagan's sense of public drama. He came across as a heroic president confronting the representatives of a narrow special interest group. The nation appreciated a chief executive who took a firm position and did not waver, as Jimmy Carter had done on a number of issues. By the end of his first year in office, Reagan had removed any lingering doubts about his ability to perform in ways that characterized a strong president.[17]

These accomplishments took place even though the Reagan White House and the larger administration had many organizational problems. The confusion about where power resided among insiders left lower-level aides searching for guidance. Peggy Noonan wondered, "Who's in charge here? I could never understand where power was in that White House; it kept moving. I'd see men in suits huddled in a hall twenty paces from the Oval Office, and I'd think, there it is, that's where they're making the decisions. But the next day they were gone and the hall was empty." Reagan was often disengaged from these maneuvers. Even though the tension between Secretary of State George Shultz and Defense Secretary Caspar Weinberger proved debilitating for the administration, the president acted as though only some outside forces could solve the problem, not his executive leadership. In Reagan's mind it was not the task of the star to discipline the crew.[18]

One influential figure in the president's calculations was his wife, Nancy Reagan. Initially, she had planned a modest role as the First Lady, but she soon discovered that there was little press interest in her pet project, the Foster Grandparents program. As criticism of her lavish lifestyle mounted, Mrs. Reagan made fun of herself at the Gridiron dinner in 1982 to disarm the press. She also became associated with the antidrug "Just Say No" program, a conservative answer to teenage addiction. Behind the scenes, she was a significant force in personnel appointments and in moving the president toward arms control in the second term. As her role in ousting Chief of Staff Donald Regan in 1987 demonstrated, she had become a more activist, conservative First Lady than any of her critics could have imagined in 1981.[19]

Despite the president's clear sense of how he wanted to handle the Soviet Union, his foreign policy team was often in turmoil. His first secretary of state, Alexander Haig, never understood Reagan's working style and regularly clashed with other White House insiders. The desire not to have another Henry Kissinger led to a succession of weak national security advisers, several of whom were clearly not up to the job. The rise in prominence of the post during the Kissinger years meant that whoever held it became a target of media scrutiny and jealousy from other parts of the foreign policy establishment. As long as a president chose wisely, the adviser could be an indispensable asset. But since the choice was entirely within a president's discretion, there were no checks and balances to ensure that wisdom and balance meshed with foreign policy expertise. Reagan's dim appreciation of these considerations led to the tenure of Richard Allen, William Clark, Robert "Bud" McFarlane, and John Poindexter, all of whom fell well short of the wise judgment that the job demanded. Only toward the end of the administration after the Iran-Contra scandal broke did Reagan get above-average talent in his national security adviser in Colin Powell.[20]

Despite these ongoing personality difficulties, the foreign policy record of the Reagan years is often cited as one of his singular achievements as president. The collapse of the Soviet Union a few years after he left office is credited to his policies: that stern confrontation with the Soviets in the first term followed by negotiations for nuclear arms reduction in the second term. The large buildup in American defense spending that continued trends from the Carter years after 1981, as well as the spending implicit in the Strategic Defense Initiative (SDI) to create a missile shield over the United States, taxed the economic resources of the Soviets to the breaking point, according to Reagan's ardent defenders.[21]

Reagan used the techniques of the celebrity presidency to sharpen the contrast with the Soviets. His famous reference to the USSR as the "evil empire" and his injunction to Mikhail Gorbachev during a speech in Berlin to "tear down this wall" demonstrated Reagan's skill at dramatizing the moral issue, as he saw it, of the Cold War. In retrospect, after he left office there came to seem a larger purpose both to his rhetoric and his policies as the Cold War wound down. Some of the change to a posture of negotiation during the second term, however, arose from the desire of Reagan intimates, especially Nancy Reagan, to have the president's historical legacy be one of a peacemaker. The shift in emphasis did not sit well with all conservative Republicans, but Reagan had so much political capital with them that their grumbling had few political consequences.[22]

Admirers of Reagan contend that the president was very involved in the overall management of Soviet-American relations during his presidency. As the records of the administration are opened, the documents may well bear out this judgment. If so, however, his greater hands-on role will also remove one key defense for his handling of the Iran-Contra affair. If he was not passive and removed from day-to-day details of one central area of foreign policy, then he may bear more historical responsibility for the disastrous outcome of that ill-fated initiative.

In other areas of foreign policy, Reagan's relaxed governing style worked less well. The effort to resolve Middle Eastern problems such as the Arab-Israeli conflict led to such reverses as the stationing of U.S. Marines in Lebanon in 1982 and the subsequent terrorist bombing in 1983 of their barracks, killing 241. Aware of the negative poll ratings that the bombings produced at home, the White House staff persuaded Reagan of the need to remove the remaining marines at an early date. Three and a half months later, the marines were evacuated to ships in the Mediterranean. The incident was one of the first major acts of terrorism directed against the United States, and the failure to respond forcefully did not escape the notice of Muslim fundamentalists who hated the West's most powerful nation. Finding an effective response to terrorism would be a continuing problem for future presidents.[23]

The invasion of the island of Grenada in October 1983 to oust a procommunist government and free American medical students there became one of the foreign policy triumphs of Reagan's first term and a major lift for his reelection chances the next year. That the adversary facing the United States was

Ronald Reagan, George Shultz, and other members of the administration being briefed on air strikes in Libya, April 1986. In moments of crisis the White House became a foreign policy nerve center, with pictures of decision making distributed to the press to show the president at work. (Courtesy of the Ronald Reagan Library.)

relatively weak in military terms only made the achievement more gratifying from a public relations point of view. A low-cost conflict bolstered presidential prestige at little apparent expense to the country or to Ronald Reagan.[24]

There was no question in 1983 and 1984 that Reagan would run for a second term, even though the basic store of ideas he had brought to the White House had largely been implemented by that time. The momentum that drives a president to seek a second term had become so powerful in terms of money, commitment of political activists, and pressure on the candidate that the hazards of another four years for most modern presidents were not explored. Whatever had not been achieved during the first four years would surely be accomplished in the second, or so the logic ran in the Reagan camp and among conservatives.

The resulting presidential campaign against Democrat Walter Mondale was largely a formality. So overwhelming was the Reagan lead that there seemed no need to articulate a vision of where a second term might go.

Modern presidents run for a second term because they can, not because they have an agenda to implement. The Reagan team might have gathered some warning signs from the president's lackluster performance in the first presidential debate. When he bounced back with a patented one-liner in the second face-off, everyone was reassured. Yet after Mondale had been disposed of, with Reagan carrying forty-nine states, the question of what to do in a second term persisted.[25]

The internecine warfare and backbiting of the Reagan White House below the president had taken a toll on the major presidential aides. Out of their fatigue came the idea to have Secretary of the Treasury Donald Regan named White House chief of staff, with James A. Baker moving into Regan's post. Made in haste and without careful thought, this decision replaced the troika arrangement with a dominant and imperious chief of staff in the Sherman Adams–H. R. Haldeman mode. A former Wall Street executive whose whim was law, Regan accumulated power for himself but did not manage the White House or the president well. Beneath the surface of the presidential operation, the inattention of Reagan to what his aides were doing allowed freelance operatives such as Colonel Oliver North to thrive. The result within a few years was the Iran-Contra scandal and its somber consequences, much like spinoffs from the main production on the set.[26]

The impact of Iran-Contra on the modern presidency was not so much the damage it did to Reagan's reputation or the machinations of North and the rest of those involved in the arms-for-hostages deal with Iran and the diversion of funds to the Nicaraguan Contras. What made the episode so troubling was the willingness of the Reagan White House to wield presidential authority to expand extraconstitutional procedures for executing ongoing clandestine operations outside the purview of either Congress or the press. Though often described as a conservative president in terms of his policies, Reagan and those around him proved to be quite radical in their willingness to dispense with those aspects of the Constitution that interfered with their foreign policy goals. As with other modern presidents, both liberal and conservative, for Reagan and his associates the constraints of the existing constitutional system were obstacles to be circumvented rather than provisions to be respected.[27]

Because the Iran-Contra scandal broke late in Reagan's second term, impeachment of the president over the affair was never a real possibility. Democrats feared the possible backlash from trying to oust a popular president who would soon be leaving office anyway. No one looked with eagerness to a repetition of the Watergate trauma. When Reagan dropped Donald Regan and replaced him with Howard Baker and then Frank Carlucci, as well as installing Colin Powell as national security adviser, a sense that grown-ups were in charge of the White House returned to Washington. The troubling aspects of the Iran-Contra case simply ebbed away without much further thought to what these related episodes revealed regarding the broadening of executive autonomy outside constitutional boundaries.[28]

Reagan's second term did have substantive accomplishments, which did not add up to the revolution that his admirers associate with his presidency. The Tax Reform Act of 1986 produced genuine, if temporary, change in that key economic policy. Reagan also deserves praise for the reduction in Cold War tensions that occurred in the last years of his presidency. At the same time, assigning credit to the incumbent for these positive changes runs up against the comments of his aides. As Frank Carlucci, the national security adviser after the Iran-Contra affair concluded, said, "The Great Communicator wasn't always the greatest communicator in the private sessions; you didn't always get clear and crisp decisions. You assumed a lot in your decisions. You had to."[29]

For Ronald Reagan, his stumbling performance in public and private during the revelations about Iran-Contra took the edge off his standing with the American people. Though he remained well liked, his image changed from that of an effective, kindly communicator of clear ideas to one of a chief executive who probably had stayed too long. As Reagan's hero Calvin Coolidge once observed, presidents who served eight years often found that "the latter parts of their term" had "often been clouded with grave disappointments." Later disclosures about Alzheimer's disease would raise questions of whether Reagan's illness began during the presidential years. More likely was the explanation that the cumulative effects of six years in a physically and emotionally demanding office had taken their toll on a man in his mid-seventies. Although Reagan had spent a great deal of time in California on his ranch while in office, he could not escape the burdens that the presidency posed, even to someone who let the details of governing float by him. By the time he left office in January 1989, he had exhausted his intellectual and physical capital. The star had burned out.[30]

At the end of the Reagan administration, talk of the revival of the presidency during his eight years was commonplace. The focus was on some of his accomplishments in foreign affairs, though less weight was given to the increase in the national debt on his watch. The greatest attention concentrated on Reagan's ability to convey optimism and confidence to the American people. "He was a first-class communicator," said President Gerald Ford, and the media agreed with the verdict.[31]

Oddly enough, despite the restoration of confidence that Reagan was said to have supplied to the nation, within a year or two of his departure the optimistic mood had evaporated on the domestic scene. While George H. W. Bush benefited from national pride over victory in the Gulf War, the early 1990s, with their economic recession, saw a renewal of fears about the nation's future. The spell that Reagan had cast was temporary, and his revival of respect for the modern presidency proved transitory as well and was not transferable to subsequent presidents.

Although Ronald Reagan might have been reelected in 1988 in the absence of the two-term limit, his presidency was winding down as far as new ideas were concerned. His successor, George H. W. Bush, could not say publicly that he intended to govern in a non-Reagan style, but there was little doubt among Republicans of his overall intentions in that regard. Lacking Reagan's skills as a political communicator, Bush intended to provide the clear and direct leadership that Reagan had not supplied to the White House staff. Competence would be valued. Charisma would be discounted.

George Herbert Walker Bush had been preparing to run for president for two decades. The son of a Connecticut senator, Prescott Bush, the younger Bush had moved to Texas after service in World War II and graduation from Yale to seek his fortune in the oil business. After some years in West Texas, he relocated to Houston and became an active participant in the Republican politics of that growing city. Handsome but inarticulate, Bush was more moderate than many of his fellow Texas Republicans. He believed in birth control and had advocated a mild civil rights stance in college. Yet when he ran for the Senate in 1964, he denounced the 1964 Civil Rights Act and took positions pleasing to the right wing of the Texas GOP. After a loss in his first try for statewide office, he won a House seat in 1966 and then sought another Senate opening in 1970. Defeat at the hands of Lloyd Bentsen moved Bush into another track of Republican preferment. He was named ambassador to the United Nations, head of the American Public Liaison Office in China, and later director of the Central Intelligence Agency during the Ford administration. The presidency was the natural capstone to a distinguished record and Bush sought the big prize in 1980. He fell before the Reagan tide but bounced back to become the running mate. In none of these posts did Bush display a penchant for ideological purity or a clear sense of what a future presidential agenda might be. Richard Nixon in a private conversation called Bush "soft and unsophisticated."[32]

The presidential campaign set the terms for Bush's administration in one key area of domestic economic policy. Anxious to label the Democrats as lavish spenders intent on raising taxes at every opportunity, Bush decided to make an explicit pledge against any future tax increase when he addressed the Republican National Convention in 1988. His acceptance speech declared that if the Democrats pressed him to raise taxes, he would respond: "Read my lips, no new taxes." The remark delighted his audience and mollified the Republican conservatives who feared that Bush might have latent tendencies toward moderation. Of course, it also meant that, should economic or political conditions change, Bush would have painted himself into a fiscal corner. But in the modern presidential campaign, winning came first; governance came second. Bush did not fully realize how much the no-new-taxes pledge had defined his public personality in 1988.[33]

To win the contest over his Democratic rival, Governor Michael Dukakis of Massachusetts, Bush allowed his campaign to play the race card for its full electoral potential. His key political adviser, Lee Atwater of South Carolina, encouraged Republican surrogates to attack Dukakis about his policy of allowing convicted felons weekend furloughs. One of these convicts, William J. Horton Jr., had fled the state and committed additional assaults before being recaptured. That Horton, who was soon renamed "Willie" by GOP operatives, was black enhanced his value as a symbol of Democratic softness on the crime issue. In running for office, Bush was quite willing to do what he believed victory demanded of him. As an incumbent, he could then govern with less attention to these kinds of tactics.[34]

During the 1988 campaign, there was some attention to Bush's lack of a quality he called "the vision thing," his sense of where the nation ought to go in the future. When his Democratic opponent, Dukakis, said that the election was "not about ideology, it's about competence," he allowed Bush to

Presidential campaigns in the late twentieth century sought pleasing images for the nightly news. Here George H. W. Bush attracts an enthusiastic crowd as he seeks the presidency in 1988. (Photograph by Dirck Halstead, the Dirck Halstead Collection, Center for American History, University of Texas at Austin.)

embrace enough of the Reagan legacy to convince conservatives that he was a better choice than any Democrat. The larger question lingered of whether Bush would simply be a caretaker for what Reagan had done or be able to set forth his own sense of where he wanted the country to go.[35]

In office, however, Bush believed that the logic of the continuous campaign did not apply to him. The election race for 1992 was three and a half years away, and in the meantime there was the business of government to conduct. While Bush and his team did not ignore political considerations in shaping policy, neither did they pay as much heed to the subject on a daily basis as Reagan's men had done. Since much went right for Bush in the area of foreign policy in 1989 and 1990, the focus on substance did not seem to drag down his chances to secure another four years of power in 1992.[36]

To emphasize the contrast with Reagan, President Bush tried to interact with the press on a more regular basis. He held more frequent press conferences in the White House briefing room, where he showed his mastery of both

The White House provides an attractive backdrop for presidential success as here when George H. W. Bush and Mikhail Gorbachev sign a treaty between the United States and the Soviet Union in June 1990 (Courtesy of the George Bush Presidential Library.)

foreign policy and domestic matters in a way that would have been alien to Reagan and his handlers. In the heady early days of the administration, Bush won praise for his talents in this area. Over the long haul of his four years, his inability to spell out his vision for the country in effective addresses to individual groups or to the American people at large undercut the work he did in wooing the media at the beginning of his presidency. As one of his aides put it, "He thought that you should be able to just work your ass off and people would love you," without spending undue attention on how ideas were conveyed to the voters.[37]

The Bush administration sent another signal of its divergence from the Reagan years in the way Barbara Bush handled her role as First Lady. After the lavish displays and the controversies of Nancy Reagan's tenure, Barbara Bush presented herself as a reassuring, grandmotherly presence in the White House. The public learned that she was "the Silver Fox" in the Bush family, saw her endorse literacy, and watched her avoid flaps with the press with a sure hand. In 1990 when students at Wellesley College objected to her as a commencement speaker because her fame derived from her husband, Mrs. Bush brought Raisa Gorbachev to the event and wowed her critics. Her popularity remained high for four years, and she did not venture into public issues until 1992. By the time of the Republican National Convention, she let slip her disagreements with her husband's policy on abortion, but even that spate of controversy did not damage her standing. As her published memoir and diary excerpts revealed, she was a more acerbic figure than the press understood, but her time as First Lady was an unalloyed public relations success.[38]

The general thrust of the Bush presidency in 1989 and 1990 was that Reaganism did not require followers of the former president to be in charge to realize the optimal results in the White House. Indeed, it was probably better if individuals more seasoned in matters of governing replaced the Reagan team. Thus, the transition in 1988 and 1989 had more elements of a transfer of power from one party to another than a shift from one conservative Republican administration to another. These trends heightened conservative dislike of Bush and fueled suspicions of his ultimate intentions.[39]

With the Soviet Union collapsing in 1989 and 1990, the president and his foreign policy team of James A. Baker as secretary of state and Brent Scowcroft as national security adviser managed the end of the Cold War with evident skill. Bush had wanted the former senator John G. Tower of Texas as his secretary of defense, but the nomination had failed because of Tower's personal lapses with alcohol and women. Bush's next choice was Richard "Dick" Cheney, a Wyoming congressman. Working with the chairman of the Joint Chiefs of Staff, General Colin Powell, Cheney emerged as one of the strongest members of the Bush cabinet.[40]

The Bush administration contributed to the onset of the crisis with Iraq when it sent mixed signals about its attitude toward that country's claims on the oil-rich neighbor of Kuwait. Once the Iraqis invaded Kuwait at the end of July 1990, however, Bush was in his element as an international diplomat in mobilizing a multinational coalition to oust Saddam Hussein's army from its conquest. The resulting Gulf War produced a smashing coalition victory that drove the aggressor back into Iraq and shattered temporarily much of his armed force.[41]

This decisive triumph turned out to be a mixed blessing for Bush's reputation as president. With television covering the carnage as the Iraqi army collapsed, and the major war aim of freeing Kuwait was achieved, the president and his advisers believed that their choice lay between stopping the fighting promptly or pursuing a thrust to the Iraqi capital of Baghdad to seize Saddam Hussein and topple his then-fragile regime. The Bush White House opted for the first alternative and brought the war to an end after one hundred hours. In so doing, they allowed large elements of the Iraqi forces to escape, buttressing Hussein's political grip on his country. More intense destruction of the Iraqi military, rather than the occupation of territory, would have served the national interest of the United States over the ensuing decade. Indeed by 2002, the president's son, George W. Bush, was formulating plans for his administration to finish the task the elder Bush had left undone.[42]

Success in the Gulf War lifted George H. W. Bush's approval ratings in the polls to over 90 percent. With the 1992 presidential election twenty months away, President Bush seemed unbeatable, and major Democratic contenders decided not to challenge him in 1992. A grateful nation would surely accord the president who had won the war and expunged the memories of the Vietnam defeat the second term he very much wanted.

Although he was adept at foreign policy, Bush's performance in the domestic arena left Republican conservatives unhappy and the mass of voters convinced that the president was out of touch with their concerns. His modest aspirations in this area came through in his pledge to "first, do no harm" and his emphasis on volunteering through his Thousand Points of Light program. The key defining episode was Bush's reversal on his no-new-taxes pledge in 1990. In the Democratic Congress, the fate of the Bush budget that year was in doubt when the majority insisted that increased taxes be included along with cuts in spending. The White House announced that the no-new-taxes pledge could not be sustained. Outraged Republican conservatives such as Congressman Newt Gingrich assailed the administration for its heresy.[43]

Later that year, with the congressional elections approaching, the White House worked out a budget agreement with Congress that put new taxes in place. In the long run this deal started the rehabilitation of the government's financial position that continued during the 1990s. But fiscal responsibility was now a lesser element for Bush's party than reduced taxes. Conservative displeasure with Bush mounted, and some on the right urged that a challenge to the president's renomination occur, either within or without the Republican party.[44]

The problem with the Bush presidency in the domestic sphere was that he offered neither the allure of celebrity nor the mode of continuous campaigning to offset his lack of personal charisma as an executive. He saw his role much like that of William Howard Taft following Theodore Roosevelt. The policies of the Reagan years had been good and now had to be administered in a sensible and prudent way. But the expectations for presidential activism, or at least the appearance of that quality, were now so ingrained that merely carrying forward what Reagan had accomplished was not enough to satisfy the conservative base of the Republicans. If the Reagan revolution were not extended, it would recede.

George Bush was an active president — some would say hyperactive — in his approach to the day-to-day business of running the country. But his temperament made him suspicious of ideological crusades and sweeping social change. As a result, he shrank the presidency back to a human scale that did not go well on television or satisfy Republican partisans. Affable and pleasant in person, Bush at his best was an adequate speaker whose addresses often seemed dull and detached. He abhorred dramatics and failed to fill the screen of the home television. To the extent that the modern presidency required the skills of an actor, he came up short.

Bush believed, as William Howard Taft had done, that his substantive record would make its own case with the voters. In choosing key aides, therefore, he gave little weight to how these men and women would appear as the public face of his administration. In some instances, such as Secretary of Defense Cheney, the selection did fuse competence in private with effectiveness in public. Bush was less successful with his White House chief of staff, John Sununu. A former governor of New Hampshire who had engineered Bush's key primary victory in the state over Senator Robert Dole, Sununu had large claims on the Bush White House. Never one to suffer those he perceived as fools, he brought an imperious style and an ample belief in his own ability to the job.[45]

Sununu proved to be a strong administrator who took maximum advantage of the perquisites of his position. His dealings with Congress were not as effective, and he alienated key lawmakers with his contemptuous attitude toward them, regardless of party. During the budget deal crisis of 1990, Sununu said of Trent Lott of Mississippi, a key Senate Republican, that he had "become an insignificant figure in this process." Lott responded, "He just stuck the wrong pig." The position of chief of staff, often allocated as a political reward, as in the case of Sununu, needed qualities of tact and skill in Washington that Bush, despite his own personal experience, undervalued. There were few tears when Sununu had to leave his job amid revelations that he had used White House services for personal errands.[46]

As the economy worsened during 1991 and into early 1992, Bush came to seem increasingly out of touch with the concerns of working Americans. While the downturn was not as severe as it seemed at the time, Bush could not convey a credible sense of personal involvement with problems on the minds of the voters. By 1992, his disapproval rating on the management of the economy stood at 80 percent in one Gallup poll. Bush proclaimed that his message was "I care," but no amount of reassurance could persuade the public that the president had their interests at heart.[47]

An instructive example of Bush's slowness in recognizing the public's attitude came when Los Angeles erupted in rioting during spring 1992, following the acquittal of white policemen accused of beating the black motorist Rodney King. Several days elapsed before the White House responded to the situation, and the press contrasted Bush's insensitivity on racial matters to the empathy of his Texas predecessor, Lyndon B. Johnson, with the aspirations of black Americans. Given Bush's use of the race card in his 1988 presidential campaign and his policies as president, little specific action to address the black-white divide was to be expected. But the prolonged absence of even a hint of rhetorical recognition of the problem underlined his presidential detachment.[48]

When it came time to plan for the 1992 reelection campaign, the president did not engage the matter until the last moment in political terms. As one aide said, Bush "felt that what he was elected to do was to govern, not to be out campaigning." He rejected the notion of a continuous campaign for president while governing the country. In the process, he allowed his opponents, Ross Perot and Bill Clinton, to define him in ways that highlighted his worst qualities. He felt entitled to another term on the basis of his record and did not relish the interaction with the voters that would be necessary to carve out an electoral success. His lackluster performance in the televised debates underscored his uneasiness about having to run for president again under those circumstances.[49]

George H. W. Bush could never accept that the American people would turn to a Ross Perot or worse yet to a Bill Clinton in the 1992 race over the president's proven record of achievement and devotion to the national interest. What Ronald Reagan remembered and George Bush forgot was that the executive office was no longer allowed to put aside electoral politics between presidential campaigns. The process of raising money and running for the White House began as soon as one four-year cycle came to an end. Just as professional sports and mass entertainment no longer had well-defined chronological seasons, the dance of American presidential politics had morphed into a perpetual marathon. In trying to separate governance from campaigning, George H. W. Bush only emphasized how interwoven these twin forces had become by the early 1990s. Even mastery of continuous campaigning, however, did not guarantee success in office or immunity from political enemies. As Bush's successor Bill Clinton would soon discover, the politics of the 1980s had added a new dimension to the modern presidency. Labeled "the politics of personal destruction," this added pressure on presidents would make the last chief executive of the twentieth century a target for animus that, combined with Clinton's personal faults, produced a major crisis for the modern presidency in the two years before the 2000 presidential contest.

10

Perils of the Modern Presidency
Bill Clinton

None of the modern presidents fused the elements of political celebrity with continuous campaigning in a more distinct manner than did William Jefferson Clinton between 1993 and 2001. The union of these key elements produced some striking substantive achievements in the domestic sphere and some creditable results overseas. Because Clinton's personal character fed off celebrity and the sexual energy that came with national power, he brought the moral sensibility of a rock star to the Oval Office as well. The combination of a successful politician and persistent sexual adventurer drove his enemies to distraction and in time gave them a weapon to seek his destruction. The result was a presidential soap opera of international proportions.

In his policies, Bill Clinton was a moderate Democrat who sought to mute the liberal image of his party. As president, he turned the Democrats toward a commitment to fiscal responsibility and even balanced budgets. Declaring that "the era of big government is over," he sought to trim the size of the federal establishment and to concentrate on modest programs that were efficient, economical, and popular. The White House emphasized its commitment to fostering creative business and expanding American trade. In foreign affairs, Clinton operated as a prudent Wilsonian, involving the nation in peacekeeping missions but always seeking to minimize the potential loss of American lives in such ventures. Though his partisan foes rarely recognized it, the Clinton administration followed the broad outlines of the foreign policy of the preceding Bush administration.[1]

[213]

If Clinton was in fact a mainstream president in his policies, why did his pursuit of these conventional goals arouse such intense hatred among Americans on the right? Some of that passion remains elusive. The Clintons were the first baby boomers to occupy the White House, and they brought with them some of the baggage of the 1960s. Although their behavior in that decade had been conventional compared with some of the extremes on the left and right, the Clintons were depicted as the personification of the era when Americans abandoned the values of the postwar years in favor of hedonism and irresponsibility. For conservatives, to see Bill and Hillary Clinton in the presidency was to see a great nation giving in to its worst impulses.

Some of Bill Clinton's political opponents went further. To them, the new president was not just a clever politician but a demonic figure who intended to seize absolute power. To that end, he had aided drug dealers, abused women, and now proposed to terminate democracy as it had existed in the United States for two centuries. In some circles, he was believed to be a Mafia-like serial murderer who exterminated all who stood in his path. Yet these same critics chastised Clinton for being irresolute in office, not a quality usually associated with a ruthless tyrant.[2]

His wife, Hillary Rodham Clinton, aroused equal fury among her conservative critics. Remembering her youthful allegiance to Barry Goldwater and her minor role in the impeachment of Richard M. Nixon, they depicted her as power hungry, the leader of a lesbian cabal, and unfaithful to her husband with his friend Vincent Foster. Her ultimate goal was, in this scenario, to run for president herself and maintain the Clintonian stranglehold on political decency for several generations. When Mrs. Clinton was assigned to deal with the issue of health care in 1993, many of these fears became even more intense; and her program, which was not presented with great skill, came under withering assault from the right.[3]

As president, Bill Clinton did a good deal to validate some of the criticism against him. An admirer of the youthful image of John F. Kennedy, Clinton also shared Kennedy's sexual adventurism and disregard for propriety. As a politician, Clinton proved more adept than his foes when he had to extricate himself from a tight corner. Swift changes of position enabled him to escape political traps. Time after time, the president eluded his pursuers from predicaments over the budget, government shutdowns, and welfare reform. When he did so, he left his adversaries and much of the press convinced that he had not been entirely honest with them. The label "Slick Willie," bestowed on him by an unfriendly Arkansas newspaper columnist, came to seem an essential ingredient of his presidential style.[4]

From his teenage years on, Bill Clinton had been marked for political success, and some friends even envisioned the presidency for him one day. His father died before he was born, and young Clinton grew up in Arkansas amid a dysfunctional family, with an abusive stepfather and a party-loving, gambling mother. Nonetheless, his charm, natural eloquence, and quick mind took him to Georgetown, a Rhodes scholarship, and the Yale Law School. In each educational setting he impressed most of his teachers. At Yale he met Hillary Rodham, whom he married in 1975. In 1976 Clinton was elected attorney general of Arkansas and moved up to become governor two years later.[5]

Though turned out of office in 1980, Clinton bounced back to regain the governorship in 1982. Over the next decade, he became identified as a New Democrat who wanted to move his party toward the center, away from the liberalism that voters by then disliked. He was soon recognized as a rising Democratic star. In the background, there were whispers in Arkansas political circles about his personal life and his easy way with his marriage vows. Such considerations kept him out of the race for the Democratic nomination in 1988. When no prominent Democrat came forward to challenge George H. W. Bush for 1992, Clinton sensed his opportunity. He announced his candidacy late in 1991.

The nonstop race that ensued demonstrated Clinton's mastery of continuous campaigning and his intuitive sense of how to package his personality and program to the voters. His presidential campaign became a combination of personal soap opera along with adroit national politics. More than any of his rivals in 1992, Clinton approached politics as a twenty-four-hour exercise. No Republican charge went unanswered from the Democratic war room in Little Rock; some were answered even before the Republicans officially released them. The candidate poured his prodigious energies into handshaking, speechmaking, and television appearances. As the days unwound toward November 1992, the rhythms of the campaign provided a coherent structure for the Clinton team.[6]

When Clinton promised voters that he would feel their pain as president and be an activist chief executive, the candidate himself does not seem to have given much thought to how he would operate the office he was so desperately seeking. Some planning about the transition occurred during fall 1992, but Clinton understandably did not have time to give that problem much attention. Once he won, as he had done so often in the past, he would figure out how he wished to function as president.

Clinton and the Democrats won a decisive victory in November 1992 over Bush and the dispirited Republicans as well as Ross Perot and his makeshift organization. At the end of the campaign, the voters broke for Clinton and the prospect of change. The winner received only a plurality of the popular vote and in that sense was a minority president. Republicans grumbled that Bush had been closing the gap in the final days in the polls before the Iran-Contra special prosecutor, Lawrence Walsh, announced indictments of Ronald Reagan's secretary of defense, Caspar Weinberger, and others. In the euphoria of Democratic victory, this sense of Republican grievance seemed only a footnote to Clinton's stunning success.[7]

The problem that the Walsh episode presented to the Clinton presidency was more significant than it seemed at the time. Viewing themselves as the natural governing party, the Republicans now saw the presidency as their inherent possession, not a gift of the American people to be renewed at four-year intervals. Rather than focusing on their own mistakes in office as the reason for Bush's defeat in 1992, the Republicans questioned Clinton's legitimacy as president. Congressman Richard Armey (R-Tex.) described Clinton to his Democratic colleagues in the House as "your president," and the Senate GOP leader, Robert Dole (R-Kans.), said after the election that Clinton's minority status entitled his programs to less respect from the political opposition on that account. This Republican mind-set was well summed up in the talk-show host Rush Limbaugh's daily reminder during the Clinton years, "America Held Hostage."[8]

Beyond partisan opposition, Clinton also confronted political and covert insurgencies against his right to hold power. The extent to which there was, in the words of Hillary Clinton, a "vast right-wing conspiracy" against the president is still a topic of controversy. But the evidence indicates that wealthy conservatives such as Richard Mellon Scaife did fund projects to gather damaging evidence of alleged Clinton wrongdoing with an eye toward an ultimate impeachment inquiry. The extent to which Clinton himself furnished real evidence to justify their probes is in doubt for his financial affairs, less so for his sexual shenanigans. Few sitting presidents have had their years before the

For a president who had strained relations with the military, a picture of Bill Clinton with the troops on the White House lawn created precisely the kind of impression to offset such criticism of his leadership. (Photograph by Dirck Halstead, the Dirck Halstead Collection, Center for American History, University of Texas at Austin.)

White House scrutinized to the degree that his were. The Clinton White House thus faced a level of organized opposition that represented a new form of political assault on the presidency as an institution. Precedent suggests that these weapons, once deployed on one side of the partisan divide, will most likely be relied on again by another side in some future political dispute.[9]

The press did not like Clinton, whom they regarded as a liar for his tricky way with the language, and the media readily joined in the ideological assaults on the administration. Reporters applied investigative probing to Clinton and his wife that they had not devoted to previous presidents for the years before they took office. The *New York Times* was especially assiduous in exploring Clinton's financial affairs, though it was less accurate than persistent. Following the lead of the *Times,* other inquiries and the resulting congressional hearings delved deeply into the documentary record of the Clintons to the point that much material historians would usually not see for years was spread on the public record. The constant drumbeat of press attention and the expectation of scandal around the next corner supplied an ongoing background irritant for the Clinton White House that shaped how decisions were made and policy formulated.[10]

For all the burdens that these elements imposed on Clinton, he compounded his problems with his own loose approach to the presidency. More brilliant than disciplined himself, he relied on the permanent White House staff to instill the order that he and his people could not provide. In his management of the presidency, he appointed a boyhood friend, Thomas Franklin "Mack" McClarty III, as his first chief of staff. An Arkansas businessman, McClarty was out of his depth in the job and did little to impose constraints on the president and others. Eventually, McClarty had to be replaced in 1994 by the former congressman Leon Panetta, who was more experienced in the ways of Washington and more willing to impose order on the workings of the White House and the more than eight hundred people who directly served the president and vice president.[11]

The evident disarray of the Clinton operation was apparent during the aftermath of the election and into the confused transition period. The president-elect allowed the issue of gays in the military to become a hot subject that defined his presidency as culturally liberal even before it began. A series of embarrassing revelations regarding illegal aliens and the nonpayment of Social Security taxes for domestic workers torpedoed the nominations of two female candidates for the post of attorney general. Few presidencies, even that of Jimmy Carter, have had a shakier start than Bill Clinton's did in January 1993.[12]

Part of the problem was a dearth of executive talent among Democrats. Out of office for the preceding twelve years, they had not had a chance to groom skilled administrators, and those associated with the Carter presidency did not have distinguished pedigrees either. The new secretary of defense, Congressman Les Aspin of Wisconsin, though a bright and talented lawmaker, was no administrator, as he quickly proved. The secretary of the treasury, the former senator from Texas Lloyd M. Bentsen Jr., had a business background that helped him perform capably, but some of the others took time to get oriented. The demands of running a presidential administration at the end of the twentieth century were outpacing the capacity of even skilled politicians to take over and run complex organizations.

The siege of the Branch Davidian complex outside Waco, Texas, that ended in a fiery raid with significant casualties among those inside stamped the

Clinton administration as inept in April 1993. Though the roots of the problem lay in the Bush administration, Clinton and his new attorney general, Janet Reno of Florida, were blamed for the fiasco, as conspiracy theories proliferated on the right and among those hypercritical of the president about what had happened. The episode illustrated the difficulty for a new administration in mastering the unexpected problems arising from ongoing investigations with which they were unfamiliar. For the Clinton presidency, it was another blow to its legitimacy with a significant minority of the population.[13]

The larger problems of the Clinton presidency were an outgrowth of his character. He did not like to delegate power to subordinates or to accept the discipline of a schedule. The new president became notorious for his lack of punctuality, and every public event seemed to run late. Rudeness toward an audience in that regard became a Clinton trademark, but any hard feelings usually vanished when he began to speak. The president's rock-star sensibility ensured that he could not conform to a schedule. That in turn contributed to the impression of self-indulgence and egotism that he conveyed.[14]

Clinton's formidable capacity to focus on a problem when he had to and to find a last-minute solution often extricated him from a tight corner during his presidency. There was, however, always the spirit of a collegiate all-nighter about his presidency that never went away during his eight years in office. The hectic frenzy of his last days contributed to the scandal over his final pardons. Continuous campaigning suited his working style, since he fed off crises and their ultimate resolution.

Like Jimmy Carter and his aides, Clinton and his team came to Washington suspicious of the capital city and unconcerned about winning over its longtime residents. The president and his wife spent little time cultivating opinion makers in and out of the media. As a result, the permanent Washington establishment regarded the president and the new First Lady as pushy Arkansas parvenus out of touch with the city's ethos. That disdain drove much of the press coverage from journalists, who might otherwise have supported Clinton's substantive policies. Such episodes as the firing of the staff of the White House Travel Office in spring 1993 confirmed for many insiders that the Clintons had no real sense of how things ought to be done in the presidency.[15]

A similar attitude governed relations between Clinton and Congress. Democratic during the first two years and Republican thereafter, Capitol Hill did not like the president, and the feeling was mutual. The inept handling of cabinet selections got things off to a bad start. In working with the initial Democratic majority, Clinton had the worst of the available alternatives. The leadership proved unable to deliver on its promises in the case of an ill-fated package to stimulate the economy. Clinton thus lost any chance to push for issues such as campaign finance reform that could have reshaped the political dialogue.[16]

The president did use the Democratic majority to pass, by the narrowest of margins, his economic package during summer 1993. Although the budget as adopted laid the basis for the improvement of the government's finances during the 1990s, it came at a high political cost for the president's party in Congress. Popular unhappiness with higher taxes and the Clinton administration in general led to the massive defeats of Democrats in the 1994 congressional elections, when Republicans regained the House for the first time in half a century. Although Democrats had to support Clinton for the next six years, a vein of mutual suspicion ran through their relations.[17]

Once the Republicans took over in 1995, Clinton found a useful foil for his political skills in Speaker of the House Newt Gingrich and his right-wing allies. Overly impressed with his feat in becoming Speaker, Gingrich galvanized Democrats and proved to be an inept leader. Because of their profound dislike of Clinton, the House Republicans underestimated his abilities and allowed themselves to be drawn into battles over the closing of the federal government in 1995 and 1996, which Clinton easily won. Time after time the president drove the Republican Congress to distraction with his timely escapes from their efforts to trap him. Republican congressional frustration with Clinton was a large element in driving the passions behind his impeachment in 1998 and 1999.[18]

The arrival of the Republican majority in Congress did lead to the adoption of a change in the presidency that many chief executives, including Clinton, had sought — the line-item veto power over appropriations. In 1996 the Republicans gave the president such authority, and the measure went into effect in 1997. When the law reached the Supreme Court, however, the justices ruled that it was unconstitutional because it imparted to the president sole power to alter statutes already passed. The apparent presidential panacea for curbing congressional expenditures soon faded from the national agenda.[19]

Clinton and his administration also pursued changes in the way that the government operated, much as William Howard Taft, Warren G. Harding, Dwight D. Eisenhower, and Richard Nixon had done before him. The Na-

For much of his presidency, Bill Clinton had to confront a Republican House and Senate. Here he confers with Senator Bob Dole and future Speaker of the House Newt Gingrich in the Oval Office in 1993. (Courtesy of the Library of Congress.)

tional Performance Review, or "reinventing government," targeted government agencies, rather than the presidency itself, for scrutiny and management revision. The overall goal was to convince the public that government could be made to work better and at a lower cost through tools of modern management. The history of the National Performance Review remains to be written, but its momentum had run out by the time the Clinton presidency ended. The administration of George W. Bush came in with ambitious plans to transform the Defense Department and with little respect for Clinton's administrative legacy.[20]

Few presidents have been more gifted orators than Bill Clinton at his best, and the president often relied on his skills at the podium to turn the tables on his enemies or to shore up his own support. Even more than during the Reagan years, Clinton's major speeches became dramatic events in their own right as the president adapted, improvised, and reshaped his words on the fly to evoke the desired response from his audiences. The process by which the words were composed, however, had more of the nature of the campaign trail than a measured deliberative process within the White House.

In speechwriting as in everything else, Clinton displayed a propensity to micromanage and to leave decisions to the last minute. Confident of his own abilities, he involved himself deeply in the process of framing remarks, drew in outsiders to critique the product of his speechwriters, and often spent time tinkering with the text, almost to the point where his talk began. Sometimes he even went beyond that point and improvised on the themes of the speech as it rolled through the teleprompter.[21]

As a result, Clinton's State of the Union messages, for example, ran longer and longer as his presidency continued. Where Reagan and the elder George Bush sought to finish in under an hour, even allowing for applause, Clinton regularly exceeded the sixty-minute mark. Although pundits fretted about the president's verbosity, the public seemed to like the level of information that he provided about national problems. Clinton continued and expanded Reagan's practice of recognizing guests in the gallery. The precise placing of these individuals and their symbolic significance, both dignitaries and typical Americans, became a closely watched and analyzed aspect of every State of the Union event.

To maximize the political impact of the State of the Union, the Clinton team added a new follow-up to the address itself. In the days immediately following the televised speech, the president would fly to well-planned rallies where, before cheering, friendly crowds, he would reprise the themes of the State of the Union. No longer a report to Congress and the nation about the affairs of the government, the State of the Union became more like the acceptance speech at a partisan national gathering that then launched the candidate on to the hustings. Even the Republican opposition in the House chamber became a kind of prop for Clinton's use. Televised reaction shots of the lawmakers also provided fodder for commentary. For Clinton, who thrived on these experiences, it was a return to what he did best. The continuous campaign had enveloped the State of the Union in its all-consuming embrace.[22]

After taking what he deemed to be a statesmanlike position on the economy in 1993 and 1994 at great political cost, Clinton found that such a strategy did not serve his interest in being reelected in 1996. Moving outside even his own White House staff, he turned to a longtime political consultant, Richard "Dick" Morris, for his salvation. The emergence of Morris put a good deal of strain on relationships within the White House as the new political guru crossed jurisdictional lines and offended many longtime Clinton allies. Under Morris's tutelage, Clinton reshaped making policy into a poll-driven enterprise that framed issues in terms of their direct salience with voters in 1996. Morris argued that Clinton should rely on targeted initiatives aimed at specific groups to counteract the perception that the president was a liberal, out of touch with regular Americans. Proposals on school uniforms, modest gun control measures, and other programs aimed at soccer moms soon followed.[23]

To win reelection in 1996 with these ideas, Clinton needed to preempt potential Republican challengers in 1995 before the actual election commenced. That strategy required a lavish television advertising campaign at immense cost. Paying for such strikes on the opposition's base demanded in turn ample campaign funds to offset the inherent fund-raising superiority of the GOP. Clinton and his political aides thus used the allure of the White House to raise money on a scale that dwarfed the excesses of Richard Nixon in 1971 and 1972 and previous efforts by Ronald Reagan during the 1980s.

The White House emerged as combination casino and tourist attraction for well-heeled donors. Sleepovers in the Lincoln Bedroom, coffees with the president, and photo opportunities for generous givers became key parts of

Clinton's daily routine. The president and the Democrats also reached out to foreign corporations for donations, with the result that money came in from foreign governments such as China through dummy businesses and middlemen. The implicit argument of the Democrats was that they had to remain competitive with their Republican foes, and, in effect, that justified the attitude of anything goes in what had become the sordid world of American politics. Perhaps so, but moral scruples seemed discounted in the fundraising saturnalia of Clinton's reelection drive in 1995 and 1996.

As a political strategy, the actions of Clinton and his party worked to perfection. The president's advertising in key states put the Republicans on the defensive, and they never regained the initiative for their presidential candidate, Senator Robert Dole, in the 1996 race. Not until the end of the campaign, when word of the Democratic fund-raising spree leaked out to the press, did the negative political fallout of what Clinton had done become clear. The public revulsion at the more egregious examples of dunning donors, and the links to foreign governments, contributed to the Democratic failure to regain the House of Representatives in 1996.[24]

Republican denunciations of Clinton's actions were loud and long after the 1996 election, but the effectiveness of his tactics did not escape GOP notice. The evidence remains fragmentary on the current public record, but the Bush-Cheney administration has also used the facilities of the presidency and the vice presidency to welcome fund-raisers and to obtain their largesse. By late summer 2002, President George W. Bush had raised over $100 million, almost three times as much as Bill Clinton compiled in a similar period in his presidency. The continuous campaign has reached out to make the physical locations of the modern presidency an integral part of the way politicians spread campaign funds around Washington.

Bill Clinton's most lasting contribution to the conduct of the modern presidency arose from the extensive probes into his personal life, prepresidential career, and behavior in the White House, which continued throughout his tenure. In the process of resolving these issues, some scandalous and some not, permanent changes occurred in the legal and constitutional place of the presidency in the American political system that, if carried out consistently in the future, will impact all future chief executives.

The charges that a former Arkansas state employee, Paula Jones, made against Clinton about an alleged sexual encounter in a Little Rock hotel in

1991 claimed that the then governor had asked her to perform sexual acts for him. Her civil lawsuit, filed in 1994, asserted that her refusal to do so had resulted in reprisals against her in the workplace. The case itself as a civil rights suit was not strong on its merits, because the alleged damages Jones had suffered were minimal and unconnected to Governor Clinton. Nonetheless, the litigation made its way through the federal court system. The president's lawyers sought to have it dismissed or postponed on the grounds that fighting the suit would interfere with Clinton's ability to function as president. The U.S. Supreme Court heard the case and in 1997 ruled unanimously in *Clinton v. Jones* that the suit could proceed while Clinton was in office.[25]

In their ruling, the Supreme Court justices displayed a high degree of ignorance about how the presidency worked on a day-to-day basis and the impact of such a suit on Clinton's presidency. The Court decided that any effects would be minimal and easily handled within the president's regular duties. That might have been true had this been a garden-variety civil case, but beneath the surface was the reality that the *Jones* case was designed to trap Clinton into perjury or other misdeeds on which an impeachment charge could be based. The anti-Clinton forces thus had every incentive to make the process of dealing with the president on Jones's behalf as time-consuming and complex as they could. Though the likelihood of civil suits against the presidency in the future remains small, the capacity for other such filings to hamstring future presidents persists unless the Supreme Court reconsiders its ruling in *Clinton v. Jones* in the future.

Before Bill Clinton became president, the activities of a chief executive before taking office were not usually the subject of a congressional inquiry. Thus, Lyndon Johnson's television empire, Richard Nixon's activities in the Eisenhower administration, Jimmy Carter's peanut business, Ronald Reagan's gubernatorial record, or George H. W. Bush's performance in Congress and during the Ford administration, to name a few, were either not considered or deemed out of bounds for legislative scrutiny. Bill and Hillary Clinton's financial linkage to the ill-fated Whitewater land deal of their onetime friend, James McDougal, seemed in a different category to Republicans. They were eager for political payback after Democratic attacks on Republicans over alleged scandals during the Reagan-Bush years. Clinton's finances could plausibly be tied to the savings and loan scandals of the 1980s and thus made to seem a legitimate subject of congressional inquiry. If that were not enough, implications of a continuing cover-up could also be invoked. The whole package proved too tempting a target to ignore, whatever the long-range negative impact on the presidency might be.[26]

The result was a welter of inquiries into the Clinton record in Arkansas. Despite all the digging, however, a smoking gun of clear impropriety, much less an actual crime by either of the Clintons, remained elusive. The workings of Arkansas politics and the interaction of politicians and local businesses had sordid aspects, but all of these deals never quite added up to any substantive evidence against the Clintons. Critics found enough innuendo and "troubling questions," however, to justify calls, predominantly from Republicans, for a special prosecutor or independent counsel under the statute that the Democrats had relied on so often in the past.[27]

The suicide of the White House counsel Vincent Foster during summer 1993 added the scent of possible foul play to the mix. Some of the more overheated Clinton critics suggested then and later that the president had been behind Foster's death. When the first independent counsel to probe Foster's demise, Robert Fiske, concluded that Foster had indeed killed himself, the uproar over the report led conservative federal judges to name the more partisan Kenneth Starr in Fiske's place. With Starr, there now existed a legal operation to probe all aspects of the Clinton White House whenever a credible Republican allegation arose. The attorney general, Janet Reno, could not usually deny Starr jurisdiction without spurring more charges of a cover-up. To avoid such allegations, Justice had to broaden Starr's charter at periodic intervals. No previous presidency, not even that of Richard Nixon, had faced an ongoing criminal investigation of its activities that monitored its every move in that light.[28]

The logic of such an inquiry meant that every White House document was the subject of a potential subpoena from the independent counsel. Keeping a diary or detailed records could lead a White House aide to potential legal peril and mounting attorney's fees. The ultimate impact was to make all presidential communications of whatever kind subject to legal exposure and ultimate publication. For Clinton, there was in the end no haven of confidentiality except those that arose from his talks with lawyers and were thus covered by attorney-client privilege.[29]

Clinton's use of executive privilege to shield himself from queries about his intimate personal affairs further eroded the utility of the concept as a resource for modern presidents. Kenneth Starr cited the reliance of the Clinton lawyers on the privilege as one element in the impeachment referral to Congress in 1998. As Starr's document put it, "The President repeatedly and unlawfully invoked the Executive Privilege to conceal evidence of his personal misconduct from the grand jury." When presented with the charge, congressional Republicans decided not to include it in the impeachment allegations against Clinton lest the privilege be weakened for other presidents. Still, Clinton's handling of the matter had diminished the effectiveness of the privilege in general. When the administration of George W. Bush took over, it saw one of its tasks in rebuilding presidential power to be in reviving the doctrine of executive privilege. Whether those efforts would operate when a future president came under serious allegations of wrongdoing remains to be seen.[30]

The presence of all these legal proceedings about their prepresidential affairs and the Clinton's performance in office swept up both the president and his wife. The issue of whether documents in the custody of or associated with Vincent Foster and Whitewater had been withheld from prosecutors brought Hillary Rodham Clinton to testify before a federal grand jury in early 1996, an unprecedented step for the wife of a president to have to take. The idea that a First Lady could be indicted, convicted, and jailed always had a certain surreal quality. What would have been the political fallout of such a trial? If convicted, would she have had Secret Service protection in prison, for example? Commentators such as William Safire of the *New York Times* threw around the possibility of an indictment in a cavalier manner, and repeated leaks emerged from Starr's office about Mrs. Clinton's legal fate, none of which proved to be accurate predictions.[31]

Of course, Clinton himself, by his sexual recklessness with Monica Lewinsky, brought on his own impeachment and trial before the Senate in 1998 and 1999. Whether his private acts with a White House intern shed any real light on the civil rights suit of Paula Jones faded in significance before the issue of whether Clinton had lied under oath in his deposition in Jones's case and in his testimony to Starr's lawyers in August 1998. Clinton's dexterity with words tripped him up in the end, as in his statement about the exact definition of the word "is" in the context of his sexual conduct with Lewinsky.[32]

Presidential bandying over the precise meaning of language was great fodder for Clinton's congressional and conservative critics, who advanced the view that anything other than the plainest speaking was evidence of executive evasion. Such a lofty standard apparently applied only to Bill Clinton and his predicament in 1998, not to other politicians of both parties, who knew how decisive linguistic disputes could be in Washington's backrooms. In later years, moreover, the standards of terminological exactitude that had been imposed on President Clinton were waived for his successor, George W. Bush, and his Republican colleagues.

The effort to impeach and then convict Bill Clinton convulsed American politics in 1998 and 1999 as the Republicans sought to oust their hated adversary from office. Their preferred route was to put such pressure on him that he would feel compelled to resign. Yet there was always a certain degree of unreality about the Republican impeachment campaign that suggested its ambivalent purposes. Removing Clinton would put Vice President Albert Gore in office as an incumbent before the 2000 election, and that was not a scenario that commended itself to Republicans. While the Republican control of the House of Representatives, though diminished after the 1998 elections, ensured that articles of impeachment could pass, the real test would come in the Senate, where a two-thirds vote was needed for conviction.[33]

The Senate in 1999 had fifty-five Republicans and forty-five Democrats, which meant that the anti-Clinton forces, assuming that the Republicans remained united, needed at least twelve Senate Democrats to vote for Clinton's conviction. The mathematics of the situation were never in doubt. Yet the Republicans in the House and Senate did not act as though they understood the process on which they had embarked. To build the necessary momentum in the Senate, the Republicans had to create a bipartisan majority in the House and thus make the removal of Clinton not a political struggle but a moral undertaking. That had been the key to Richard Nixon's ouster a generation earlier. Instead, the House Republicans were as relentlessly partisan as they could be and did not give potential Democratic converts to their cause much reason to vote for the impeachment resolutions. Hardball was emotionally satisfying to the House Republicans, but it virtually guaranteed that their campaign could not prevail in the Senate. They never created a climate in which the Democratic senators were under pressure to desert the president, and they never sought to foster such an atmosphere.

In the Senate, it was evident from the outset of the trial that the president was going to be acquitted. Had Robert Byrd of West Virginia, who disliked Clinton personally, come out against him, for example, the senator might have

Here Bill Clinton represents the modern chief executive in the Oval Office at the center of his presidency as an institution. (Photograph by Dirck Halstead, the Dirck Halstead Collection, Center for American History, University of Texas at Austin.)

swayed Democratic votes toward conviction. But neither the impeachment managers from the House nor the Republican leadership in the Senate ever displayed a coherent strategy for assembling the needed Democratic votes for conviction. Impeachment became another spasm of Clinton-bashing that turned in on itself.

The unfortunate effect of this sordid episode was more harmful to the modern presidency itself than to the remainder of Bill Clinton's second term. To be a viable part of the constitutional process, presidential impeachment should not be used lightly, nor, once begun, is it good for such an effort to fail. The prospect of impeachment, like the political equivalent of a nuclear weapon, should deter presidents from their worst impulses. If impeachment is seen merely as a potential annoyance, acted upon out of partisanship, then it loses much of its credibility and deterrent capacity. Either the Republicans in 1998 and 1999 were serious and lacked sufficient acumen to achieve their goals, or they were playing games with the Constitution for temporary political advantage. Either way, they discredited impeachment as part of the constitutional system of checks and balances.

In 2001 and 2002, after the terrorist attacks of 11 September 2001, conservatives assailed Bill Clinton for his alleged failures to deal with the threat that Muslim extremists such as Osama bin Laden posed. Though there were many legitimate criticisms to be made of how Clinton dealt with terrorism during his eight years as president, the critics failed to recognize one important element limiting his performance, for which they bore some responsibility. Lyndon Johnson often remarked that the United States has only one president at a time. That was as true as ever from 1993 to 2001.

Yet when President Clinton proposed measures to deal with domestic terrorism after the Oklahoma City bombings in 1995, and following various acts of international terrorism during the rest of his administration, there was no rallying around the chief executive or broad assertions of national resolve. Similarly, when the Clinton administration launched cruise missile attacks aimed at Osama bin Laden in 1998, these initiatives were widely derided as clumsy efforts to divert attention from the president's legal problems and imminent impeachment. With Clinton, such motives could never be ruled out, but if he was doing the right thing for the wrong reasons, that was better than doing nothing at all about terrorism. For his political enemies, whatever he did was wrong by definition. Conservative critics who scolded him for doing too much in 1998 berated him three years later for having done too little.[34]

The downside of the continuous campaign and the politicizing of the presidency that followed in its wake was that every presidential decision was seen only through a partisan lens. In the domestic context, such a perspective was often illuminating. By the end of the 1990s, however, with terrorism a growing issue, a partisan take on every event worked to forestall needed policies on the world scene as much as it fostered them. Bipartisanism came to represent a synonym for surrender to most politicians, and thus the term lost most of its substantive meaning for presidents.

By 2000 the Clinton model of the modern presidency had fallen into disrepute, at least as far as the two major presidential candidates were concerned. Texas's governor George W. Bush made it a theme of his campaign that he would change the tone in Washington and would end the politics of personal destruction. In the process, dignity and honor would reappear at the White House. Vice President Albert Gore Jr. sought to embrace the substantive benefits of Clinton's legacy while distancing himself from the sordid aspects of his boss's tenure in the White House. On the substantive side, however, both candidates outdid themselves in promises to preserve the nation's fiscal health as Clinton and Congress had restored it in the 1990s. For Bush, times were so good that there was enough money even for a major tax cut. Gore's tax plan for reductions was more modest. Both of them pledged to pay down the debt and preserve Social Security.

For the first time in some years, however, the campaign did not include major promises to pare back the size of the presidency itself, such as trimming the White House staff. Bush's pledges to return dignity to the White House left alone the operating structure of the executive. Nor did Gore promise significant changes in the size of or approach to the presidency. While there was the usual anti-Washington tone to the campaign, there was no attack on the executive power as such. To that extent, the modern presidency had emerged as the abiding fact of governmental life in Washington by 2000. The presidency might gain in power in the years ahead. There no longer seemed to be much viable sentiment for returning the institution to anything like the size and scope that had prevailed during the first half of the century. Indeed, after he was in office, George W. Bush asserted that rehabilitating presidential power was one of the key goals of his administration.

Bill Clinton's ambiguous legacy to the presidency had one more act to play out in the month after the disputed presidential election of 2000 was finally resolved in favor of George W. Bush. Aware as he had not been for the preceding eight years of his historical legacy, Clinton turned to an indisputable area of constitutionally sanctioned presidential authority, the power to pardon. The process occurred with all the deliberate consideration of a state fair gambling tent on a Saturday night. In a hasty manner that undercut many of the achievements of his White House tenure, Clinton handed out pardons to some unsavory characters. The most notable of these miscreants was a fugitive financier, Marc Rich. Indicted on multiple criminal charges, Rich had fled to Switzerland. His former wife, a major Clinton contributor, pleaded for clemency, which the outgoing president granted. When announced, the pardon evoked a wave of national disgust. Criminal investigations ensued, and then protest died away as time passed and the public's attention turned to the war on terrorism during fall 2001. Clinton had, however, cast a cloud over the presidential pardoning power.[35]

What Bill Clinton's legacy to the presidency will be remains to be determined in the years following his departure from office. Whenever his presidential papers become available, opinion is likely to polarize along the ideological divide that shaped so much of his White House record in the first place. Republicans and conservatives appear determined to run against his presidency in the manner that they believe Democrats used Herbert Hoover and the Great Depression during the 1930s and 1940s. Given the generally good economic times during Clinton's two terms, this tactic may prove to be a hard sell to the public, especially in light of the shortness of historical memory in contemporary society. Tying Clinton to the intelligence failures over terrorism is also risky since the record of the other parts of the political system was not noticeably better in that regard before 11 September 2001.

When the stock market plummeted in summer 2002 amid revelations of corporate wrongdoing in such failed companies as Enron, WorldCom, Adelphia, and Global Crossing, Republicans blamed Clinton for a climate of moral permissiveness that encouraged chief executive officers to jettison moral principles. So attuned were these businessmen to Clinton's libido that when he dallied with Monica Lewinsky, corporate moguls in turn felt free to manipulate stocks, falsify income for their companies, and enrich themselves at the stockholders' expense. The conservative indictment of Clinton thus presumed that hard-headed businessmen, many of them large contributors to Republican campaigns, were so impressionable that the mere news of presidential philandering sent them off their ethical rails and into elaborate criminal schemes. This formulation conveniently ignored Republican deregulatory legislation of the 1990s, some of which was passed over Clinton's veto, that probably had more impact on corporate behavior than the president's sex life ever did.

Clinton's impact on the modern presidency will be seen in the light of his successor's ability to win the struggle with terrorism and maintain the nation's economic health. Should George W. Bush achieve both objectives, Clinton will most likely be relegated to the middle rank among twentieth-century chief executives. He will be praised for his economic record and criticized for his moral failings. Should Bush win abroad and leave the economy with renewed government deficits, sluggish growth, and massive entitlements not paid for, Clinton will probably look better in retrospect.

As an instrument to conduct foreign policy among nation-states, to pursue American interests, and to manage a diverse economy and society, the modern presidency had become a sophisticated and complex political institution by the early 1990s. It was a tool that Bill Clinton wielded with as much skill as any of his immediate predecessors. What was less clear was whether the modern presidency, with its celebrity trappings and devotion to continuous campaigning, enabled the occupant of the White House to address serious issues in a responsible manner. The experience of Bill Clinton indicated that the modern presidency was not up to the tasks that American society faced even before the war on terrorism escalated with the attacks of 11 September 2001.

Presidential scholarship always lags behind presidential actions, and the institution has undergone apparent changes since the inauguration of George Walker Bush on 20 January 2001 and the terrorist attacks of 11 September 2001. In fundamental ways, the Bush administration has shown itself adept at some features of the presidency, such as continuous campaigning, media events, and political fundraising. Whether it has yet adapted to the altered political environment that the United States faces in the wake of terrorism is beyond the scope of this book.

Despite his loss of the popular vote in the 2000 election and the disputed circumstances of his ultimate victory, George W. Bush came into office as if he had a decisive mandate. He secured congressional passage of his tax cut program and implemented other phases of his conservative agenda by executive orders in a host of areas. Notwithstanding campaign criticism of Bill Clinton for partisanship, excessive reliance on polls, and fund-raising, Bush practiced these same arts while denying that he was doing so. The new president traveled widely and emphasized public appearances. Whenever possible he spent time at the Western White House in Crawford, Texas. By the end of August 2001, however, his poll numbers suggested a serious softening of his support.

The events of 11 September changed the Bush presidency. After an initial uncertain start for Bush, his well-received speech to Congress on 20 September, his promises of decisive action to defeat terrorism and to capture Osama bin Laden, and the triumph in the war in Afghanistan sent his poll numbers soaring to over 90 percent. After a year of war, Bush's approval ratings remained in the 60 percent range, and his popularity helped carry the Republicans to an election victory in November 2002 when they regained control of the Senate.

The White House, under Karl Rove's skillful management, capitalized on Bush's popularity to maximize his effectiveness as a Republican fund-raiser and to advocate for his war policy and domestic programs. The reliance on presidential travel intensified, and there was no letup in the number of photo opportunities at elementary schools, rallies, and White House events. Public service announcements for stock car races and telephoned greetings to charitable events remained as integral parts of the presidential schedule. One notable detail was the use of poster-sized slogans displayed behind the president at public events. Congressional leaders soon adopted the technique.

The 2004 presidential election loomed with its customary effect on executive behavior. A free-trade president increased quotas on foreign steel, an opponent of campaign-finance reform signed the McCain-Feingold campaign-reform bill, and an executive determined to reform education accepted a watered-down bill on that subject. At the same time, although he is a proponent of smaller government, Bush signed an expensive subsidy bill for farmers. The war on terrorism was a national priority only to the extent that it did not inconvenience any substantial bloc of potential voters.

During late spring 2002, revelations about intelligence failures by the CIA and the FBI roused controversy about the events leading up to 11 September. While debate about whether the FBI and the CIA had properly briefed the president continued, the infighting between the two agencies diverted Washington and sparked congressional probes. The president proposed the creation of a Homeland Security Department that would coordinate the war on terrorism, and the administration advocated a preemptive strike on Iraq as well. The Bush White House and its Justice Department also asserted sweeping legal powers to combat terrorism at home, without checks from courts or Congress.

For George W. Bush these steps were also part of an effort to revive presidential power after three decades of alleged neglect and executive weakness, relative to Congress and the press. The indictment seemed more grounded in political considerations than in historical evidence. The modern presidency has all the authority needed to run the government. What is lacking is the time and the will, both of which are consumed by the demands of continuous campaigning, the desire for reelection, addressing the needs of interest groups, and appeasing the curiosity of the media and the public about matters of presidential personality and trivia.

The modern presidency has evolved into a perennial campaign, combined with the essential features of a television network and a Hollywood studio. It is demanding labor to elect a president and stage symbolic events, interspersed with policy issues and ritual meetings. Yet these latter activities ought not be confused with real governance. In a job where thinking is essential, all the features of the contemporary presidency conspire toward mindless repetition of tried-and-true staged events. Even presidential vacations must have an allotment of campaign-style appearances and presidential announcements, lest the chief executive be seen as inactive and aloof.

None of the twentieth-century presidents started out to have the institution evolve in the way it has. Relying on the mass media to glamorize the office, as Theodore Roosevelt, Franklin Roosevelt, John F. Kennedy, and Ronald Reagan did, made sense as a way of communicating with the people and creating support for programs. But once the practitioners of celebrity politics were in the White House, their influence was impossible to restrain or control.

Similarly, the idea that four years was not long enough to learn the job of president and accomplish real change was always persuasive to men who began in any case with ample egos. Achieving greatness and ranking high among presidents proved hypnotic temptations, once a chief executive sat in the White House. Pursuing a second term thus became a corollary of being elected in the first instance. That most second terms ended badly seemed clear only in retrospect. As the mechanisms of politics became tied to the mass media, especially with the arrival of television, the need to raise money, attend to one's public image, and espouse popular policies swept aside all other considerations.

The world environment of the twentieth century, dangerous and bloody as it was, allowed presidents to operate as leaders of a country within an international order composed of other nation-states who at least operated by a rough set of rules. Terrorism as an instrument of policy existed on the margins of politics and diplomacy. If a president spent time on building his domestic base or seeing to his reelection, there was no disconnect with those purposes and the real business of his office. Now, however, the United States faces, in the words of John F. Kennedy in 1961, "a long twilight struggle" with terrorism that may well extend for decades. The nation can no longer afford what has been business as usual in the management of the Oval Office for the past half century. Presidents will have to reduce the time they spend on distracting trivia in order to husband their energies for the serious priority of protecting the nation.

The traditional practices of the late-twentieth-century presidency are now hallowed by custom and the self-interest of operatives from both political parties. Pollsters, consultants, and pundits grow rich off the presidential status quo, with its predictable rhythms. A popular television show such as *West Wing* glamorizes these activities and legitimizes them for a mass audience. But a better justification is needed than just custom for activities that waste a president's time and cost money for electoral or cosmetic reasons. The American people are not participants in the process. They serve only as unpaid extras or props.

The bubble that surrounds the president, an outgrowth of a reasonable need for security, mocks the notion that presidential travel keeps the chief executive in touch with the people. Getting the feel of public opinion from the backseat of an armored limousine is an improbable feat. Presidents and the nation would be better served by less travel for travel's sake, fewer events produced to build up poll numbers, and more engagement with the nitty-gritty of making Washington function in a dangerous world.

There is only so much that can be done to reshape the modern presidency in its current incarnation. Radical rethinking of what the nation needs from its chief executive is imperative. The president cannot be a movie star, rock idol, or perennial candidate any longer because none of these roles meets the demands of the twenty-first century. In these respects, the modern presidency, dominated by celebrity and campaigning, has outlived its usefulness and has become a liability to the person who holds the post and to the nation that the president of the United States is supposed to serve.

1. THE AGE OF CORTELYOU

1. For the situation of the Cleveland presidency during his second term, see R. Hal Williams, *Years of Decision: American Politics in the 1890s* (Prospect Heights, Ill.: Waveland Press, 1993), 96, and Stephen Ponder, *Managing the Press: Origins of the Media Presidency, 1897–1933* (New York: St. Martin's Press, 1998), 3–4.

2. David S. Barry, "News-Getting at the Capitol," *Chautauquan* 26(1897): 282.

3. C. C. Buel, "Our Fellow-Citizen of the White House: The Official Cares of a President of the United States," *Century Magazine* 53(1897): 653

4. Pete Daniel and Raymond Smock, *A Talent for Detail: The Photographs of Miss Frances Benjamin Johnston, 1889–1910* (New York: Harmony Books, 1974), 71, 73, show the looseness of McKinley's protection before he was shot in 1901. See also Margaret Leech, *In the Days of McKinley* (New York: Harper and Brothers, 1959), 131.

5. John Sherman, *John Sherman's Recollections of Fifty Years in the House, Senate and Cabinet*, 2 vols. (Chicago: Werner, 1895), 1: 375.

6. "Cleveland, the 'Strong Man,'" *Literary Digest* 14(1897): 290.

7. Lewis L. Gould, "The President in the Age of the Politico," in *Every Four Years*, ed. Robert C. Post (New York: Norton, 1980), 123–27; R. Hal Williams, "James Abram Garfield, 1881," in *The American Presidents*, ed. Melvin I. Urofsky, (New York: Garland, 2000), 219–24.

8. Lewis L. Gould, "Benjamin Harrison," in Urofsky, ed., *The American Presidents*, 246–54; Homer Socolofsky and Allan B. Spetter, *The Presidency of Benjamin Harrison* (Lawrence: University Press of Kansas, 1987).

9. H. Wayne Morgan, *William McKinley and His America* (Syracuse, N.Y.: Syracuse University Press, 1963), offers the best one-volume life of McKinley. Morgan is preparing a revised and updated edition for the Kent State University Press.

10. Lewis L. Gould, *The Presidency of William McKinley* (Lawrence: University Press of Kansas, 1980), 3, 7.

11. Ibid., 135–36.

12. *Speeches and Addresses of William McKinley from March 1, 1897, to May 30, 1900* (New York: Doubleday and McClure, 1900), 125.

13. Leech, *In the Days of McKinley*, 348–50.

14. Jules Cambon to Theophile Delcassé, 13 July 1901, United States, vol. 8, Archives of the Ministry of Foreign Affairs, Paris; John A. Kasson to Edward S. Ready, 29 April 1901, Papers of the Reciprocity Commissioner, Records of the Department of State, Record Group 59, National Archives, Washington, D.C.

15. Gould, *Presidency of William McKinley*, 39.

16. Benjamin Temple Ford, "A Duty to Serve: The Governmental Career of George Bruce Cortelyou" (Ph.D. diss., Columbia University, 1963), provides biographi-

cal information but is thin on analysis of Cortelyou's role. James Creelman's "Mr. Cortelyou Explains President McKinley," *Pearson's Magazine* 19(1908): 569–85, is important for understanding their working relationship.

17. "Suavity and Stenography," *Stenographer* 19 (August 1904): 443. This article reprints an essay on Cortelyou by James Creelman that appeared in the *New York World* on 26 June 1904.

18. Otis B. Goodall, "George Bruce Cortelyou," *Phonographic Magazine* 15(1901): 50. Professor Ephraim Smith kindly shared these Cortelyou articles with me.

19. Gould, *Presidency of William McKinley*, 37–38; Ponder, *Managing the Press*, 5–6.

20. Francis E. Leupp, "The President — And Mr. Wilson," *Independent* 76(1913): 394; "Suavity and Stenography," 443.

21. George B. Cortelyou diary, 16 April 1898, George B. Cortelyou Papers, Box 52, Manuscript Division, Library of Congress.

22. Richard T. Loomis, "The White House Telephone and Crisis Management," *United States Naval Institute Proceedings*, 45(1969): 64–65. For an example, see memorandum of phone conversation, 13 August 1900, Cortelyou Papers, Box 64, dealing with events in China during the aftermath of the Boxer Rebellion.

23. DeB. Randolph Keim, "The President's War," *Frank Leslie's Popular Monthly* 50(1900): 120, 121.

24. David S. Barry, "George Bruce Cortelyou," *World's Work* 5(1903): 3340.

25. Robert Bacon and James Brown Scott, eds., *The Military and Colonial Policy of the United States: Addresses and Reports by Elihu Root* (Cambridge: Harvard University Press, 1916), 252.

26. *Pittsburgh Post*, 8 March 1900, clipping in Papers of Bernard Moses, Bancroft Library, University of California, Berkeley. See also Lewis L. Gould, "William McKinley and the Expansion of Presidential Power," *Ohio History* 87(1978): 15.

27. "Developments in China," *Literary Digest* 21(1900): 3; Arthur M. Schlesinger Jr., *The Imperial Presidency* (Boston: Houghton Mifflin, 1973), 88–89.

28. Goodall, "George Bruce Cortelyou," 50.

29. Perry Belmont, "The President's War Power and an Imperial Tariff," *North American Review* 170(1900): 434; David Yancy Thomas, *A History of Military Governments in Newly Acquired Territory of the United States* (New York: Columbia University Press, 1904), 320.

30. James P. Pfiffner, *The Modern Presidency* (New York: St. Martin's Press, 1994), 1.

31. The best study of Roosevelt's rise to national prominence remains William H. Harbaugh, *The Life and Times of Theodore Roosevelt* (New York: Oxford University Press, 1975).

32. Lewis L. Gould, *The Presidency of Theodore Roosevelt* (Lawrence: University Press of Kansas, 1991), 102–3, 104. Edmund Morris, *Theodore Rex* (New York: Random House, 2001), deals with Roosevelt's presidency in some selected aspects but constructs the narrative based on the premise that it reflects only what Roosevelt knew at the time of his tenure in the White House. Stephen Skowronek, *The Politics*

Presidents Make: Leadership from John Adams to George Bush (Cambridge: Belknap Press of Harvard University Press, 1993), 228–59, presents an analysis that differs from the one offered here.

33. William Seale, *The President's House: A History,* 2 vols. (Washington, D.C.: White House Historical Association, 1986), 2: 682–83.

34. William Allen White, *Masks in a Pageant* (New York: Macmillan, 1930), 307.

35. Gould, *Presidency of Theodore Roosevelt,* 138, 142–44.

36. The tacit assumption that Congress did not need to meet and that the new president would not speak to the nation before submitting his annual message to Congress in early December underlined the slower pace of political life in 1901.

37. "Theodore Roosevelt," *American Monthly Review of Reviews* 34(1901): 438

38. White, *Masks in a Pageant,* 308.

39. Barry, "George Bruce Cortelyou," 338.

40. "Suavity and Stenography," 443, and Barry, "George Bruce Cortelyou," 339.

41. Seale, *President's House,* 2: 688–89.

42. Ponder, *Managing the Press,* 24.

43. William Loeb to George B. Cortelyou, 17 October 1905, and Cortelyou memorandum, 18 October 1905, Box 62, Cortelyou Papers.

44. Walter E. Clark to Erastus Brainerd, 26 January 1906, Erastus Brainerd Papers, University of Washington Library, Seattle.

45. Gould, *Presidency of Theodore Roosevelt,* 161–62.

46. Ibid., 294–96.

47. Ibid., 147–71, 199–206.

48. Ibid., 298.

49. Theodore Roosevelt, *Addresses and Presidential Messages of Theodore Roosevelt, 1902–1904* (New York: Putnam, 1904), 121.

50. On Roosevelt's diplomatic style, see Richard H. Collin, *Theodore Roosevelt's Caribbean: The Panama Canal, the Monroe Doctrine, and the Latin American Context* (Baton Rouge: Louisiana State University Press, 1990), 545–62, and Raymond Esthus, *Theodore Roosevelt and the International Rivalries* (Waltham, Mass.: Ginn-Blaisdell, 1970).

51. On Roosevelt and the Hepburn Act, John Morton Blum's *The Republican Roosevelt* (Cambridge: Harvard University Press, 1954), 73–105, remains an indispensable starting point for understanding Roosevelt as a legislative leader.

52. J. Hampton Moore, *Roosevelt and the Old Guard* (Philadelphia: Macrae Smith, 1925), 219.

53. James D. Richardson, comp., *A Compilation of the Messages and Papers of the Presidents,* 10 vols. (Washington, D.C.: Bureau of National Literature, 1911), 10: 7628.

54. The two important books on Brownsville are John D. Weaver's *The Brownsville Raid* (1970; reprint, College Station: Texas A&M University Press, 1992), and idem, *The Senator and the Sharecropper's Son: Exoneration of the Brownsville Soldiers* (College Station: Texas A&M University Press, 1997).

55. Theodore Roosevelt to Charles Hallam Keep, 2 June 1905, in *The Letters of Theodore Roosevelt*, ed. Elting E. Morison et al., 8 vols. (Cambridge: Harvard University Press, 1951–1954), 4: 1201. See also Peri Arnold, *Making the Managerial Presidency: Comprehensive Reorganization Planning, 1905–1996*, 2d ed., rev. (Lawrence: University Press of Kansas, 1998), 23–26. Arnold's book is a valuable, well-researched treatment of its subject that has been of great assistance in tracing the issue of reorganization as it relates to the modern presidency. The standard sources on the Keep Commission are Harold T. Pinkett, "The Keep Commission, 1905–1909: A Rooseveltian Effort for Administrative Reform," *Journal of American History* 52(1965): 297–312, and Oscar Kraines, "The President Versus Congress: The Keep Commission: First Comprehensive Presidential Inquiry into Administration," *Western Political Quarterly* 23(1970): 5–54.

56. Gould, *Presidency of Theodore Roosevelt*, 197–98. For examples of Roosevelt's consultations with Garfield, see entries for 1 November 1907, 9 November 1907, James R. Garfield Diaries, James R. Garfield Papers, Manuscript Division, Library of Congress.

2. THE LAWYER AND THE PROFESSOR

1. Frederick C. Howe to Robert M. La Follette, 14 December 1910, La Follette Family Papers, Manuscript Division, Library of Congress.

2. Robert C. Hilderbrand, *Power and the People: Executive Management of Public Opinion in Foreign Affairs, 1897–1921* (Chapel Hill: University of North Carolina Press, 1981), 73–74.

3. Alexander Walker, *Stardom: The Hollywood Phenomenon* (Middlesex, U.K.: Penguin Books, 1970), 15–23, and Richard Schickel, *Intimate Strangers: The Culture of Celebrity* (Garden City, N.Y.: Doubleday, 1985), 34–40. For the effect of these forces on Theodore Roosevelt's postpresidential career, see Lewis L. Gould, "The Price of Fame: Theodore Roosevelt as a Celebrity, 1909–1919," *Lamar Journal of the Humanities* 10(1984): 5–18.

4. Taft badly needs a modern biography. Henry F. Pringle's *The Life and Times of William Howard Taft*, 2 vols. (New York: Farrar and Rinehart, 1939) is the best treatment of his political rise; the anecdote about the "how is the horse" telegram is in ibid., 1: 235–36. Paolo E. Coletta's *The Presidency of William Howard Taft* (Lawrence: University Press of Kansas, 1973), is now dated, and Donald F. Anderson, *William Howard Taft: A Conservative's Conception of the Presidency* (Ithaca, N.Y.: Cornell University Press, 1973), does not do justice to Taft's political thought. For Roosevelt's comment, see the *New York Times*, 4 April 1905.

5. *Chicago Tribune*, 7 October 1908.

6. William Howard Taft, *Our Chief Magistrate and His Powers* (New York: Columbia University Press, 1916), 144.

7. William Howard Taft to Helen Herron Taft, 3 October 1909, William Howard Taft Papers, Manuscript Division, Library of Congress.

8. George von Lengerke Meyer diary, 4 January 1909, George von Lengerke Meyer Papers, Massachusetts Historical Society, Boston. Meyer had been a member of Roosevelt's cabinet and stayed on as secretary of the navy for Taft. See Lewis L. Gould, *Reform and Regulation: American Politics from Roosevelt to Wilson,* 3d ed. (Prospect Heights, Ill.: Waveland Press, 1996), 155.

9. Oscar King Davis, *Released for Publication* (Boston: Houghton Mifflin, 1925), 99; Mabel Boardman to F. B. Tracy, 18 September 1911, James T. Williams Jr. Papers, Duke University Library, Durham, N.C. (second quotation).

10. Stacy A. Cordery, "Helen Herron Taft," in *American First Ladies: Their Lives and Their Legacy,* ed. Lewis L. Gould, 2d ed. (New York: Garland, 2001), 213–25.

11. For Taft's problems with Carpenter, see Stephen Ponder, *Managing the Press: Origins of the Media Presidency, 1897–1933* (New York: St. Martin's Press, 1998), 51–53, 58–59. The Charles D. Hilles Papers, Sterling Library, Yale University, attest to the efficiency and political skill shown during his tenure in the White House.

12. William Howard Taft to William Allen White, 20 March 1909, in William Allen White, *The Autobiography of William Allen White* (New York: Macmillan, 1946), 451.

13. Taft to Helen Herron Taft, 3 October 1909, Taft Papers; *Presidential Addresses and State Papers of William Howard Taft from March 4, 1909, to March 4, 1910* (New York: Doubleday, Page, 1910), 226.

14. See Archibald Butt, *Taft and Roosevelt: The Intimate Letters of Archie Butt, Military Aide,* ed. Lawrence F. Abbott, 2 vols. (Garden City, N.Y.: Doubleday, Doran, 1930) 2: 439, 457, on Taft's golf playing and his image.

15. On the new president's decision to work with Speaker Cannon, see Taft to Joseph L. Bristow, 5 December 1908, Taft to Horace Taft, 27 July 1909, Taft Papers, and Stanley Solvick, "William Howard Taft and the Payne-Aldrich Tariff," *Mississippi Valley Historical Review* 50(1963): 424–42. See also George Kibbe Turner, "How Taft Views His Own Administration: An Interview with the President," *McClure's Magazine* 35(1910): 211 (quotation).

16. For the legislative situation that Taft and Aldrich confronted in 1909, see Lewis L. Gould, "Western Range Senators and the Payne-Aldrich Tariff," *Pacific Northwest Quarterly* 64(1973): 49–56. The Dolliver quotation is in White, *Autobiography,* 426.

17. The best study of the Ballinger-Pinchot controversy is James L. Penick Jr.'s *Progressive Politics and Conservation: The Ballinger-Pinchot Affair* (Chicago: University of Chicago Press, 1968).

18. For Taft's relations with Congress during the remainder of the 1909–1910 session, see Herbert F. Margulies, *Reconciliation and Revival: James R. Mann and the House Republicans in the Wilson Era* (Westport, Conn.: Greenwood Press, 1996), 19–34.

19. For these events, see Gould, *Reform and Regulation,* 139–147.

20. See *Index to the William Howard Taft Papers,* 5 vols. (Washington, D.C.: Library of Congress, 1972), 1: xi–xii, for the Taft filing system.

21. The best source for Taft's reorganization efforts is Peri Arnold, *Making the Managerial Presidency: Comprehensive Reorganization Planning, 1905–1996*, 2d ed., rev. (Lawrence: University Press of Kansas, 1998), 26–28.

22. Ibid., 35.

23. Ibid., 43–44. "The Administration on Trial: Spending the People's Money," *Metropolitan Magazine* (1912): 771–74.

24. "Copy of a Letter Sent by the President to the Secretary of the Treasury Relating to the Submission of a Budget to Congress," with Franklin MacVeagh, to Taft, 24 October 1912, Series 6, Case File 3868, Reel 441, Taft Papers.

25. Arnold, *Making the Managerial Presidency*, 45–51.

26. Mencken is quoted in David Burner, *The Politics of Provincialism: The Democratic Party in Transition, 1918–1932* (New York: Knopf, 1968), 68, n. 2.

27. Kendrick Clements, *The Presidency of Woodrow Wilson* (Lawrence: University Press of Kansas, 1992), 8.

28. Gould, *Reform and Regulation*, 149–50.

29. For Wilson's campaign speeches, see John Wells Davidson, ed., *A Crossroads of Freedom: The 1912 Campaign Speeches of Woodrow Wilson* (New Haven: Yale University Press, 1956). John Milton Cooper Jr., *The Warrior and the Priest: Woodrow Wilson and Theodore Roosevelt* (Cambridge: Belknap Press of Harvard University Press, 1983), compares the two presidential candidates.

30. On the smallness of Wilson's White House operation, see Clements, *Presidency of Woodrow Wilson*, 34; Ponder, *Managing the Press*, 83–84; and John Morton Blum, *Joe Tumulty and the Wilson Era* (Boston: Little, Brown, 1956).

31. Walter Prescott Webb and Terrell Webb, eds., *Washington Wife: Journal of Ellen Maury Slayden, from 1897–1919* (1962; reprint, New York: Harper and Row, 1963), 202.

32. Robert C. Hilderbrand, *Power and the People*, 94.

33. On Wilson's press conferences, see also W. Dale Nelson, *Who Speaks for the President? The White House Press Secretary from Cleveland to Clinton* (Syracuse, N.Y.: Syracuse University Press, 1998), 29–32. Robert C. Hilderbrand, ed., *The Papers of Woodrow Wilson*, vol. 50, *The Complete Press Conferences, 1913–1919* (Princeton: Princeton University Press, 1985), provides a full record of Wilson's formal interaction with the press corps. See also Elmer E. Cornwell Jr., "The Press Conferences of Woodrow Wilson," *Journalism Quarterly* 39(summer 1962): 292–300.

34. Ponder, *Managing the Press*, 77–90.

35. Michael E. McGerr, *The Decline of Popular Politics: The American North, 1865–1928* (New York: Oxford University Press, 1986), 165.

36. There are numerous accounts of Wilson's working habits; see Clements, *Presidency of Woodrow Wilson*, 13. The issue of Wilson's health has aroused a large controversy among doctors, political scientists, and historians. The best recent guide to the voluminous literature is John Milton Cooper Jr.'s *Breaking the Heart of the World: Woodrow Wilson and the Fight for the League of Nations* (New York: Cambridge University Press, 2001), 122–23, 198–205.

37. Clements, *Presidency of Woodrow Wilson*, 35–44; David Sarasohn, *The Party of Reform: Democrats in the Progressive Era* (Jackson: University Press of Mississippi, 1989), 168–73; Elizabeth Sanders, *Roots of Reform: Farmers, Workers, and the American State, 1877–1917* (Chicago: University of Chicago Press, 1999), 282–97.

38. A. Maurice Low, "The South in the Saddle," *Harper's Weekly* 57(8 February 1913): 20; Joel Williamson, *The Crucible of Race: Black-White Relations in the American South Since Emancipation* (New York: Oxford University Press, 1984), 365–371.

39. Sarasohn, *Party of Reform*, 169, 172–73; Gould, *Reform and Regulation*, 176.

40. Lewis L. Gould, *Progressives and Prohibitionists: Texas Democrats in the Wilson Era* (Austin: University of Texas Press, 1973), 160–65. On the significance of this successful episode for Wilson's later decision to make a speaking tour on behalf of the League of Nations in 1919, see Cooper, *Breaking the Heart of the World*, 156–57.

41. John Milton Cooper Jr., *Pivotal Decades: The United States, 1900–1920* (New York: Norton, 1990), 242–43.

42. Wilson's campaign speeches can be followed in *The Papers of Woodrow Wilson*, vol. 38, 1916, ed. Arthur S. Link et al., 69 vols. (Princeton: Princeton University Press, 1982), 306 (quotation). Relatively little attention has been given to the end of this tradition against incumbents campaigning on their own behalf. The advantages of being in office as a candidate for reelection were thus much enhanced by this change in unwritten practice.

43. On the success of the Democratic campaign in 1916, see also McGerr, *Decline of Popular Politics*, 162–67.

44. S. E. High to Claude Kitchin, 21 September 1916, Claude Kitchin Papers, Southern Historical Collection, University of North Carolina, Chapel Hill.

45. On Wilson's wartime performance, see Robert H. Ferrell, *Woodrow Wilson and World War I, 1917–1921* (New York: Harper and Row, 1985), 13–47, and Clements, *Presidency of Woodrow Wilson*, 143–62. Kendrick A. Clements, in "Woodrow Wilson and Administrative Reform," *Presidential Studies Quarterly* 28(1998): 320–36, makes clear Wilson's lack of interest in efforts to reform the operation of the presidency itself.

46. For Republican comments about Wilson's aloof attitude toward their party, see James F. Vivian, ed., *William Howard Taft: Collected Editorials, 1917–1921* (New York: Praeger, 1990), 23, and James T. Williams to Sumner Williams, 1 May 1918, James T. Williams Papers, Duke University Library, Durham, N.C. Williams was a Republican reporter who commented about the treatment of Leonard Wood.

47. Woodrow Wilson to Garrett Droppers, 12 December 1916, in Link et al., eds., *Papers of Woodrow Wilson*, Vol. 40, 1916–1917, 219.

48. On Wilson's political situation in Congress after 1916, see Margulies, *Reconciliation and Revival*, 165–66, and Seward Livermore, *Politics Is Adjourned: Woodrow Wilson and the War Congress, 1916–1918* (Middletown, Conn.: Wesleyan University Press, 1966), 10–14.

49. Burner, *Politics of Provincialism*, 32–34; Gould, *Reform and Regulation*, 204–5.

50. Bayard Henry to James Bryce, 1 August 1918, Papers of Lord Bryce, American Correspondence, Bodleian Library, Oxford; Livermore, *Politics Is Adjourned*, 169–72; Margulies, *Reconciliation and Revival*, 187.

51. On the Committee on Public Information, see Hilderbrand, *Power and the People*, 142–64, and Stephen Vaughn, *Holding Fast the Inner Lines: Democracy, Nationalism and the Committee on Public Information* (Chapel Hill: University of North Carolina Press, 1980).

52. Clements, *Presidency of Woodrow Wilson*, 153–55.

53. Charles D. Hilles to Taft, 28 October 1918, and Luther Bowen to Taft, 30 October 1918, Taft Papers, provide a sense of the Republican reaction to Wilson's appeal. See also Livermore, *Politics Is Adjourned*, 224–27.

54. On Wilson's problems with domestic issues after 1918, see Clements, *Presidency of Woodrow Wilson*, 205–20.

55. Cooper, *Breaking the Heart of the World*, 34–37, persuasively analyzes Wilson's decision not to take a major Republican figure with him to Paris. There is little evidence, however, that the president and his few close advisers ever devised an explicit strategy for getting the needed two-thirds vote. That is, they did not pursue a course that tabulated the number of senators on whom the administration could count and the number of Republicans needed to reach a winning majority.

56. For Wilson's handling of the League issues with the press in Paris, see Hilderbrand, *Power and the People*, 182–84.

57. Cooper, *Breaking the Heart of the World*, 140–57, offers a more favorable evaluation of the decision to make a speaking tour and the impact of the trip. For less positive appraisals of the trip's effect on senators, see Ralph Stone, *The Irreconcilables: The Fight Against the League of Nations* (Lexington: University Press of Kentucky, 1970), 128–31, and Herbert F. Margulies, *The Mild Reservationists and the League of Nations Controversy in the Senate* (Columbia: University of Missouri Press, 1989), 94–97.

58. Burner, *Politics of Provincialism*, 59.

59. The latest analysis of Edith Wilson's role in 1919 and 1920 is in Phyllis Lee Levin, *Edith and Woodrow: The Wilson White House* (New York: Scribner's, 2001).

60. See two memoranda by Cary Travers Grayson, 25 March 1920, in Link et al., eds., *Papers of Woodrow Wilson*, vol. 65, 1920, 123–24, and Burner, *Politics of Provincialism*, 68.

61. Kirk H. Porter and Donald Bruce Johnson, *National Party Platforms, 1840–1968* (Urbana: University of Illinois Press, 1966), 230, 233; Republican National Committee, *Republican Campaign Text-Book, 1920* (New York: Republican Congressional Committee, 1920), 19; White, *Autobiography*, 597.

62. Arthur Willert, *Washington and Other Memories* (Boston: Houghton Mifflin, 1972), 16; "The Wilson Administration," *Outlook* 127(1921): 367.

3. THE MODERN PRESIDENCY RECEDES

1. "Mr. Harding for Simplicity," *Nation* 112(19 January 1921): 72.

2. See David Jacobs and John Milton Cooper, "Warren Gamaliel Harding: A Babbitt in the White House," in *American Heritage Illustrated History of the Presidents,* ed. Michael Beschloss, (New York: Crown, 2000), 353. The standard studies of the Harding presidency are Robert K. Murray, *The Harding Era: Warren G. Harding and His Times* (Minneapolis: University of Minnesota Press, 1969), and Eugene P. Trani and David L. Wilson, *The Presidency of Warren G. Harding* (Lawrence: University Press of Kansas, 1977). Phillip Payne is at work on a new biography of Harding, *Our Worst President? The Harding Scandals and the Making of History.*

3. Carl Sferrazza Anthony, *Florence Harding: The First Lady, the Jazz Age, and the Death of America's Most Scandalous President* (New York: Morrow, 1998), 263.

4. "Tremendous Problems That Face Harding," *Literary Digest* 65(5 March 1921): 7, and Robert H. Ferrell, "The Nation's Worst President? Warren G. Harding and Woodrow Wilson Compared," *Indiana Magazine of History* 94(1998): 344–48.

5. Stephen Ponder, *Managing the Press: Origins of the Media Presidency, 1897–1933* (New York: St. Martin's Press, 1998), 112.

6. On presidential–press relations during Harding's presidency, see Lindsay Rogers, "The White House 'Spokesman,'" *Virginia Quarterly Review* 2(July 1926): 356–57; Oswald Garrison Villard, "The Press and the President: Should the President Be Quoted Directly or Indirectly?" *Century* 111(December 1925): 199–200; and "How the White House Became a Glass House," *Literary Digest* 88(20 February 1926): 38, 40, 45.

7. Anthony, *Florence Harding,* 271, 278–79; Ponder, *Managing the Press,* 113–14.

8. "Judson Welliver, Newspaperman, 72," *New York Times,* 15 April 1943, summarizes Welliver's life. See also Harry Slattery to Warren G. Harding, 9 January 1922, Warren G. Harding Papers, Roll 136, File 6, Folder 38, Ohio Historical Society, Columbus. For a sample of his writing, see Judson Welliver, "Dolliver: The Leader of Insurgency," *Munsey's Magazine* 46(September 1912): 874–77. For Welliver's salary in the White House, see Rudolph Forster to W. M. Stewart, 30 June 1925, with accompanying table, Calvin Coolidge Papers, Case File 3B, Reel 7, Manuscript Division, Library of Congress.

9. Robert K. Murray, *The Harding Era: Warren G. Harding and His Times* (Minneapolis: University of Minnesota Press, 1969), 122–23.

10. William Allen White, *The Autobiography of William Allen White* (New York: Macmillan, 1946), 619.

11. Kirk H. Porter and Donald Bruce Johnson, *National Party Platforms, 1840–1968* (Urbana: University of Illinois Press, 1972), 223; Peri Arnold, *Making the Managerial Presidency: Comprehensive Reorganization Planning, 1905–1996,* 2d ed., rev. (Lawrence: University Press of Kansas, 1996), 52–53.

12. Arnold, *Making the Managerial Presidency,* 54(quotation).

13. Donald Wilhelm, "Executive Reforms at Washington: How President Harding's Plans for Reorganizing the Administration of National Government Will Operate," *World's Work* 43(November 1921): 631, and Edward Goedeken, "Charles G. Dawes Establishes the Bureau of the Budget," *Historian,* 50(November 1987): 40–53.

14. Arnold, *Making the Managerial Presidency,* 63.

15. Ibid., 66–69. For the impact of these plans on one member of Harding's cabinet, see David H. Stratton, *Tempest over Teapot Dome: The Story of Albert B. Fall* (Norman: University of Oklahoma Press, 1998), 211–18.

16. Arnold, *Making the Managerial Presidency,* 71–74.

17. For Coolidge's rise to national prominence, see Donald R. McCoy, *Calvin Coolidge: The Quiet President* (New York: Macmillan, 1967), 1–101, and Robert Sobel, *Coolidge: An American Enigma* (Washington, D.C.: Regnery, 1998), 1–158 (the famous quotation appears on 144). Coolidge's use of ghostwriters is discussed in Robert Lincoln O'Brien to Solomon B. Griffin, 7 August 1923, Robert Lincoln O'Brien Papers, Lewis L. Gould Collection of American Political History, Center for American History, University of Texas, Austin. O'Brien had worked for Grover Cleveland and was a prominent newspaperman in Massachusetts.

18. See McCoy, *Calvin Coolidge,* 92. Robert H. Ferrell, *The Presidency of Calvin Coolidge* (Lawrence: University Press of Kansas, 1998), 19–24, has relatively little to say about Coolidge's press relations. For Welliver's work in the Coolidge White House, see Welliver to Everett Sanders, 8 September 1925, Coolidge Papers, Case File 36, Reel 39.

19. Ponder, *Managing the Press,* 119–20.

20. Ibid., 120–21; Charles Merz, "The Silent Mr. Coolidge," *New Republic* (2 June 1926): 51–54.

21. See Howard H. Quint and Robert Ferrell, eds., *The Talkative President: The Off-the-Record Press Conferences of Calvin Coolidge* (Amherst: University of Massachusetts Press, 1964), for Coolidge's style with the press corps. Essary is quoted in John L. Blair, "Coolidge, the Image-Maker: The President and the Press, 1923–1929," *New England Quarterly* 46(December 1973): 502.

22. Blair, "Coolidge, the Image-Maker," 502.

23. George Durno to Calvin Coolidge, 7 November 1923, and Calvin Coolidge to George E. Durno, 12 November 1925, Case File 36, Reel 39 (White House Press Association); Everett Sanders to George R. Holmes, 18 November 1926, Case File 144B (release dates); R. Z. Henle to Coolidge, 27 December 1927, Case File 36, Reel 39 (press conference questions), all in Coolidge Papers.

24. Blair, "Coolidge, the Image Makers," 504 (quotation), and 505 (inclusion in social events).

25. Ponder, *Managing the Press,* 123, discusses Coolidge's radio broadcasts. The Republican National Convention was broadcast in 1924 as was the gathering of the Democrats. See Louise M. Benjamin, "Broadcast Campaign Precedents from the 1924 Presidential Election," *Journal of Broadcasting and Electronic Media* 31(1987): 453–54.

26. Daniel J. Leab, "Coolidge, Hays and 1920s Movies: Some Aspects of Image and Reality," in *Calvin Coolidge and the Coolidge Era,* ed. John Earl Haynes (Washington, D.C.: Library of Congress, 1998), 101.

27. Ibid., 103. See also Ishbel Ross, *Grace Coolidge and Her Era: The Story of a President's Wife* (New York: Dodd, Mead, 1962), 164–65.

28. Leab, "Coolidge, Hays and 1920s Movies," 103, 120.

29. Ross, *Grace Coolidge and Her Era,* 162–63, 194 (quotation).

30. McCoy, *Quiet President,* 390.

31. The literature on Herbert Hoover is vast and grows yearly. A good recent treatment of his relations with Coolidge in the 1920s that offers an intelligent analysis of Hoover's style is George H. Nash's "The 'Great Enigma' and the 'Great Engineer': The Political Relationship of Calvin Coolidge and Herbert Hoover," in Haynes, ed., *Calvin Coolidge and the Coolidge Era,* 149–82. The two most influential biographies of Hoover are Joan Hoff Wilson, *Herbert Hoover: Forgotten Progressive* (Boston: Little, Brown, 1975), and David Burner, *Herbert Hoover: A Public Life* (New York: Knopf, 1979). Mark M. Dodge, ed., *Herbert Hoover and the Historians* (West Branch, Iowa: Herbert Hoover Presidential Library, 1989), provides a good collection of essays that reflects what historians have said about Hoover's rise and presidency. Stephen Skowronek, *The Politics Presidents Make: Leadership from John Adams to George Bush* (Cambridge: Belknap Press of Harvard University Press, 1993), 260–85, offers a sympathetic treatment of Hoover's predicament in the White House.

32. See Saul Braun and Lewis L. Gould, "Herbert Clark Hoover: The Great Engineer," in Beschloss, ed., *American Heritage Illustrated History of the Presidents,* 370, and Kent Schofield, "The Public Image of Hoover in the 1928 Campaign," *Mid-America* 51(1969): 278–93. The best treatment of Hoover during the 1928 campaign is in Allan Lichtman, *Prejudice and the Old Politics: The Presidential Election of 1928* (Chapel Hill: University of North Carolina Press, 1979).

33. Charles Walcott and Karen M. Hult, "Management Science and the Great Engineer: Governing the White House During the Hoover Administration," *Presidential Studies Quarterly* 20(summer 1990): 558.

34. Louis W. Liebovich, *Bylines in Despair: Herbert Hoover, the Great Depression, and the U.S. News Media* (Westport, Conn.: Praeger, 1994), 107–20, discusses the problems the president had with his staff about handling the press. Walcott and Hult, "Management Science and the Great Engineer," 558–63, also consider the workings of the Hoover staff.

35. Paul Y. Anderson, "Hoover and the Press," *Nation* 133(14 October 1931): 382.

36. Lewis L. Gould, "A Neglected First Lady: A Reappraisal," in *Lou Henry Hoover: Essays on a Busy Life,* ed. Dale C. Mayer (Worland, Wyo.: High Plains, 1994), 64–67; Liebovich, *Bylines in Despair,* 135.

37. See Liebovich, *Bylines in Despair,* 140–41, on the changes in newspapers. Ponder, *Managing the Press,* 143–48, makes the same point.

38. Harold Brayman, "Hooverizing the Press," *Outlook and Independent* (24 September 1930): 123, discusses Hoover's positive start with the press and how things went wrong. See also Ponder, *Managing the Press,* 149.

39. Bess Furman, *Washington By-Line: The Personal History of a Newspaperwoman* (New York: Knopf, 1949), 57–61.

40. Anderson, "Hoover and the Press," 382.

41. "Six Months of Hoover's Presidential Engineering," *Literary Digest* (21 September 1929): 14.

42. See Martin Fausold, *The Presidency of Herbert C. Hoover* (Lawrence: University Press of Kansas, 1985), 156; Martin Carcasson, "Herbert Hoover and the Presidential Campaign of 1932: The Failure of Apologia," *Presidential Studies Quarterly* 28(1998): 349–65; also useful is William Allen White, "Herbert Hoover — The Last of the Old Presidents or the First of the New?" *Saturday Evening Post,* 4 March 1933, 6–7, 53.

4. THE MODERN PRESIDENCY REVIVES AND GROWS

1. J. William Youngs, *Eleanor Roosevelt: A Personal and Public Life* (Boston: Little, Brown, 1985), 153.

2. The interaction between Roosevelt and Hoover can be traced in George McJimsey, *The Presidency of Franklin Delano Roosevelt* (Lawrence: University Press of Kansas, 2000), 26–217, 30–31. When I spoke with the veteran Washington newsman Gould Lincoln about this episode in the early 1960s, he was adamant in his belief that Roosevelt had been at fault in not working more closely with Hoover, a sign of the passions that the controversy still aroused.

3. William Allen White, *The Autobiography of William Allen White* (New York: Macmillan, 1946), 635.

4. See Fred I. Greenstein, *The Presidential Difference: Leadership Style from FDR to Clinton* (New York: Free Press, 2000), 12, and James P. Pfiffner, *The Modern Presidency* (New York: St. Martin's Press, 1994), 1. William E. Leuchtenburg, "Franklin D. Roosevelt: The First Modern President," in *The FDR Years: On Roosevelt and His Legacy* (New York: Columbia University Press, 1995), 1–34, makes the historical case but does not really address the ways in which Roosevelt's predecessors laid the foundation for what occurred under the New Deal. Mark J. Rozell and William D. Pederson, *FDR and the Modern Presidency: Leadership and Legacy* (Westport, Conn.: Praeger, 1997), offer a variety of perspectives on Roosevelt's role in the White House. David K. Nichols, *The Myth of the Modern Presidency* (University Park: Pennsylvania State University Press, 1994), 3–10, questions whether Roosevelt was especially influential in reshaping the presidency and finds that many earlier chief executives "exhibited many of the attributes of the modern activist Presidency" (3). Stephen Skowronek, *The Politics Presidents Make: Leadership from John Adams to George Bush* (Cambridge: Belknap Press of Harvard University Press, 1993), 313–19, locates Roosevelt's impact on the modern presidency in his second term.

5. See Joseph Alsop, *FDR: 1882–1945, A Centenary Remembrance* (New York: Washington Square Press, 1982), 92–93, and Charles E. Walcott and Karen M. Hult, *Governing the White House from Hoover Through LBJ* (Lawrence: University Press of Kansas, 1995), 32–33, 62–63, 77, 97–99.

6. Numerous accounts attest to Roosevelt's lack of a systematic philosophy of politics; see Frank Freidel, *Franklin D. Roosevelt: A Rendezvous with Destiny* (Boston: Little, Brown, 1990), and McJimsey, *Presidency of Franklin Delano Roosevelt*, 12, 17, 20–26.

7. Geoffrey C. Ward, "Roosevelt, Theodore," in *Franklin D. Roosevelt: His Life and Times, An Encyclopedic View*, ed. Otis L. Graham Jr. and Meghan Robinson Wander (Boston: Hall, 1985), 375.

8. A good modern treatment of Roosevelt's service in the Wilson administration would be helpful. Frank Freidel's *Franklin D. Roosevelt: The Apprenticeship* (Boston: Little, Brown, 1952) remains the best synthesis of Roosevelt's initial experience in a presidential setting. John Milton Cooper Jr., *Breaking the Heart of the World: Woodrow Wilson and Fight for the League of Nations* (New York: Cambridge University Press, 2001), 405–9 discusses Roosevelt's attitude toward his Wilsonian legacy in foreign policy. Frank Freidel, *Franklin D. Roosevelt: The Ordeal* (Boston: Houghton Mifflin, 1954), deals with Roosevelt's role in the 1920 election campaign and his attitudes toward Wilson during the 1920s.

9. Geoffrey C. Ward, *A First-Class Temperament: The Emergence of Franklin Roosevelt* (New York: Harper and Row, 1989), and Frank Freidel, *Franklin D. Roosevelt: The Triumph* (Boston: Houghton Mifflin, 1956), examine Roosevelt's emergence as a presidential hopeful.

10. See William E. Leuchtenburg, *Franklin D. Roosevelt and the New Deal, 1932–1940* (New York: Harper and Row, 1963), 169–70. See also Richard Thayer Goldberg, *The Making of Franklin D. Roosevelt: Triumph over Disability* (Cambridge, Mass.: Abt Books, 1981).

11. William Seale, *The President's House: A History*, 2 vols. (Washington, D.C.: White House Historical Society, 1986), 2: 901.

12. Ibid., 2: 925(quotation), and 927 (air-conditioning).

13. Allida M. Black, "Anna Eleanor Roosevelt," in *American First Ladies: Their Lives and Their Legacy*, ed. Lewis L. Gould, 2d ed. (New York: Routledge, 2001), 292–299; Blanche Wiesen Cook, *Eleanor Roosevelt*, vol. 2, *1933–1938* (New York: Viking, 1999), 30–99.

14. McJimsey, *Presidency of Franklin Delano Roosevelt*, 31; Leuchtenburg, *Franklin D. Roosevelt and the New Deal*, 41–42.

15. See John Gunther, *Roosevelt in Retrospect* (New York: Harper, 1950), 22–23; W. Dale Nelson, *Who Speaks for the President? The White House Press Secretary from Cleveland to Clinton* (Syracuse, N.Y.: Syracuse University Press, 1998), 70–74; Raymond Clapper, "Why Reporters Like Roosevelt," *Review of Reviews and World's Work* (June 1934): 14–17; and John H. Crider, "The President's Press Con-

ference," *American Mercury* 59(October 1944): 481–87. For a reminiscence of a Roosevelt press conference, see Clifton Daniel, Oral History Interview, 3 May and 4 May 1972, Harry S. Truman Library, Independence, Mo., 23–24.

16. *Fortune,* quoted in Gary Giddins, *Bing Crosby: A Pocketful of Dreams, The Early Years, 1903–1940* (Boston: Little, Brown, 2001), 652 n. 5.

17. Lois Scharf, "Rutherfurd, Lucy Page Mercer," in Graham and Wander, eds., *Franklin D. Roosevelt,* 380–81; Cook, *Eleanor Roosevelt,* 2: 28, 46–48.

18. See McJimsey, *Presidency of Franklin D. Roosevelt,* 134–35; R. M. Eisinger and J. Brown, "Polling as a Means Toward Presidential Autonomy: Emil Hurja, Hadley Cantril and the Roosevelt Administration," *International Journal of Public Opinion Research* 10(1998): 237–56; and Melvin G. Holli, *The Wizard of Washington: Emil Hurja, Franklin Roosevelt and the Birth of Public Opinion Polling* (New York: Palgrave, 2002). Steven Casey, *Cautious Crusade: Franklin D. Roosevelt, American Public Opinion, and the War Against Nazi Germany* (New York: Oxford University Press, 2001), examines how polls and other measures of public opinion affected Roosevelt's policy toward his major wartime adversary.

19. See Walcott and Hult, *Governing the White House,* 77–78, 238–39, and Harold C. Relyea, "The White House Office," in *The Executive Office of the President: A Historical, Biographical, and Bibliographical Guide,* ed. Harold C. Relyea (Westport, Conn.: Greenwood Press, 1997), 46–50.

20. Matthew J. Dickinson, *Bitter Harvest: FDR, Presidential Power and the Growth of the Presidential Branch* (New York: Cambridge University Press, 1996), 64–69.

21. Ibid., 81.

22. Leuchtenberg, *Franklin D. Roosevelt and the New Deal,* 328–29, discusses the president's administrative style, as does Freidel, *Franklin D. Roosevelt,* 120–21, 124–25.

23. There is not a good synthesis of Roosevelt's relations with Congress throughout his presidency. For a brief overview, see Walcott and Hult's *Governing the White House,* 32–35, which makes clear how many people could be involved with the process at any one time. Freidel, *Franklin D. Roosevelt,* 97–99, discusses the president's interaction with Capitol Hill at the outset of the administration.

24. Leuchtenburg, *Franklin D. Roosevelt and the New Deal,* 148–49, examines White House aides who dealt with Congress, such as Benjamin Cohen and Thomas G. "Tommy the Cork" Corcoran. See also McJimsey, *Presidency of Franklin Delano Roosevelt,* 146–47.

25. The literature on the Court fight is voluminous, but most sources concur that Roosevelt's relations with Congress were never again as harmonious as they had once been. See McJimsey, *Presidency of Franklin Delano Roosevelt,* 172–74.

26. Roosevelt's performance as a party leader has been much written about, but more could be done. See McJimsey, *Presidency of Franklin Delano Roosevelt,* 181–82. Sean J. Savage, *Roosevelt: The Party Leader, 1932–1945* (Lexington: University of Kentucky Press, 1991), provides a good start.

27. Harvard Sitkoff, *A New Deal for Blacks: The Emergence of Civil Rights as a National Issue* (New York: Oxford University Press, 1978) offers an overall look at Roosevelt's record. McJimsey, *Presidency of Franklin Delano Roosevelt*, 162–64, gives more credit to Eleanor Roosevelt than to the president for progress on civil rights. Kenneth O'Reilly, *Nixon's Piano: Presidents and Racial Politics from Washington to Clinton* (New York: Free Press, 1995), 109–44, is critical of Roosevelt.

28. Peri Arnold, *Making the Managerial Presidency: Comprehensive Reorganization Planning, 1905–1996,* 2d ed., rev. (Lawrence: University Press of Kansas, 1998), 89–90. See also Dickinson, *Bitter Harvest,* 71–85; Walcott and Hult, *Governing the White House,* 238–40; and Peri Arnold, "Executive Reorganization and the Executive Office of the President," in Relyea, ed., *Executive Office of the President,* 412–13. The standard historical account of this process is Richard Polenberg's *Reorganizing Roosevelt's Government* (Cambridge: Harvard University Press, 1966).

29. Dickinson, *Bitter Harvest,* 110–13, 111 (quotation).

30. Arnold, *Making the Managerial Presidency,* 107–15.

31. Relyea, "The Executive Office Concept," in Relyea, ed., *Executive Office of the President,* 23–25, and Arnold, *Making the Managerial Presidency,* 114–15.

32. Melvin Urofsky, "Corcoran, Thomas Gardiner," in *The Scribner Encyclopedia of American Lives,* vol. 1, *1981–1985,* ed. Kenneth T. Jackson et al. (New York: Charles Scribner's Sons, 1998), 182–84; and Ellis Hawley, "Cohen, Benjamin Victor," in ibid., 167–69.

33. Douglas M. Charles, "Informing FDR: FBI Political Surveillance and the Isolationist Internationalist Foreign Policy Debate, 1939–1945," *Diplomatic History* 24(spring 2000): 211–32; Joseph E. Persico, *Roosevelt's Secret War: FDR and World War II Espionage* (New York: Random House, 2001), 34–40.

34. William Doyle, *Inside the Oval Office: The White House Tapes from FDR to Clinton* (New York: Kodansha International, 1999), 6–44.

35. McJimsey, *Presidency of Franklin D. Roosevelt,* 219, summarizes Roosevelt's record on Japanese relocation. Greg Robinson, *By Order of the President: FDR and the Internment of Japanese Americans* (Cambridge: Harvard University Press, 2001), provides a recent, critical appraisal of the president's role.

36. For the comparison of Roosevelt's actions in this case and terrorism in 2001–2002, see Dana Milbank, "In War, It's Power to the President," *Washington Post,* 20 November 2001; William Safire, "Kangaroo Courts," *New York Times,* 26 November 2001; and Safire, "'Voices of Negativism,'" *New York Times,* 6 December 2001. For the World War II episode itself, see Persico, *Roosevelt's Secret War,* 198–205.

37. McJimsey, *Presidency of Franklin Delano Roosevelt,* 215–21. For Roosevelt and world affairs, the best source is Robert Dallek, *Franklin D. Roosevelt and American Foreign Policy, 1932–1945* (New York: Oxford University Press, 1979). Also informative is Warren F. Kimball, *Forged in War: Roosevelt, Churchill and the Second World War* (New York: William Morrow, 1997).

38. William E. Leuchtenberg, *In the Shadow of FDR: From Harry Truman to George W. Bush* (Ithaca, N.Y.: Cornell University Press, 2001), examines how various presidents used and misused Roosevelt's legacy. For Lyndon Johnson's invocation of World War II precedents in the Vietnam era, see Michael Beschloss, ed., *Reaching for Glory: Lyndon Johnson's Secret White House Tapes, 1964–1965* (New York: Simon and Schuster, 2001), 187. In his 2002 State of the Union message, President George W. Bush employed the phrase "axis of evil" to characterize Iran, Iraq, and North Korea in an effort to rouse support for military actions against these countries for their support of terrorism.

39. Seale, *President's House*, 2: 995–96; "Shangri-La," in Graham and Wander, eds., *Franklin D. Roosevelt*, 385.

40. "Third Term," in Graham and Wander, eds., *Franklin D. Roosevelt*, 423–24; McJimsey, *Presidency of Franklin Delano Roosevelt*, 285–86.

41. Thomas T. Spencer, "Franklin D. Roosevelt Library and Museum," in Graham and Wander, eds., *Franklin D. Roosevelt*, 151–52; Fritz Veit, *Presidential Libraries and Collections* (Westport, Conn.: Greenwood Press, 1987), 57–65; and Paula Span, "Monumental Ambition," *Washington Post Magazine*, 17 February 2002, 24–30 (for a modern look at the presidential library system, see 37–39).

5. THE PRESIDENCY IN THE COLD WAR ERA

1. Alonzo L. Hamby, *Man of the People: A Life of Harry S. Truman* (New York: Oxford University Press, 1995), offers a comprehensive and favorable account of Truman's background and career. More recent critical assessments are Michael J. Hogan's *A Cross of Iron: Harry S. Truman and the Origins of the National Security State, 1945–1954* (New York: Cambridge University Press, 1998) and Arnold A. Offner's *Another Such Victory: President Truman and the Cold War, 1945–1953* (Stanford: Stanford University Press, 2002).

2. Hamby, *Man of the People*, 539, 549, 639.

3. William Doyle, *Inside the Oval Office: The White House Tapes from FDR to Clinton* (New York: Kodanska International, 1999), 45–67.

4. The literature on Truman and the decision to drop the atomic bomb is too vast to discuss here. Hamby, *Man of the People*, 331–37, makes a strong case for the president's decision. McGeorge Bundy, *Danger and Survival: Choices About the Bomb in the First Fifty Years* (New York: Random House, 1988), looks at the policy decisions that presidents faced about nuclear weapons. The impact on individual presidents of their proximity to the ultimate weapons that could destroy humanity has not been much examined.

5. Francis H. Heller, ed., *The Truman White House: The Administration of the Presidency, 1945–1953* (Lawrence: University Press of Kansas, 1980), 19–21.

6. Peri Arnold, *Making the Managerial Presidency: Comprehensive Reorganization Planning, 1905–1996*, 2d ed. rev. (Lawrence: University Press of Kansas, 1998), 118–59.

7. Heller, ed., *Truman White House,* discusses the positive aspects of Truman's executive style. Andrew J. Dunar, *The Truman Scandals and the Politics of Morality* (Columbia: University of Missouri Press, 1984), looks at the downside of the president's performance.

8. Hamby, *Man of the People,* 467, 471–72.

9. For the physical changes in the White House during the Truman years, see William Seale, *The President's House,* 2 vols. (Washington, D.C.: White House Historical Association, 1986), 2: 1025–51.

10. Jack Gould, "Political Leaders Acclaim TV but Warn Against Its Misuse," *New York Times,* 25 June 1951.

11. W. Dale Nelson, *Who Speaks for the President? The White House Press Secretary from Cleveland to Clinton* (Syracuse, N.Y.: Syracuse University Press, 1998), 97–108; Donald R. McCoy, *The Presidency of Harry S. Truman* (Lawrence: University Press of Kansas, 1984), 189–90; Franklin D. Mitchell, *Harry S. Truman and the News Media: Contentious Relations, Belated Respect* (Columbia: University of Missouri Press, 1998).

12. Mitchell, *Truman and the News Media,* 31–55, discusses the opposition of the news media to Truman during the 1948 election.

13. Ibid., 81–100; Nelson, *Who Speaks for the President?,* 101–2.

14. Mitchell, *Truman and the News Media,* 98–99.

15. Susan Hartmann, *Truman and the Eightieth Congress* (Columbia: University of Missouri Press, 1971); McCoy, *Presidency of Harry S. Truman,* 91–101, 164–74.

16. See Hamby, *Man of the People,* 364–66, 433–35, and McCoy, *Presidency of Harry S. Truman,* 167–71. Michael R. Gardner, *Harry Truman and Civil Rights: Moral Courage and Political Risks* (Carbondale: Southern Illinois University Press, 2002), provides a new and favorable study of Truman's performance in this area.

17. McCoy, *Presidency of Harry S. Truman,* 295–96; Hamby, *Man of the People,* 445–46, 640–41.

18. Charles E. Walcott and Karen M. Hult, *Governing the White House from Hoover Through LBJ* (Lawrence: University Press of Kansas, 1998), 35–37; Heller, ed., *Truman White House,* 225–30.

19. McCoy, *Presidency of Harry S. Truman,* 116–17; Hamby, *Man of the People,* 309–10.

20. Hamby, *Man of the People,* 309–10.

21. See David F. Rudgers, *Creating the Secret State: The Origins of the Central Intelligence Agency, 1943–1947* (Lawrence: University Press of Kansas, 2000), 90–92; Christopher Andrew, *For the President's Eyes Only: Secret Intelligence and the American Presidency from Washington to Bush* (New York: Harper Perennial, 1995), 148–98; and Anna Kasten Nelson, "President Truman and the Evolution of the National Security Council," *Journal of American History* 72(1985): 360–78. Rhodri Jeffreys-Jones, *Cloak and Dollar: A History of American Secret Intelligence* (New Haven: Yale University Press, 2002), 156–60, is critical of the process by which the CIA was created.

22. There is an extensive literature pro and con on the containment policy. Michael J. Lacey, ed., *The Truman Presidency* (New York: Cambridge University Press, 1989), 205–44, provides contrasting perspectives on various aspects of the president's foreign policy.

23. McCoy, *Presidency of Harry S. Truman*, 214–15.

24. Arthur H. Vandenberg Jr., with Joe Alex Morris, eds., *The Private Papers of Senator Vandenberg* (Boston: Houghton Mifflin, 1952), 451.

25. See Hamby, *Man of the People*, 537–39. Barton J. Bernstein, "The Truman Administration and the Korean War," in Lacey, ed., *Truman Presidency*, 425–27, is critical of Truman's decision. Robert Dallek, "Declaring War Is More Than a Formality," *Washington Post*, 4 May 2002, places these developments in the context of the war on terrorism and a possible encounter with Iraq.

26. McCoy's *Presidency of Harry S. Truman*, 221–48, is good on Korea's impact on the administration's political standing.

27. The McCarthy period and its effect on the nation have been examined from many perspectives, most of them critical of Truman. Andrew, *For the President's Eyes Only*, 178–81, discusses the Venona decrypts of Soviet espionage. Jeffreys-Jones, *Cloak and Dollar*, 159, 164, puts McCarthy in the context of intelligence operations.

28. For Dewey's problems as a presidential candidate, see Richard Norton Smith, *Thomas E. Dewey and His Times* (New York: Simon and Schuster, 1982), 524–27, 528–29, 535–36. Hamby's *Man of the People* is good on the 1948 election. Press coverage of the campaign is examined in Mitchell, *Truman and the News Media*, 30–55. Zachary Karabell, *The Last Campaign: How Harry Truman Won the 1948 Election* (New York: Vintage Books, 200), and Gary A. Donaldson, *Truman Defeats Dewey* (Lexington: University Press of Kentucky, 1999), provide recent examinations of this campaign.

29. The deterioration in Truman's political fortunes during the second term is traced in McCoy, *Presidency of Harry S. Truman*, 163–310, and in Hamby, *Man of the People*, 488–508, 534–74.

30. Hamby, *Man of the People*, 629–31, notes Truman's importance in solidifying the presidential library system as part of the institution of the presidency itself. Richard Kirkendall supplied a significant element in stimulating scholarly interest in Truman with two books, *The Truman Period as a Research Field* (Columbia: University of Missouri Press, 1967) and his subsequent *Truman Period as a Research Field: A Reappraisal* (Columbia: University of Missouri Press, 1974).

31. For an evaluation of Truman as commander in chief, see D. Clayton James, "Harry S. Truman: The Two War Chief," in *Commander in Chief: Presidential Leadership in Modern Wars*, ed. Joseph G. Dawson, (Lawrence: University Press of Kansas, 1993), 107–26.

32. The major work on Eisenhower revisionism is by Fred I. Greenstein, *The Hidden-Hand Presidency: Eisenhower as Leader* (1992; reprint, Baltimore: Johns Hopkins University Press, 1994), but see also Robert A. Divine, *Eisenhower and the Cold*

War (New York: Oxford University Press, 1981). See also Richard H. Immerman, "Confessions of an Eisenhower Revisionist: An Agonizing Reappraisal," *Diplomatic History* 14(1990): 319–42. The beginning of Eisenhower revisionism appeared in "The Underestimation of Dwight D. Eisenhower," originally in *Esquire* 68(September 1967) and reprinted in Murray Kempton's *Rebellions, Perversities and Main Events* (New York: Times Books, 1994), 437–46.

33. Dwight D. Eisenhower, *The White House Years: Mandate for Change, 1953–1956* (Garden City, N.Y.: Doubleday, 1963), 87.

34. See Chester J. Pach Jr. and Elmo Richardson, *The Presidency of Dwight D. Eisenhower* (Lawrence: University Press of Kansas, 1991), 45–48. The best biography of Eisenhower as president remains Stephen E. Ambrose's *Eisenhower*, vol. 2, *The President* (New York: Simon and Schuster, 1984).

35. See Duane Tanabaum, *The Bricker Amendment Controversy: A Test of Eisenhower's Political Leadership* (Ithaca, N.Y.: Cornell University Press, 1988), and Gayle B. Montgomery and James W. Johnson, *One Step from the White House: The Rise and Fall of Senator William F. Knowland* (Berkeley: University of California Press, 1998), 143–45. On Bricker, see Walter Johnson, ed., *Selected Letters of William Allen White, 1899–1943* (New York: Henry Holt, 1947), 444.

36. Greenstein, *Hidden-Hand Presidency*, 86; Byron C. Hulsey, *Everett Dirksen and His Presidents: How a Senate Giant Shaped American Politics* (Lawrence: University Press of Kansas, 2000), 56–58, 64–65.

37. Doyle, *Inside the Oval Office*, 68–92.

38. On Eisenhower's staffing approach to the presidency, see Greenstein, *Hidden-Hand Presidency*, 100–113, and Pach and Richardson, *Presidency of Dwight D. Eisenhower*, 36–41.

39. Greenstein, *Hidden-Hand Presidency*, 138–50.

40. Samuel Kerell and Samuel L. Popkin, eds., *Chief of Staff: Twenty-five Years of Managing the Presidency* (Berkeley: University of California Press, 1986), 68–69, 76–77.

41. See Robert H. Ferrell, ed., *The Diary of James C. Hagerty: Eisenhower in Mid-Course, 1954–1955* (Bloomington: Indiana University Press, 1983), 16. For more on Eisenhower's use of these new approaches to presidential press conferences, see Craig Allen, *Eisenhower and the Mass Media: Peace, Prosperity, and Prime-Time TV* (Chapel Hill: University of North Carolina Press, 1993), 47–63.

42. Ferrell, ed., *Diary of James C. Hagerty*, 169.

43. W. Dale Nelson, *Who Speaks for the President?*, 118–24; Clarence G. Lasby, *Eisenhower's Heart Attack: How Ike Beat Heart Disease and Held on to the Presidency* (Lawrence: University Press of Kansas, 1997), 64–65, 75–83.

44. Allen, *Eisenhower and the Mass Media*, 38–39, discusses Eisenhower's use of polls.

45. See Nigel Bowles, *The White House and Capitol Hill: The Politics of Presidential Persuasion* (Oxford: Clarendon Press, 1987), 16–18, and Walcott and Hult, *Governing the White House*, 38–43. See also Kenneth E. Collier, *Between the Branches:*

The White House Office of Legislative Affairs (Pittsburgh, Pa.: University of Pittsburgh Press, 1997), 29–56.

46. John Hart, *The Presidential Branch* (New York: Pergamon Press, 1987), 121; Greenstein, *Hidden-Hand Presidency*, 113–24.

47. Walcott and Hult, *Governing the White House*, 167–73, and David M. Barrett, with Christopher Ryan, "National Security," in *The Executive Office of the President: A Historical, Biographical, and Bibliographical Guide*, ed. Harold C. Relyea (Westport, Conn.: Greenwood Press, 1997), 185–88.

48. Greenstein, *Hidden-Hand Presidency*, 155–227.

49. For the doctrine of executive privilege, see Herbert Brownell, with John P. Burke, *Advising Ike: The Memoirs of Attorney General Herbert Brownell* (Lawrence: University Press of Kansas, 1993), 257–58; Pach and Richardson, *Presidency of Dwight D. Eisenhower*, 70–71; and Mark J. Rozell, *Executive Privilege: Presidential Power, Secrecy, and Accountability*, 2d ed., rev. (Lawrence: University Press of Kansas, 2002).

50. Lasby, *Eisenhower's Heart Attack*, 326–27.

51. Pach and Richardson, *Presidency of Dwight D. Eisenhower*, 159–85.

52. See Andrew, *For the President's Eyes Only*, 209–11, 251–56; Pach and Richardson, *Presidency of Dwight D. Eisenhower*, 87–93, 222–25; and Derek Leebaert, *The Fifty-Year Wound: The True Price of America's Cold War Victory* (Boston: Little, Brown, 2002), 169–75. For conservative Republican unhappiness with Eisenhower's moderate policies, see Mary C. Brennan, *Turning Right in the Sixties: The Conservative Capture of the GOP* (Chapel Hill: University of North Carolina Press, 1995), 21–27, and Rick Perlstein, *Before the Storm: Barry Goldwater and the Unmaking of the American Consensus* (New York: Hill and Wang, 2001), 33–34. See also Douglas B. Harris, "Dwight D. Eisenhower and the New Deal: The Politics of Preemption," *Presidential Studies Quarterly* 27(1997): 333–42, for a defense of Eisenhower's position. For Barry Goldwater's critique of Eisenhower, see "The Preservation of Our Basic Institutions: Effects of Governmental Spending and Taxation," *Vital Speeches of the Day*, 15 May 1957, 455–59.

53. Kirk Porter and Donald Bruce Johnson, *National Party Platforms, 1840–1968* (Urbana: University of Illinois Press, 1972), 594, 600.

54. Arthur M. Schlesinger Jr., *Robert Kennedy and His Times* (Boston: Houghton Mifflin, 1978), 219.

6. THE SOURING OF THE MODERN PRESIDENCY

1. The best study of Kennedy's political rise is Herbert S. Parmet's *Jack: The Struggles of John F. Kennedy* (New York: Dial Press, 1980).

2. Charles O. Jones, ed., *Preparing to Be President: The Memos of Richard E. Neustadt* (Washington, D.C.: American Enterprise Institution, 2000), 54–60, makes the case for the merits of Roosevelt's presidential style to Kennedy. Kennedy advanced an activist interpretation of the office in "The Presidency in 1960," 14 January 1960,

at the National Press Club, but did not discuss in detail how this view of the office would work in practice. <www.jfklibrary.org/io11460.htm.> provides the speech's text.

3. W. Dale Nelson, *Who Speaks for the President? The White House Press Secretary from Cleveland to Clinton* (Syracuse, N.Y.: Syracuse University Press, 1998), 128.

4. Jack Gould to Lester Markel, 30 April 1963, in archives of the *New York Times*, New York City.

5. Arthur Gelb and Barbara Gelb, "Culture Makes a Hit at the White House," *New York Times*, 28 January 1962, reprinted in *The Kennedys: A New York Times Profile*, ed. Gene Brown, (New York: Arno Press, 1980), 78. Bruce Miroff, "The Presidency and the Public: Leadership as Spectacle," in *The Presidency and the Political System*, ed. Michael Nelson, 6th ed. (Washington, D.C.: CQ Press, 2000), 307–9, examines Kennedy's use of the mechanisms of celebrity to advance his policies.

6. The ways in which the Kennedy administration used the cultural possibilities of the White House remain to be explored in depth; Gelb and Gelb, "Culture Makes a Hit at the White House," give the flavor of contemporary coverage. See also Betty Boyd Caroli, "Jacqueline Lee Bouvier Kennedy Onassis," in *American First Ladies: Their Lives and Their Legacy*, ed. Lewis L. Gould, 2d ed. (New York: Routledge, 2001), 324–29.

7. As a graduate student at Yale University in the early 1960s and the son of a *New York Times* reporter, I heard stories about Kennedy's alleged first marriage and the "disappearance" of copies of the *Social Register* with the damaging information. Other rumors included Joseph P. Kennedy's supposed payment of $1 million to Mrs. Kennedy to stay in the marriage and the reconciliation of the couple after the death of their stillborn son in summer 1963. Richard Reeves, *President Kennedy: Profile of Power* (New York: Simon and Schuster, 1993), and Thomas C. Reeves, *A Question of Character: A Life of John F. Kennedy* (New York: Free Press, 1991) discuss Kennedy's personal behavior.

8. The most notable of the muckraking books about Kennedy was Victor Lasky's *J.F.K.: The Man and the Myth* (New York: Macmillan, 1963). For Bradlee, see Benjamin Bradlee, *Conversations with Kennedy* (New York: Norton, 1975).

9. Nigel Bowles, *The White House and Capitol Hill: The Politics of Presidential Persuasion* (Oxford: Clarendon Press, 1987), 18–23, and Patricia Heidotting Conley, *Presidential Mandates: How Elections Shape the National Agenda* (Chicago: University of Chicago Press, 2001), 150–53. Kennedy had promised during the campaign to achieve a "one hundred days" to equal that of Roosevelt. See James Reston, "Kennedy's Victory by Close Margin," *New York Times*, 10 November 1960.

10. Charles E. Walcott and Karen M. Hult, *Governing the White House from Hoover Through LBJ* (Lawrence: University Press of Kansas, 1995), 173–78; David M. Barrett, with Christopher Ryan, "National Security," in *The Executive Office of the President: A Historical, Biographical, and Bibliographical Guide*, ed. Harold C. Relyea, (Westport, Conn.: Greenwood Press, 1997), 188–91.

11. For the impact of the Bay of Pigs on the Kennedy presidency, see John Morton Blum, *Years of Discord: American Politics and Society, 1961–1974* (New York: Norton, 1991), 38–42. See also James N. Giglio, *The Presidency of John F. Kennedy* (Lawrence: University Press of Kansas, 1991), 48–63, and James T. Patterson, *Grand Expectations: The United States, 1945–1974* (New York: Oxford University Press, 1996), 492–96.

12. The Cuban Missile Crisis has generated an extensive historical literature. Important for firsthand evidence of what the participants in the administration thought at the time is Ernest R. May and Philip D. Zelikow's *The Kennedy Tapes: Inside the White House During the Cuban Missile Crisis* (Cambridge: Belknap Press of Harvard University Press, 1997). A recent study of the episode is Robert Weisbrot's *Maximum Danger: Kennedy, the Missiles, and the Crisis of American Confidence* (Chicago: Ivan Dee, 2001). Thomas Preston, *The President and His Inner Circle* (New York: Columbia University Press, 2001), 97–136, offers a favorable evaluation of Kennedy's style in this episode.

13. Lawrence Freedman, *Kennedy's Wars: Berlin, Cuba, Laos, and Vietnam* (New York: Oxford University Press, 2000), provides a good synthetic treatment of Kennedy's decision-making about Vietnam.

14. Ibid., 382–97.

15. Ibid., 150–52, 157–59, 232–33.

16. William Doyle, *Inside the Oval Office: The White House Tapes from FDR to Clinton* (New York: Kodansha International, 1999), 93–137.

17. For polling during the Kennedy years, see Walcott and Hult, *Governing the White House*, 61, 67–68, 69.

18. With *The Other Side of the Sixties: Young Americans for Freedom and the Rise of Conservative Politics* (New Brunswick, N.J.: Rutgers University Press, 1997), 151–68, John Andrew III began his look at presidents and the Internal Revenue Service. In *Power to Destroy: The Political Use of the IRS from Kennedy to Nixon* (Chicago: Ivan Dee, 2002), 11–44, Andrew supplies much more fascinating detail on this sordid aspect of presidential power.

19. Bowles, *White House and Capitol Hill*, 18–25; Kenneth E. Collier, *Between the Branches: The White House Office of Legislative Affairs* (Pittsburgh, Pa.: University of Pittsburgh Press, 1997), 57–78.

20. In 2002, Kennedy ranked second only to Lincoln in a popular evaluation of presidents (*Washington Post National Weekly Edition*, 25 February–3 March 2002, 34). In 1990, Kennedy had the highest approval rating, 84 percent, in the Gallup poll for all the presidents from Franklin D. Roosevelt through Ronald Reagan. See James P. Pfiffner, *The Modern Presidency* (New York: St. Martin's Press, 1994), 221. The same was true during the 1980s. See Barbara Perry, "John Fitzgerald Kennedy," in *The American Presidents*, ed. Melvin I. Urofsky, (New York: Garland, 2000), 395.

21. Richard Schickel, *Intimate Strangers: The Culture of Celebrity* (Garden City, N.Y.: Doubleday, 1985), 168–76; Giglio, *Presidency of John F. Kennedy*, 4–6.

22. Robert Dallek, *Flawed Giant: Lyndon Johnson and His Times, 1961–1973* (New York: Oxford University Press, 1998), 63–66.

23. For Johnson's rise to power, there are now several helpful biographical studies. Robert Dallek's *Lone Star Rising: Lyndon Johnson and His Times, 1908–1960* (New York: Oxford University Press, 1991) is the most balanced. Robert A. Caro's *The Years of Lyndon Johnson*, 3 vols. (New York: Knopf, 1982–2002), is the most critical in tone and approach.

24. Michael Beschloss, ed., *Reaching for Glory: Lyndon Johnson's Secret White House Tapes, 1964–1965* (New York: Simon and Schuster, 2001), 442.

25. Larry Berman, "Johnson and the White House Staff," in *Exploring the Johnson Years*, ed. Robert A. Divine (Austin: University of Texas Press, 1981), 187–213; Emmette S. Redford and Richard T. McCulley, *White House Operations: The Johnson Presidency* (Austin: University of Texas Press, 1986), 69–76; Walcott and Hult, *Governing the White House*, 248–50.

26. See Redford and McCulley, *White House Operations*, 61. Johnson's preference for generalists could cause problems. When he designated Bill Moyers to handle negotiations with the billboard industry in 1965 over what became the Highway Beautification Act of 1965, Moyers's lack of expertise in the field enabled the industry lobbyist Phillip Tocker to get the better of him on specific details. See Lewis L. Gould, *Lady Bird Johnson and the Environment*, 1st ed. (Lawrence: University Press of Kansas, 1988), 148–51, 167.

27. The White House tapes are replete with Johnson's involvement in matters great and small; see Beschloss, ed., *Reaching for Glory*, 200–201, 261–62.

28. Michael R. Beschloss, ed., *Taking Charge: The Johnson White House Tapes, 1963–1964* (New York: Simon and Schuster, 1997), 547–53; Doyle, *Inside the Oval Office*, 144–145.

29. Lewis L. Gould, *Lady Bird Johnson: Our Environmental First Lady*, 2d ed. (Lawrence: University Press of Kansas, 1999), 55–56.

30. Bruce E. Altschuler, *LBJ and the Polls* (Gainesville: University of Florida Press, 1990).

31. Andrew, *Power to Destroy*, 138–65, examines Johnson's use of the IRS.

32. Lewis L. Gould, "'Never a Deep Partisan': Lyndon Johnson and the Democratic Party, 1963–1969," in *The Johnson Years: LBJ at Home and Abroad*, ed. Robert A. Divine (Lawrence: University Press of Kansas, 1994), 21–52.

33. David Culbert, "Johnson and the Media," in Divine, ed., *Exploring the Johnson Years*, 214–48; Nelson, *Who Speaks for the President?*, 144–65; Kathleen J. Turner, *Lyndon Johnson's Dual War: Vietnam and the Press* (Chicago: University of Chicago Press, 1985).

34. Beschloss, ed., *Taking Charge*, 308.

35. Max Frankel, *The Times of My Life and My Life with the* Times (New York: Random House, 1999), 278–86; Turner, *Lyndon Johnson's Dual War,* 60–62.

36. Culbert, "Johnson and the Media," 230–31, discusses the origin of the phrase "credibility gap."

37. See Bowles, *White House and Capitol Hill,* 25–33, for an overview; the remainder of the book is a detailed look at Johnson's relations with Congress. See also Collier, *Between the Branches,* 79–108.

38. Dallek, *Flawed Giant,* 299–311, 533–36.

39. Ibid., 111–21, 411–18.

40. Johnson's efforts to avoid having to make difficult decisions about Vietnam during 1964 are evident in Beschloss, ed., *Taking Charge,* 257–60, 262–63, 319–20, 394–95.

41. For a history of the 1964 election that is critical of Johnson and his campaign, see Rick Perlstein, *Before the Storm: Barry Goldwater and the Unmaking of the American Consensus* (New York: Hill and Wang, 2001), 412–14, 432–38. Some of Johnson's critics such as Perlstein seem to believe that any hardball campaign tactics were inherently unfair. Also negative on Johnson is Steven F. Hayward, *The Age of Reagan: The Fall of the Old Liberal Order, 1964–1980* (Roseville, Calif.: Prima, 2001), 50–57.

42. Dallek, *Flawed Giant,* 143–56, and 238 (quotation); Cal Thomas, "George McGovern Was Right," 15 November 2001, <TownHall.com>

43. Dallek, *Flawed Giant,* 99; Beschloss, ed., *Reaching for Glory,* 213.

44. Lewis L. Gould, *1968: The Election That Changed America* (Chicago: Ivan Dee, 1993), 46–51.

7. THE RISE OF THE CONTINUOUS CAMPAIGN

1. Tom Wicker, *One of Us: Richard Nixon and the American Dream* (New York: Random House, 1991), 283.

2. *Public Papers of the Presidents of the United States: Lyndon Johnson, 1966,* 2 vols., (Washington, D.C.: Government Printing Office, 1967), 2: 133.

3. Wicker, *One of Us,* 285; H. R. Haldeman, *The Haldeman Diaries: Inside the Nixon White House* (New York: G. P. Putnam's Sons, 1994), 260.

4. Joan Hoff's *Nixon Reconsidered* (New York: Basic Books, 1994) is an essential source for Nixon revisionism. Steven F. Hayward, *The Age of Reagan: The Fall of the Old Liberal Order, 1964–1980* (Roseville, Calif.: Prima, 2001), 232–34, 286–87, examines Nixon's achievements from a conservative perspective. Gareth Davies's "The Great Society After Johnson: The Case of Bilingual Education," *Journal of American History* 88 (March 2002): 1405–29, is as much about the question of Nixon's relative liberalism in office as it is about the subject of its title. Dean J. Kotlowski, *Nixon's Civil Rights: Politics, Principle, and Policy* (Cambridge: Harvard University Press, 2001), offers a balanced but sympathetic look at Nixon's record in this controversial area.

5. Wicker, *One of Us,* 31.
6. A critical interpretation of Nixon's early years is Roger Morris's *Richard Milhous Nixon: The Rise of an American Politician* (New York: Holt, 1990). Nixon is vigorously defended in Irwin F. Gellman's *The Contender: Richard Nixon: The Congress Years, 1946–1952* (New York: Free Press, 1999). Richard Nixon's *RN: The Memoirs of Richard Nixon* (New York: Grosset and Dunlap, 1978) is revealing, often in ways the author did not intend. See Jeffrey Kimball, *Nixon's Vietnam War* (Lawrence: University Press of Kansas, 1998), 10, for quotation.
7. See Melvin Small, *The Presidency of Richard Nixon* (Lawrence: University Press of Kansas, 1999), 59, 204. Michael A. Genovese, *The Nixon Presidency: Power and Politics in Turbulent Times* (Westport, Conn.: Greenwood Press, 1990), provides an earlier treatment of the administration. Nixon's address, "The Nature of the Presidency," was broadcast on 19 September 1968 over the NBC and CBS Radio Networks (New York: Nixon/Agnew Campaign Committee, 1968), pamphlet in author's collection. Among other things, he said, "We have had enough of discord and division, and what we need now is a time of healing, of renewal, and of realistic hope."
8. Small, *Presidency of Richard Nixon,* 37, 42, 48; Samuel Kernell and Samuel Popkin, *Chief of Staff: Twenty-five Years of Managing the Presidency* (Berkeley: University of California Press, 1986), 65–67; and Shirley Anne Warshaw, *Powersharing: White House–Cabinet Relations in the Modern Presidency* (Albany: State University of New York Press, 1996), 39–43, 46–51 (Warshaw's analysis is sometimes undercut by her own evidence of Nixon's dislike for the cabinet).
9. Peri Arnold, *Making the Managerial Presidency: Comprehensive Reorganization Planning, 1905–1996,* 2d ed., rev. (Lawrence: University Press of Kansas, 1998), 274–84.
10. For Nixon's flirtations with Moynihan and Connally, see Small, *Presidency of Richard Nixon,* 45–46 (Moynihan), and 207–9 (Connally); see also Haldeman, *Haldeman Diaries,* 132–33, 215–16, 289–90. Arthur M. Klebanoff, *The Agent: Personalities, Publishing and Politics* (New York: Texere, 2001), 46–47, offers the perspective of one of Moynihan's staff members during this period.
11. Arnold, *Making the Managerial Presidency,* 282–83; Allen J. Matusow, *Nixon's Economy: Booms, Busts, Dollars and Votes* (Lawrence: University Press of Kansas, 1998), 76; Hoff, *Nixon Reconsidered,* 59–60.
12. Small, *Presidency of Richard Nixon,* 48–49, 270–71.
13. Kimball, *Nixon's Vietnam War,* 63–86, gives a thorough treatment of the "madman" approach. Derek Leebaert, *The Fifty-Year Wound: The True Price of America's Cold War Victory* (Boston: Little, Brown, 2002), 379–92, is critical of Nixon's foreign policy record.
14. Haldeman, *Haldeman Diaries,* 52, 58–59.
15. Small, *Presidency of Richard Nixon,* 50–55.
16. See Haldeman, *Haldeman Diaries,* 39, 52, 119, 120, 121. In fairness to Nixon, his mentor, Dwight D. Eisenhower, also communicated with his wife with memos; see Eisenhower to Mamie Eisenhower, 28 July 1955, in *The Papers of Dwight David*

Eisenhower, The Presidency: The Middle Way, ed. Louis Galambos et al. (Baltimore: Johns Hopkins University Press, 1996), 1796–97.

17. On Haldeman and his role, see Small, *Presidency of Richard Nixon,* 42–44; Kernell and Popkin, eds., *Chief of Staff,* 21–23, 88–89, 170–71.

18. Haldeman, *Haldeman Diaries,* 86, 95, 108, offers good glimpses of Nixon's working style.

19. John Anthony Maltese, *Spin Control: The White House Office of Communications and the Management of Presidential News,* 2d ed., rev. (Chapel Hill: University of North Carolina Press, 1994), 48–52.

20. Small, *Presidency of Richard Nixon,* 42–43.

21. Haldeman, *Haldeman Diaries,* 31, 107, 116, 118, 151, 156 (quotation) 229, 246, 335, 339.

22. Nixon, 29; Maltese, *Spin Control,* 24.

23. W. Dale Nelson, *Who Speaks for the President? The White House Press Secretary from Cleveland to Clinton* (Syracuse, N.Y.: Syracuse University Press, 1998), 168–69.

24. Maltese, *Spin Control,* 44–45; Nelson, *Who Speaks for the President?,* 174–75.

25. Maltese, *Spin Control,* 45; Stanley Kutler, ed., *Abuse of Power: The New Nixon Tapes* (New York: Free Press, 1997), 8.

26. Maltese, *Spin Control,* 27 (both quotations).

27. Ibid., 61.

28. Ibid., 41; Haldeman, *Haldeman Diaries,* 104.

29. See Maltese, *Spin Control,* 72–74. For a reporter's perspective on Nixon and the press, see Jack Germond, *Fat Man in the Middle Seat: Forty Years of Covering Politics* (New York: Random House, 1999), 87–97, and Max Frankel *The Times of My Life and My Life with the* Times (New York: Random House, 1999), 314–16.

30. See Kutler, ed., *Abuse of Power,* 31, 32. An excellent new study of Nixon's use and abuse of the Internal Revenue Service to punish his political enemies is John Andrew III's *Power to Destroy: The Political Use of the IRS from Kennedy to Nixon* (Chicago: Ivan Dee, 2002), 225–37. Andrew has some intriguing new information about Nixon's links to organized crime figures through Bebe Rebozo. John L. Bullion, *In the Boat with LBJ* (Plano: Republic of Texas Press, 2001), 328–29, notes that his father, Lyndon Johnson's tax lawyer, was audited in four of the five years that Nixon was president.

31. J. Anthony Lukas, *Nightmare: The Underside of the Nixon Years* (1976; reprint, Athens: Ohio University Press, 1998), 47–60; Small, *Presidency of Richard Nixon,* 72, 236–37.

32. Richard Reeves, *President Nixon: Alone in the White House* (New York: Simon and Schuster, 2001), 348–49; Haldeman, *Haldeman Diaries,* 124.

33. Haldeman, *Haldeman Diaries,* 74; Small, *Presidency of Richard Nixon,* 237–38.

34. Small, *Presidency of Richard Nixon,* 250–253; Andrew, *Power to Destroy,* 201–24.

35. Small, *Presidency of Richard Nixon,* 233–34, makes clear the busywork aspect of much of the tracing of press coverage in the Nixon White House.

36. See Reeves, *President Nixon*, 31. Small, *Presidency of Richard Nixon*, 158–59, shows how the administration responded to domestic unrest from 1969 to 1971.

37. Christopher Andrew, *For the President's Eyes Only: Secret Intelligence and the American Presidency from Washington to Bush* (New York: Harper, 1975), 368–69; Hoff, *Nixon Reconsidered*, 288–94.

38. Small, *Presidency of Richard Nixon*, 251, 279; Kutler, ed., *Abuse of Power*, 26–27.

39. Kutler, ed., *Abuse of Power*, 27–30; Andrew, *For the President's Eyes Only*, 379–81.

40. Instances where one political party intervened to shape the outcome of the national nominating process for the other party are rare, and none was conducted on the systematic scale of Nixon's men in 1972. Small, *Presidency of Richard Nixon*, 253–54, notes the uniqueness of the Nixon effort. The White House said that the alleged dirty tricks of Democratic operatives in previous campaigns justified their response. Though Democrats such as Dick Tuck had played pranks on Republican candidates, their activities had not involved influencing whom the GOP decided to nominate for any office.

41. For the background of Nixon's taping operation, see Kutler, ed., *Abuse of Power*, xiii–xxiii, and Kutler, *The Wars of Watergate: The Last Crisis of Richard Nixon* (New York: Knopf, 1990), 367–71. See also William Doyle, *Inside the Oval Office: The White House Tapes from FDR to Clinton* (New York: Kodansha International, 1999), 193–96.

42. Arthur M. Schlesinger Jr., *The Imperial Presidency* (Boston: Houghton Mifflin, 1973); William Goldsmith, ed., *The Growth of Presidential Power*, 3 vols. (New York: Chelsea House, 1974).

43. Haldeman, *Haldeman Diaries*, 533.

44. Bob Woodward, *Shadow: Five Presidents and the Legacy of Watergate* (New York: Simon and Schuster, 1999), looks at the impact of the independent counsel statute on the presidencies that followed Nixon. Jeffrey Toobin, *A Vast Conspiracy: The Real Story of the Sex Scandal That Nearly Brought Down a President* (New York: Random House, 1999), 67–70, gives a brief account of the special prosecutor/independent counsel system. See also Kutler, *Wars of Watergate*, 581–85.

45. On the problems surrounding Nixon's personal papers, see Kutler, *Wars of Watergate*, 563–64, 592–94.

46. Doyle, *Inside the Oval Office*, 193–96; Kutler, *Wars of Watergate*, 592–94.

47. Small, *Presidency of Richard Nixon*, 302–3; Kutler, *Wars of Watergate*, 592 (quotation).

48. Ibid., 303–8.

8. THE MODERN PRESIDENCY UNDER SIEGE

1. For Ford's approach to the presidency, see John Robert Greene, *The Presidency of Gerald R. Ford* (Lawrence: University Press of Kansas, 1995), 21–28. His relationship with Democrats in Congress is evident in Samuel Kernell and Samuel L. Popkin, eds., *Chief of Staff: Twenty-five Years of Managing the Presidency* (Berkeley: University of California Press, 1986), 9, 171–72. See also Herbert J. Storing,

ed., *The Ford White House* (Lanham, Md.: University Press of America, 1986), 76–77.

2. Greene, *Presidency of Gerald R. Ford,* 17 (quotation), 43–45.

3. Background on Ford's legislative career can be found in James Cannon, *Time and Chance: Gerald Ford's Appointment with History* (New York: HarperCollins, 1994), and Greene, *Presidency of Gerald R. Ford,* 1–17.

4. On the unique problems that Ford confronted during his brief vice presidency, see Greene, *Presidency of Gerald R. Ford,* 13–16.

5. John Anthony Maltese, *Spin Control: The White House Office of Communications and the Management of Presidential News,* 2d ed., rev. (Chapel Hill: University of North Carolina Press, 1992, 1994), 117–23, discusses Ford's public image. See also Steven F. Hayward, *The Age of Reagan: The Fall of the Old Liberal Order, 1964– 1980* (Roseville, Calif.: Prima, 2001), 395–97.

6. On the negative perceptions of Ford's intelligence, see Greene, *Presidency of Gerald R. Ford,* 22, 61–62.

7. For Betty Ford, see John Pope, "Elizabeth Ann (Betty) Bloomer Ford," in *American First Ladies: Their Lives and Their Legacy,* ed. Lewis L. Gould, 2d ed. (New York: Routledge, 2001), 363–76.

8. The cultural shift in the 1970s that *Saturday Night Live* represented is touched on in James L. Baughman, *The Republic of Mass Culture: Journalism, Filmmaking, and Broadcasting in America Since 1941* (Baltimore: Johns Hopkins University Press, 1992), 181, 195, which examines the coverage that Ford received. Bruce J. Schulman, *The Seventies: The Great Shift in American Culture, Society, and Politics* (New York: Da Capo, 2002), 49–52, gives a good sense of the changes that came with Nixon's impeachment and Ford's arrival at the White House.

9. Henry Kissinger, *Years of Renewal* (New York: Simon and Schuster, 1999), 169; Kernell and Popkin, eds., *Chief of Staff,* 149.

10. Greene, *Presidency of Gerald R. Ford,* 64–66.

11. Kissinger, *Years of Renewal,* 175; Kernell and Popkin, eds., *Chief of Staff,* 74.

12. Michael Kramer and Sam Roberts, *"I Never Wanted to Be Vice President of Anything": An Investigative Biography of Nelson Rockefeller* (New York: Basic Books, 1976), 364–377.

13. The events surrounding Ford's pardon of Nixon have been intensely scrutinized; see Greene, *Presidency of Gerald R. Ford,* 42–52.

14. W. Dale Nelson, *Who Speaks for the President? The White House Press Secretary from Cleveland to Clinton* (Syracuse, N.Y.: Syracuse University Press, 1998), 186– 90; Greene, *Presidency of Gerald R. Ford,* 53–58.

15. Ford's problems are discussed in Greene, *Presidency of Gerald R. Ford,* 101–16, and in Hayward, *Age of Reagan,* 395–446.

16. Greene, *Presidency of Gerald R. Ford,* 191; Peter G. Bourne, *Jimmy Carter: A Comprehensive Biography from Plains to Post Presidency* (New York: Scribner's, 1997), 271–72, 278, 326, 336; Hayward, *Age of Reagan,* 451, 453, 455, 489–91.

17. For conservative attitudes toward Ford, his administration, and his wife, see David W. Reinhard, *The Republican Right Since 1945* (Lexington: University Press of Kentucky, 1983), 228–34; see also John Pope, "Elizabeth Ann (Betty) Bloomer Ford," 370–73, and Hayward, *Age of Reagan,* 465 (quotation).

18. The passions that the Ford-Reagan contest aroused are evident in Raleigh E. Milton, reporter, *Official Report of the Proceedings of the Thirty-first Republican National Convention Held in Kansas City, Missouri, August 16, 17, 18, 19, 1976* (n.p.: Dulany-Vernon, 1976). See also Greene, *Presidency of Gerald R. Ford,* 170–173.

19. In addition to Bourne's *Jimmy Carter,* Burton I. Kaufman, *The Presidency of James Earl Carter, Jr.* (Lawrence: University Press of Kansas, 1993), offers a critical appraisal of Carter's record. Hayward, *Age of Reagan,* 485–601, is negative in his overall assessment but gives Carter his due. Herbert D. Rosenbaum and Alexej Ugrinsky, eds., *The Presidency and Domestic Policies of Jimmy Carter* (Westport, Conn.: Greenwood Press, 1994), includes more than thirty essays and commentary about the domestic agenda of the Carter presidency.

20. See Kaufman, *Presidency of James Earl Carter,* 5–11, and Bourne, *Jimmy Carter,* 166–236. Betty Glad, *Jimmy Carter: In Search of the Great White House* (New York: Norton, 1980), provides a thorough review of Carter's political career in Georgia.

21. Kaufman, *Presidency of James Earl Carter,* 9–10; Bourne, *Jimmy Carter,* 419–21.

22. On the religious aspect of Carter's appeal and its role in the campaign, see Bourne, *Jimmy Carter,* 304–7; Kaufman, *Presidency of James Earl Carter,* 12; and Hayward, *Age of Reagan,* 487–89. See also Michael J. Adee, "American Civil Religion and the Presidential Rhetoric of Jimmy Carter," in Rosenbaum and Ugrinsky, eds., *The Presidency and Domestic Policies of Jimmy Carter,* 74–82.

23. For the ambivalence that journalists felt about Carter during the 1976 campaign, see Jack Germond, *Fat Man in a Middle Seat: Forty Years of Covering Politics* (New York: Random House, 1999), 128–31, and Leslie Stahl, *Reporting Live* (New York: Simon and Schuster, 1999), 59–60, 62–63, 115–16.

24. On Carter's problems as a campaigner, see Bourne, *Jimmy Carter,* 345–49, and Kaufman, *Presidency of James Earl Carter,* 16–18. Since Carter won the presidency, his poor performance (he nearly gave up a thirty-point lead) was soon forgotten. These same problems, however, resurfaced in the 1980 race against the more formidable challenge of Ronald Reagan.

25. The disdain of the Carter forces toward the Democratic party is one of the main themes in accounts of his presidency; see Kaufman, *Presidency of James Earl Carter,* 24–25, 28, 30; Bourne, *Jimmy Carter,* 369–71; and Jim Wright, *Balance of Power: Presidents and Congress from the Era of McCarthy to the Rise of Gingrich* (Atlanta: Turner Publications, 1996), 275–76, 278–79. See also Hayward, *Age of Reagan,* 507–8, and Thomas P. "Tip" O'Neill, *Man of the House* (New York: Random House, 1987), 310–11.

26. The Republican delegation in the Georgia Senate, for example, during Carter's governorship, under the leadership of future U.S. senator Paul Coverdell, num-

bered fewer than five lawmakers. For a Republican view of Carter during this period, see "An Oral History Interview with Paul Coverdell," 4 March 1989, Georgia State University, Atlanta, 40–42. Bourne, *Jimmy Carter*, 420, quotes Mondale.

27. Bourne, *Jimmy Carter*, 361–62, 371.

28. Ibid., 360; Kernell and Popkin, ed., *Chief of Staff*, 71–73.

29. Hamilton Jordan, *Crisis: The Last Year of the Carter Presidency* (New York: Putnam, 1982), gives his own perspective on a key phase of his White House tenure. Kaufman, *Presidency of James Earl Carter*, 146–47, looks at Jordan's performance when he became White House chief of staff.

30. See Maltese, *Spin Control*, 160–71. The emergence of journalists who were previously aligned with Republicans or Democrats in the political world began with William Safire of the *New York Times* and later came to include John McLaughlin, Tim Russert, and Chris Matthews, among others. For this development, see Edwin Diamond, *Behind the* Times: *Inside the* New York Times (New York: Villard Books, 1994), 120–21, and Germond, *Fat Man in a Middle Seat*, 185–90.

31. Bourne, *Jimmy Carter*, 421; Steven M. Gillon, "A New Framework: Walter Mondale as Vice President," in *At the President's Side: The Vice Presidency in the Twentieth Century*, ed. Timothy Walch (Columbia: University of Missouri Press, 1997), 144–54.

32. Kathy Smith, "Eleanor Rosalynn Smith Carter," in Gould, ed., *American First Ladies*, 382–92. See also Mary Finch Hoyt, *East Wing: A Memoir* (Philadelphia: Xlibris, 2001), 136–206.

33. For Eisenhower's use of Camp David, see Chester J. Pach Jr. and Elmo Richardson, *The Presidency of Dwight D. Eisenhower* (Lawrence: University Press of Kansas, 1991), 208–9. The Camp David meetings under Carter have received extensive treatment. The president writes about them in his own memoir, *Keeping Faith: Memoirs of a President* (New York: Bantam Books, 1982), 332–33, and Rosalynn Carter provides interesting excerpts from the diary she kept during the negotiating episode. See Rosalynn Carter, *First Lady from Plains* (1984; reprint, New York: Fawcett Gold Medal, 1985), 223–55. Hayward, *Age of Reagan*, 548–49, concedes that Camp David was one of Carter's few successes in office.

34. Raleigh E. Milton, reporter, *Official Report of the Proceedings of the Thirty-second Republican National Convention held in Detroit, Michigan, July 14, 15, 16, 17, 1980* (n.p.: Dulany-Vernay, 1988), 66.

35. For the events and context of Carter's 1979 speech, see Kaufman, *Presidency of James Earl Carter*, 144–46; Bourne, *Jimmy Carter*, 441–46; Hayward, *Age of Reagan*, 574–78.

36. Kaufman, *Presidency of James Earl Carter*, 146–47; Joseph A. Califano, *Governing America: An Insider's Report from the White House and the Cabinet* (New York: Simon and Schuster, 1981), 429–31.

37. The hostage crisis in Iran is covered in most accounts of the Carter years. See Kaufman, *Presidency of James Earl Carter*, 159–60, 173–76.

38. Jack W. Germond and Jules Witcover, *Blue Smoke and Mirrors: How Reagan Won and Why Carter Lost the Election of 1980* (New York: Viking, 1981), 79–92, 141–65; Hayward, *Age of Reagan*, 659(Carter quotation).

39. For the assumptions of the Carter campaign about Reagan's perceived political vulnerabilities, see Germond and Witcover, *Blue Smoke and Mirrors*, 225, 243–46. Hayward, *Age of Reagan*, 697–700, is critical of Carter's attacks on Reagan over the issues of race and international peace.

40. Germond and Witcover, *Blue Smoke and Mirrors*, 243–66, look at the Carter-Reagan campaign in depth. Hayward, *Age of Reagan*, 672–717, analyzes the election from a pro-Reagan point of view. See also Leo Ribuffo, "Jimmy Carter and the Selling of the President, 1976–1980," in Rosenbaum and Ugrinsky, eds., *The Presidency and Domestic Policies of Jimmy Carter*, 156–59.

41. Godfrey Hodgson, *All Things to All Men: The False Promise of the Modern American Presidency* (New York: Simon and Schuster, 1980), 206.

9. THE MODERN PRESIDENCY IN A REPUBLICAN ERA

1. Peggy Noonan, *What I Saw at the Revolution: A Political Life in the Reagan Era* (New York: Random House, 1990), 151; Edmund Morris, *Dutch: A Memoir of Ronald Reagan* (New York: Random House, 1999).

2. Alexander Haig, *Caveat: Realism, Reagan, and Foreign Policy* (New York: Macmillan, 1984), 85; Martin Anderson, *Revolution: The Reagan Legacy* (Stanford: Hoover Institution Press, 1990), 289–91; Colin L. Powell, with Joseph E. Persico, *My American Journey* (New York: Random House, 1995), 334.

3. There are a number of helpful biographical accounts of Reagan's early life and his rise in the movie business. The best brief study of his life and political career is William E. Pemberton's *Exit with Honor: The Life and Presidency of Ronald Reagan* (Armonk, N.Y.: Sharpe, 1997). Garry Wills, *Reagan's America: Innocents at Home* (Garden City, N.Y.: Doubleday, 1987), is informative on Reagan's performance in Hollywood. Joan Didion, *Political Fictions* (New York: Knopf, 2001), 91–94, 109–11, offers some perceptive comments on the impact of moviemaking on Reagan's style of politics.

4. Pemberton, *Exit with Honor*, 27–43; Lou Cannon, *President Reagan: The Role of a Lifetime* (New York: Simon and Schuster, 1991), 42–43, 75.

5. For Reagan's political emergence during the 1960s and his first race for governor in California, see Matthew Dallek, *The Right Moment: Ronald Reagan's First Victory and the Decisive Turning Point in American Politics* (New York: The Free Press, 2001).

6. Cannon, *President Reagan*, 51.

7. See Didion, *Political Fictions*, 105–6. On the development of stars as a distinct segment in the movie industry and in American society generally, see Alexander Walker, *Stardom: The Hollywood Phenomenon* (Middlesex, U.K.: Penguin Books, 1974), 228–51. Richard Schickel, *Intimate Strangers: The Culture of Celebrity* (Gar-

den City, N.Y.: Doubleday, 1985), 194–200, looks at Reagan in the context of his star status as "the actor."

8. On the experience of the Reagans with John Sears in 1980, see Cannon, *President Reagan*, 66–68; see also Pemberton, *Exit with Honor*, 85–86, 87–88.

9. The performance of the troika is analyzed in a number of books about the Reagan presidency. See Pemberton, *Exit with Honor*, 92–93; Cannon, *President Reagan*, 555–61; and Deborah Hart Strober and Gerald S. Strober, *Reagan: The Man and His Presidency* (Boston: Houghton Mifflin, 1998), 60–65.

10. The origin of the radio address during the postgubernatorial period is discussed in Kinon J. Skinner, Annelise Anderson, and Martin Anderson, eds., *Reagan in His Own Hand: The Writings of Ronald Reagan That Reveal His Revolutionary Vision for America* (New York: Free Press, 2001), xiii–xxvi. See also Robert C. Rowland and John M. Jones, "Until Next Week: The Saturday Radio Addresses of Ronald Reagan," *Presidential Studies Quarterly* 32 (March 2002): 84–110.

11. The introduction of heroes began with the 1982 State of the Union message, when President Reagan identified Lenny Skutnik, a government worker who had rescued a survivor of a plane crash in the icy Potomac a few weeks earlier. No similar introduction occurred in 1983, but in 1984 two guests were presented to the audience and a tradition had begun. See Noonan, *What I Saw at the Revolution*, 198–99; David Gergen, *Eyewitness to Power: The Essence of Leadership, Nixon to Clinton* (New York: Simon and Schuster, 2000), 229–30; and "Address Before a Joint Session of Congress Reporting on the State of the Union, January 26, 1982," <www.Reagan.utexas.edu/resource/speeches/1982/12682c.htm> and "Address Before a Joint Session of the Congress on the State of the Union, January 25, 1984," <www.Reagan.utexas.edu/resource/speeches/1984/12584e.htm>. For an example of a state governor using this technique, see "Governor Bob Taft, State of the State Address, February 5, 2002: Pioneering the Third Frontier," <www.state.oh.us/gov/Major Speeches/sos2002.htm>.

12. For the mechanisms by which Reagan's presidency was choreographed on a daily basis, see Cannon, *President Reagan*, 144–46; John Anthony Maltese, *Spin Control: The White House Office of Communication and the Management of Presidential News*, 2d ed., rev. (Chapel Hill: University of North Carolina Press, 1994), 190–97; and Pemberton, *Exit with Honor*, 205–6 (quotation). Lesley Stahl, *Reporting Live* (New York: Simon and Schuster, 1999), 211, gives her version of what happened. Richard Darman, *Who's in Control? Polar Politics and the Sensible Center* (New York: Simon and Schuster, 1996), does not mention this episode. Bruce Miroff, "The Presidency and the Public: Leadership as Spectacle," in *The Presidency and the Political System*, ed. Michael Nelson, 6th ed. (Washington, D.C.: Congressional Quarterly) 309–15, analyzes the Reagan presidency as a staged spectacle.

13. Mark Herstgaard, *On Bended Knee: The Press and the Reagan Presidency* (New York: Farrar Straus Giroux, 1988).

14. For the shift in Republican attitudes in the 1970s, see Steven F. Hayward, *The Age of Reagan: The Fall of the Old Liberal Order, 1964–1980* (Roseville, Calif.: Prima Press, 2001), 524–34.

15. Reagan's 1980 campaign and the responses to it are analyzed in Hayward, *Age of Reagan,* 677–717.

16. Cannon, *President Reagan,* 253–65, and Pemberton, *Exit with Honor,* 95–103, describe the events leading to the adoption of Reagan's tax program in 1981. Two good assessments of this process are found in John W. Sloan's *The Reagan Effect: Economics and Presidential Leadership* (Lawrence: University Press of Kansas, 1999), 104–51, and in James P. Pfiffner's *The Strategic Presidency: Hitting the Ground Running,* 2d ed., rev. (Lawrence: University Press of Kansas, 1996), 105–7, 123–27. See also Darman, *Who's in Control,* 70 (quotation).

17. On the PATCO episode, see Herbert R. Northrup, "The Labor Policies of the Reagan Administration," in *Ronald Reagan's America,* ed. Eric J. Schmertz, Natalie Datlof, and Alexej Ugrinsky, 2 vols., (Westport, Conn.: Greenwood Press, 1997), 1: 320–22.

18. See Noonan, *What I Saw at the Revolution,* 148. On the Shultz-Weinberger rivalry, see Cannon, *President Reagan,* 339–40, 402–6.

19. Nancy Reagan's memoir, written with William Novak, *My Turn: The Memoirs of Nancy Reagan* (New York: Random House, 1989), is instructive. The best brief treatment of her White House years is James G. Benze Jr.'s "Nancy (Anne Francis Robbins Davis) Reagan," in *American First Ladies: Their Lives and Their Legacy,* ed. Lewis L. Gould, 2d ed. (New York: Routledge, 2001), 393–408. See also James Rosebush, "The Ultimate Political Partner: Nancy Reagan's Contribution to the Reagan Presidency," in Schmertz et al., eds., *Ronald Reagan's America,* 2: 663–71.

20. On the problems of the National Security Council and the national security adviser under Reagan, see David M. Barrett, with Christopher Ryan, "National Security," in *The Executive Office of the President: A Historical, Biographical, and Bibliographical Guide,* ed. Harold Relyea, (Westport, Conn.: Greenwood Press, 1997), 203–7.

21. The literature on Reagan is filled with such claims for his presidency. For an example, see Dinesh D'Souza, *Ronald Reagan: How an Ordinary Man Became an Extraordinary Leader* (New York: Free Press, 1997), 1–5, 13–14, 129–48. A critical assessment of the Strategic Defense Initiative is Frances Fitzgerald's *Way Out There in the Blue: Reagan, Star Wars and the End of the Cold War* (New York: Simon & Schuster, 2000).

22. See Cannon, *President Reagan,* 317, 508–9, 774; D'Souza, *Ronald Reagan,* 222, plays down any positive impact by the First Lady in this area.

23. The Lebanon incident obviously has gained in significance since 11 September 2001. Cannon, *President Reagan,* 436–45, looks at these events from the perspective of the early 1990s. The policy of the United States toward Iraq in these years also was

at odds with what would become the stance of the nation in 2001 and 2002. See also Patrick E. Tyler, "Officers Say U.S. Aided Iraq in War Despite Use of Gas," *New York Times,* 18 August 2002.

24. For the Grenada episode, see Strober and Strober, *Reagan,* 240–47.

25. The 1984 campaign and the issue of Reagan's performance in the first debate against Walter Mondale are discussed in Darman, *Who's in Control?,* 125–29; the absence of "new programmatic initiatives" in the campaign is noted in ibid., 141–42. William Clark, in Strober and Strober, *Reagan,* 301, mentioned the possibility of not running again to the president. See also Cannon, *President Reagan,* 551–52.

26. Most of the major players in the Reagan presidency discuss the mistakes that arose from the Baker-Regan shuffle. Even D'Souza, *Ronald Reagan,* 16, is implicitly critical of the move, as is Noonan, *What I Saw at the Revolution,* 202. See also Strober and Strober, *Reagan,* 304–7; Cannon, *President Reagan,* 553–66; and Pemberton, *Exit with Honor,* 144.

27. The extraconstitutional aspects of the Iran-Contra episode tend to get lost in the minutiae of who did what when. D'Souza, *Ronald Reagan,* 246–48, is untroubled by these issues. Pemberton, *Exit with Honor,* 172–92, is good on the constitutional problems involved. See also Theodore Draper, *A Very Thin Line: The Iran Contra Affairs* (New York: Hill and Wang, 1991), and Stephen Skowronek, *The Politics Presidents Make: Leadership from John Adams to George Bush* (Cambridge: Belknap Press of Harvard University Press, 1993), 423–25.

28. Derek Leebaert, *The Fifty Year Wound: The True Price of America's Cold War Victory* (Boston: Little, Brown, 2002), 553–57, treats Iran-Contra as a regrettable lapse in Reagan's otherwise exemplary foreign policy record.

29. Strober and Strober, *Reagan,* 547.

30. John Earl Haynes, ed., *Calvin Coolidge and the Coolidge Era* (Washington, D.C.: Library of Congress, 1998), 11–12. Michael B. Grossman, Martha Joynt Kumar, and Francis E. Rourke, "Second-Term Presidencies: The Aging of Administrations," in Nelson, ed., *The Presidency and The Political System,* 236–40, look at Reagan's second term as an example of the problems that presidents encounter after re-election.

31. Strober and Strober, *Reagan,* 568. The return of fears about the future of the country in 1991 and 1992, linked to the brief recession, is not usually tied to the Reagan legacy.

32. There are three useful books about Bush and his political career. Herbert S. Parmet's *George Bush: The Life of a Lone Star Yankee* (New York: Scribner's 1997) was written with the former president's cooperation and is the best biography. David Mervin's *George Bush and the Guardianship Presidency* (1996; reprint, New York: St. Martin's Press, 1998), is a study of the presidency by a British scholar. John Robert Greene, *The Presidency of George Bush* (Lawrence: University Press of Kansas, 2000), gives another overview of Bush in the White House. Bush has produced two memoirs: *Looking Forward: An Autobiography* (New York: Bantam

Books, 1987) was coauthored with Vic Gold in preparation for the 1988 presidential campaign, and *A World Transformed* (New York: Knopf, 1998) is a work written jointly with Brent Scowcroft that deals with foreign policy during the Bush years. Jonathan Rauch, "Father Superior: Our Greatest Modern President," *New Republic* 222 (22 May 2000): 22–25, makes the case for the elder Bush's success as a governing president. Nixon's comment about Bush appears in a telephone conversation with Henry Kissinger, 27 April 1971, released from the Kissinger Papers at the Library of Congress.

33. Asher and Associates, reporters, *Official Report of the Proceedings of the Thirty-fourth Republican National Convention Held in New Orleans, Louisiana, August 15, 16, 17, 18, 1988* (Washington, D.C.: Republican National Committee, 1988), 554.

34. John Brady, *Bad Boy: The Life and Politics of Lee Atwater* (Reading, Mass.: Addison Wesley, 1997), 190–94, 201–2, 204–11, examines the William J. Horton case from Atwater's perspective. Jeremy D. Mayer, *Running on Race: Racial Politics in Presidential Campaigns, 1960–2000* (New York: Random House, 2002), 212–14, 218–28, is critical of Bush's use of the Horton episode.

35. The Republicans pounded on Dukakis's comment. See *Official Report . . . Thirty-fourth Republican National Convention,* 460 (Gerald Ford).

36. On the apparent divorce between campaigning and governance in Bush's mind, see Mervin, *George Bush and the Guardianship Presidency,* 52–53, 224–25.

37. Ibid., 212. For Bush's approach to the press, see Maltese, *Spin Control,* 217–21, and Greene, *Presidency of George Bush,* 146–47.

38. Myra Gutin, "Barbara Pierce Bush," in Gould, ed., *American First Ladies,* 409–23.

39. Greene, *Presidency of George Bush,* 47–48, 50–51, 54.

40. The merits of the Bush foreign policy team can be assessed in their various memoirs. See James A. Baker III, *The Politics of Diplomacy: Revolution, War, and Peace* (New York: G. P. Putnam's Sons, 1995), and Powell, with Persico, *My American Journey.*

41. The origins of the Gulf War are dealt with in Greene, *Presidency of George Bush,* 109–27. See also Rick Atkinson, *Crusade: The Untold Story of the Persian Gulf War* (Boston: Houghton Mifflin, 1993).

42. Greene, *Presidency of George Bush,* 135–36, assigns responsibility for the decision to Bush and General Norman Schwarzkopf. The ongoing debate about the fate of Iraq and its impact on the administration of George W. Bush is discussed in Dana Milbank, "Who's Pulling the Foreign Policy Strings?" *Washington Post,* 14 May 2002, and in Tony Karon, "Iraq: The GOP War with Itself," <Time.com> 21 August 2002.

43. Martin Walker, *The President We Deserve: Bill Clinton: His Rise, Falls, and Comebacks* (New York: Crown, 1996), 116–17, 119–20, considers the political context in light of Bush's standing in the polls after the Gulf War. See Parmet, *George Bush,* 496–99.

44. Eleanor Clift and Tom Brazaitis, *War Without Bloodshed: The Art of Politics* (New York: Simon and Schuster, 1996), 244–246; Darman, *Who's in Control?,* 230–66.

45. Greene, *Presidency of George Bush,* 87–88.

46. Parmet, *George Bush,* 491–93.

47. Greene, *Presidency of George Bush,* 86; Mervin, *George Bush and the Guardianship Presidency,* 74.

48. Greene, *Presidency of George Bush,* 161–63; Parmet, *George Bush,* 497.

49. Greene, *Presidency of George Bush,* 169; Mervin, *George Bush and the Guardianship Presidency,* 224 (quotation).

10. PERILS OF THE MODERN PRESIDENCY

1. See George Stephanopoulos, *All Too Human: A Political Education* (Boston: Little, Brown, 1999), 411. Martin Walker's, *The President We Deserve: Bill Clinton: His Rise, Falls, and Comebacks* (New York: Crown, 1996) is an excellent survey of Clinton's first term by a British journalist. William C. Berman, *From the Center to the Edge: The Politics and Policies of the Clinton Presidency* (Lanham, Md: Rowman and Littlefield, 2001), offers an early attempt at a synthesis of the Clinton years. Joe Klein, *The Natural: The Misunderstood Presidency of Bill Clinton* (New York: Doubleday, 2002), gives a generally favorable impressionistic account. Steven E. Schier, ed., *The Postmodern Presidency: Bill Clinton's Legacy in U.S. Politics* (Pittsburgh, Pa.: University of Pittsburgh Press, 2000), provides a collection of essays. David Gray Adler and Michael A. Genovese, eds., *The President and the Law: The Clinton Legacy* (Lawrence: University Press of Kansas, 2002), present a look at the legal ramifications of Clinton's presidency from a number of different perspectives.

2. These charges against Clinton circulated on talk radio and in general discussion in Central Texas during his presidency. For a critique of Clinton on this basis from the left, see Roger Morris, *Partners in Power: The Clintons and Their America* (New York: Holt, 1996), 325–26, 389–427. James D. Retter, *Anatomy of a Scandal: An Investigation into the Campaign to Undermine the Clinton Presidency* (Los Angeles: General Publishing Group, 1998), looks at some of the more lurid charges that were made about Clinton.

3. The various allegations and charges against Hillary Clinton are discussed in David Brock, *The Seduction of Hillary Rodham Clinton* (New York: Free Press, 1996), Joyce Milton, *The First Partner: Hillary Rodham Clinton* (New York: William Morrow, 1999), and Gail Sheehy, *Hillary's Choice* (New York: Random House, 1999). "Hillary Rodham Clinton," in *American First Ladies: Their Lives and Their Legacy,* ed. Lewis L. Gould, 2d ed. (New York: Routledge, 2001), 425–38, attempts a more balanced approach to her career.

4. There was even a "Slick Willie's Family Pool Hall" chain based on the Clinton nickname that remained in business after he had left the presidency; Paul Greenberg, *No Surprise: Two Decades of Clinton Watching* (Washington, D.C.: Brassey's, 1996), was the creator of the title.

5. The best journalistic account of Clinton's early life is David Maraniss's, *First in His Class: A Biography of Bill Clinton* (New York: Simon and Schuster, 1995); Maraniss gives a good sense of the conventional wisdom about Clinton's political

origins. See also Meredith Oakley, *On the Make: The Rise of Bill Clinton* (Washington, D.C.: Regnery, 1994), for a critical appraisal of Clinton's record as governor of Arkansas.

6. Stephanopoulos, *All Too Human*, 25–107, provides an insider's account of Clinton's presidential race. Walker, *The President We Deserve*, 118–58, gives a good overview of the election process.

7. Peter Goldman et al., *Quest for the Presidency, 1992* (College Station: Texas A&M University Press, 1994), offers a detailed and thorough narrative of the 1992 election.

8. For Armey, see David Maraniss and Michael Weisskopf, *"Tell Newt to Shut Up!"* (New York: Simon and Schuster, 1996), 73, and Elizabeth Drew, *On the Edge: The Clinton Presidency* (New York: Simon and Schuster, 1994), 21–35. Dick Morris, *Behind the Oval Office: Winning the Presidency in the Nineties* (New York: Random House, 1997), 31, describes Clinton's feelings about his lack of political legitimacy.

9. Joe Conason and Gene Lyons, *The Hunting of the President: The Ten-Year Campaign to Destroy Bill and Hillary Clinton* (New York: St. Martin's Press, 2000), 371, quotes Hillary Clinton. As with so much about Bill Clinton, the issue of whether he faced a concerted campaign to oust him from office is much disputed. While the participants in the effort against his presidency have kept silent, the evidence arrayed in the Conason and Lyons book and the materials in Jeffrey Toobin's *A Vast Conspiracy: The Real Story of the Sex Scandal That Nearly Brought Down a President* (New York: Random House, 1999) reveal that Clinton faced a degree of organized opposition that had not previously been directed against other presidents from the outset of their administrations.

10. Gene Lyons, *Fools for Scandal* (New York: Franklin Square Press, 1996), provides a vigorous critique of the *New York Times* coverage, especially by its lead reporter on Whitewater, Jeff Gerth.

11. On McClarty, see Drew, *On the Edge*, 104–6, and Walker, *The President We Deserve*, 187. For the size of the staff in the Clinton presidency, see Bradley H. Patterson Jr., *The White House Staff: Inside the West Wing and Beyond* (Washington, D.C.: Brookings Institution Press, 2000), 347–48. What Patterson calls the larger "White House staff community" came to almost six thousand people.

12. The problems of the transition are well covered in Walker, *The President We Deserve*, 162–76, and in Drew, *On the Edge*, 21–56. See also John P. Burke, *Presidential Transitions: From Politics to Practice* (Boulder: Lynne Rienner, 2000), 283–317, for a critical appraisal of Clinton's efforts. James P. Pfiffner, *The Strategic Presidency: Hitting the Ground Running* (Lawrence: University Press of Kansas, 1996), 148–82, also considers Clinton's problems in the transition.

13. Berman, *From the Center to the Edge*, 23; Drew, *On the Edge*, 131–33; Burke, *Presidential Transitions*, 328–68.

14. For examples of Clinton's problems with scheduling, length of speeches, and his inability to be punctual, see Walker, *The President We Deserve*, 202, 221, and Drew, *On the Edge*, 136.

15. On the Travel Office episode, there are a number of accounts; see Conason and Lyons, *The Hunting of the President*, 84–85, and James B. Stewart, *Blood Sport: The President and His Adversaries* (New York: Simon and Schuster, 1996), 258–68. For the attitudes of the Washington establishment, see the famous article of the *Washington Post* insider Sally Quinn, "Not in Their Back Yard," *Washington Post*, 3 November 1998, which arraigned Clinton for his alleged insensitivity to the customs of the nation's capital.

16. Clinton's troubled relations with Congress can be followed in Walker, *The President We Deserve*, 312–25, and Berman, *From the Center to the Edge*, 24–26.

17. On Clinton and the Democrats, see Walker, *The President We Deserve*, 164–67, 317–31.

18. Gingrich's problems as Speaker and the way Clinton beat him politically can be followed in Elizabeth Drew, *Showdown: The Struggle Between the Gingrich Congress and the Clinton White House* (New York: Simon and Schuster, 1996), and in Maraniss and Weiskopf, *"Tell Newt to Shut Up."*

19. Helen Dewar and Joan Biskupic, "Court Strikes Down Line-Item Veto," *Washington Post*, 26 June 1998.

20. Clinton's efforts at reinventing government are surveyed in Peri Arnold, *Making the Managerial Presidency: Comprehensive Reorganization Planning, 1905–1996*, 2d ed., rev. (Lawrence: University Press of Kansas, 1998), 365–80.

21. For Clinton's speeches, see Michael Waldman, *POTUS Speaks: Finding the Words That Defined the Clinton Presidency* (New York: Simon and Schuster, 2000); Stephanopoulos, *All Too Human*, 199–203; and Bradley H. Patterson Jr., *The White House Staff: Inside the West Wing and Beyond* (Washington, D.C.: Brookings Institution Press, 2000), 162–72. Benjamin R. Barber, *The Truth of Power: Intellectual Affairs in the Clinton White House* (New York: Norton, 2001), 104–31, offers a sympathetic and persuasive critique of Clinton's use of speaking and words during his presidency.

22. Drew, *Showdown*, 66–69, describes the 1995 State of the Union message. See also Dick Morris, *Behind the Oval Office*, 90–95.

23. Morris gives himself ample credit for the strategy that produced Clinton's 1996 reelection in *Behind the Oval Office*, 3–17.

24. For the campaign scandals in brief, see Berman, *From the Center to the Edge*, 67–68, 70. Howard Kurtz's, *Spin Cycle* (New York: Simon and Schuster, 1998) is more detailed on the issue.

25. For a critique of *Clinton v. Jones* from a conservative jurist, see Richard A. Posner, *An Affair of State: The Investigation, Impeachment, and Trial of President Clinton* (Cambridge: Harvard University Press, 1999), 225–28.

26. By 2002, the independent counsel who had succeeded Kenneth Starr, Robert Ray, announced that there was not enough evidence to sustain an indictment of either of the Clintons in the Whitewater case. See "The Great Whitewater Scandal That Never Was," London, *Independent*, 22 March 2002, and *Chicago Sun Times*, 21 March 2002. These conclusions were anticipated in Lyons, *Fools for Scandal*, 1–29.

27. Conason and Lyons, *The Hunting of the President*, 174–200.

28. There is an extensive polemical literature on the Vincent Foster suicide, most of which has been discredited because of the findings of several independent counsels that the White House aide did in fact kill himself. A good summary treatment is Dan E. Moldea's, *A Washington Tragedy: How the Death of Vincent Foster Ignited a Political Firestorm* (Washington, D.C.: Regnery, 1998).

29. Stephanopoulos, *All Too Human*, 416–17.

30. *The Starr Report: The Official Report of the Independent Counsel's Investigation of the President* (Rocklin, Calif.: Prima, 1998), 429–33; Peter Baker, *The Breach: Inside the Impeachment and Trial of William Jefferson Clinton* (New York: Scribner's, 2001), 214–15; Robert Busby, *Defending the American Presidency: Clinton and the Lewinsky Scandal* (New York: Palgrave, 2001) Bill Straub, "Bush Out to Beef up Pesidency," *Detroit News*, 20 May 2002.

31. See Conason and Lyons, *The Hunting of the President*, 189, 190, for one example of a prediction that Mrs. Clinton would soon be indicted. See also Lyons, *Fools for Scandal*, 26–27.

32. On the question of whether Clinton's testimony was needed to resolve the underlying claim of Paula Jones that she had suffered sexual discrimination in the workplace, see Posner, *An Affair of State*, 228. For the impact in September 1998 of the televised deposition of August, see Klein, *The Natural*, 177–78, and Peter Baker, *The Breach*, 105–7.

33. This evaluation of the strategy of the House Republicans is based on my own observations of the impeachment process and from the testimony in several published accounts such as Baker, *The Breach*, 188–216, especially 193, 196–97, and 210–11. Like Woodrow Wilson and the League of Nations in 1919 and 1920, the House and Senate Republicans in 1998 and 1999 seemed to believe that their argument would prevail on its own merits, without regard to the political dynamics of congressional opinion in both parties.

34. Byron York, "Clinton Has No Clothes," *National Review Online*, 17 December 2001, <www.nationalreview.com>, is critical of Clinton's record on terrorism. Bill Press, "Don't Blame It on Bill Clinton," <www.CNN.com>, defends Clinton's performance. Klein, in *The Natural*, 189–93, attempts a balanced appraisal. This debate is likely to continue for some time. David Benjamin and Steven Simon, *The Age of Sacred Terror* (New York: Random House, 2002), 256–325, offer a nuanced and balanced view of the performance of the Clinton White House.

35. Barbara Olson's *The Final Days: The Last Desperate Abuses of Power by the Clinton White House* (Washington, D.C.: Regnery, 2001) is a polemic by a confirmed Clinton critic. Since Olson died in the 11 September 2001 terrorist incident, her book has not been the subject of much real analysis. Klein, *The Natural*, 203–5, is critical without being conspiratorial.

I do not attempt to discuss all the sources used in preparing this book nor do I endeavor to mention all the important books on the presidency. Instead, I offer comments on recent books on the institution that provide insights into how the presidency has developed. Key books on each of the twentieth-century presidents are then discussed as a guide for readers to delve into the history of the occupants of the White House on their own.

Several works are useful for understanding the way historians and political scientists have seen the presidency during the past decade. James P. Pfiffner, *The Modern Presidency* (1994; reprint, New York: St. Martin's Press, 1998), offers an analytic examination that uses historical examples to illuminate specific issues. Forrest McDonald, *The American Presidency: An Intellectual History* (Lawrence: University Press of Kansas, 1994), has some provocative insights about the impact of the mass media on the institution in the twentieth century. Robert Dallek, *Hail to the Chief: The Making and Unmaking of American Presidents* (New York: Hyperion, 1996), considers common threads among all the presidents in various aspects of American history. Fred I. Greenstein, *The Presidential Difference: Leadership Style from FDR to Clinton* (New York: Free Press, 2000), covers the last two-thirds of the twentieth century in a general manner. Michael Geneovese, *The Power of the American Presidency, 1789–2000* (New York: Oxford University Press, 2001), gives a narrative account of the presidents that lacks a strong grasp of the historical context. Harold C. Relyea, ed., *The Executive Office of the President: A Historical, Biographical, and Bibliographical Guide* (Westport, Conn.: Greenwood Press, 1997), includes useful essays on various aspects of how the White House operates. Bradley H. Patterson Jr.'s *The White House Staff: Inside the West Wing and Beyond* (Washington, D.C.: Brookings Institution Press, 2000) is very good for the human perspective on White House functions and the people who serve the president. Peri Arnold's *Making the Managerial Presidency: Comprehensive Reorganization Planning, 1905–1996*, 2d ed., rev. (Lawrence: University Press of Kansas, 1998) is important for its examination of the ways in which presidents tried to reshape the workings of the White House.

A number of helpful reference works came out around 2000, and these are good places to begin for the general history of individual presidencies. Michael Beschloss, ed., *American Heritage Illustrated History of the Presidents* (New York: Crown, 2000), provides short, interpretive essays on each president, as do Alan Brinkley and Davis Dyer, eds., *The Reader's Companion to the American Presidency* (Boston: Houghton Mifflin, 2000), and Melvin I. Urofsky, ed., *The American Presidents* (New York: Garland, 2000). Philip B. Kunhardt Jr., Philip B. Kunhardt III, and Peter W. Kunhardt, *The American President* (New York: Riverhead Books, 1999), provide a more topical approach. Michael Nelson, ed., *The Presidency and the Political System,* 6th ed. (Washington, D.C.: CQ Press, 2000), offers a valuable collection of perceptive essays that will provide a good guide to recent writing and interpretations of the presidency.

For the individual presidents of the twentieth century, there are many analyses and biographies that repay further study. Only a few can be listed here. Preference has been given to volumes now in print or readily available from on-line used booksellers. Books in the University Press of Kansas series will be listed first for each chief executive.

Lewis L. Gould, *The Presidency of William McKinley* (Lawrence: University Press of Kansas, 1980), considers the role of George B. Cortelyou and the president in the creation of modern executive practices. H. Wayne Morgan's *William McKinley and His America* (Kent, Ohio: Kent State University Press, 2003) is a revised and updated version of a biography that originally appeared in 1963. Margaret Leech's, *In the Days of McKinley* (New York: Harper and Brothers, 1959) is an older examination of the presidential years that still contains much useful information about McKinley in the White House.

Lewis L. Gould, *The Presidency of Theodore Roosevelt* (Lawrence: University Press of Kansas, 1991), places Roosevelt in the context of changes in the presidency during the early twentieth century. Edmund Morris, *Theodore Rex* (New York: Random House, 2001), works from the premise that the reader should know only what Americans knew about Roosevelt between 1901 and 1909. As a result, key controversies are highlighted, but many salient aspects of what Roosevelt did as president are simply relegated to endnotes or ignored altogether. John Milton Cooper Jr., *The Warrior and the Priest* (Cambridge:

Harvard University Press, 1983), compares Roosevelt and Woodrow Wilson. John Morton Blum, *The Republican Roosevelt* (Cambridge: Harvard University Press, 1954), offers penetrating essays about Roosevelt's political career and his impact on the presidency.

Paolo Coletta's *The Presidency of William Howard Taft* (Lawrence: University Press of Kansas, 1973) has not aged well, and a new examination of Taft's presidency is needed. Most of the other books on Taft are now out of print. Henry F. Pringle, *The Life and Times of William Howard Taft*, 2 vols. (New York: Farrar and Rinehart, 1939), offers a sound biography. Donald F. Anderson's *William Howard Taft: A Conservative's Conception of the Presidency* (Ithaca, N.Y.: Cornell University Press, 1973) is based on Taft's papers and theoretical assumptions about what he should have done as chief executive.

Kendrick Clements, *The Presidency of Woodrow Wilson* (Lawrence: University Press of Kansas, 1992), provides good coverage of Wilson's impact on the presidency. An excellent new treatment of Wilson's performance during the League of Nations struggle is John Milton Cooper Jr.'s *Breaking the Heart of the World: Woodrow Wilson and the Fight for the League of Nations* (New York: Cambridge University Press, 2001), which has an abundance of information about scholarship on this important president. Phyllis Lee Levin, *Edith and Woodrow: The Wilson White House* (New York: Scribner's, 2001), offers a look at Wilson's second marriage and its effect on his performance in the White House.

Eugene P. Trani and David L. Wilson, *The Presidency of Warren G. Harding* (Lawrence: University Press of Kansas, 1977), deal with the administration in a clear and analytic manner. Robert H. Ferrell, *The Strange Deaths of President Harding* (Columbia: University of Missouri Press, 1996), debunks some of the long-standing mythology about the president, including his alleged affair with Nan Britton. Carl Sferrazza Anthony, *Florence Harding: The First Lady, the Jazz Age, and the Death of America's Most Scandalous President* (New York: William Morrow, 1998), revisits the Harding administration with gossip and anecdotes to reestablish the traditional interpretation of a scandal-ridden presidency.

Robert H. Ferrell, *The Presidency of Calvin Coolidge* (Lawrence: University Press of Kansas, 1998), takes a thoughtful look at the president's achievements in office. John Earl Haynes, ed., *Calvin Coolidge and the Coolidge Era* (Washington, D.C.: Library of Congress, 1998), provides a number of important essays about the president and the 1920s that contain much useful information. Robert Sobel, *Coolidge: An American Enigma* (Washington, D.C.: Regnery, 1998), writes from a conservative perspective and provides a clear, interpretive narrative of Coolidge's career.

Martin Fausold, *The Presidency of Herbert C. Hoover* (Lawrence: University Press of Kansas, 1985), offers a sympathetic, informed treatment of Hoover's troubled one term in office. The best biographies were written almost a generation ago. Joan Hoff Wilson's *Herbert Hoover: Forgotten Progressive* (Boston: Little, Brown, 1975) was influential in shaping attitudes toward the president among historians. David Burner, *Herbert Hoover: A Public Life* (New York: Knopf, 1979), provides a persuasive summary of Hoover's long career.

George McJimsey, *The Presidency of Franklin Delano Roosevelt* (Lawrence: University Press of Kansas, 2000), brings the complexity of Roosevelt's four terms into the space of a readable and clear narrative. A good one-volume treatment of Roosevelt's life is Frank B. Freidel's *Franklin D. Roosevelt: A Rendezvous with Destiny* (Boston: Little, Brown, 1990). Patrick J. Maney, *The Roosevelt Presence: The Life and Legacy of FDR* (Berkeley: University of California Press, 1998), balances praise and criticism for this important president.

Donald R. McCoy, *The Presidency of Harry S. Truman* (Lawrence: University Press of Kansas, 1984), surveys the administration in a credible and thorough manner. Alonzo L. Hamby, *Man of the People: A Life of Harry S. Truman* (New York: Oxford University Press, 1995), offers a comprehensive analysis that provides a balanced look at Truman's accomplishments. Michael J. Hogan, *A Cross of Iron: Harry S. Truman and the Origins of the National Security State, 1945–1954* (Cambridge: Cambridge University Press, 1998), is critical of Truman's handling of the government at home in response to the Cold War.

Chester J. Pach Jr. and Elmo Richardson, *The Presidency of Dwight D. Eisenhower* (Lawrence: University Press of Kansas, 1991), provide an account of Eisenhower in the White House that reflects the positive appraisal of his presidency that occurred in the 1980s. Fred Greenstein, *The Hidden-Hand Presidency: Eisenhower as Leader* (1992; reprint, Baltimore: Johns Hopkins University Press, 1994), reshaped the way historians thought about Eisenhower and has updated this edition. Clarence G. Lasby's *Eisenhower's Heart Attack: How Ike Beat Heart Disease and Held on to the Presidency* (Lawrence: University

Press of Kansas, 1997) is one of the most interesting and insightful books about Eisenhower to appear in recent years.

James N. Giglio, *The Presidency of John F. Kennedy* (Lawrence: University Press of Kansas, 1991), provides a reliable account of the major events of Kennedy's administration. Richard Reeves, *President Kennedy: Profile of Power* (New York: Simon and Schuster, 1993), takes a close look at Kennedy's performance. Hugh Brogan's *Kennedy* (London and New York: Longman, 1996) offers a brief look at Kennedy's career by a sympathetic British journalist.

Vaughn Bornet's *The Presidency of Lyndon Johnson* (Lawrence: University Press of Kansas, 1982) is now dated but has some interesting insights about Johnson's health and his sudden exit in 1968. Robert Dallek, *Flawed Giant: Lyndon Johnson and His Times, 1961–1973* (New York: Oxford University Press, 1998), looks at Johnson's record in foreign and domestic policy in a balanced and comprehensive way. Irving Bernstein, *Guns or Butter: The Presidency of Lyndon Johnson* (New York: Oxford University Press, 1996), goes into impressive detail about the policy choices of the Great Society.

Melvin Small, *The Presidency of Richard Nixon* (Lawrence: University Press of Kansas, 1999), provides an impressive synthesis that treats Nixon fairly and with insight. Jeffrey Kimball, *Nixon's Vietnam War* (Lawrence: University Press of Kansas, 1998), has much to say about Nixon's governing style as well as the war in Southeast Asia. Richard Reeves, *President Nixon: Alone in the White House* (New York: Simon and Schuster, 2001), looks at key episodes in the Nixon presidency to develop his thesis on his subject's presidential isolation.

John Robert Greene, *The Presidency of Gerald R. Ford* (Lawrence: University Press of Kansas, 1995), gives Ford his due as a chief executive. James Cannon's *Time and Chance: Gerald Ford's Appointment with History* (New York: HarperCollins, 1994) is a biography by a former aide. Steven F. Hayward, *The Age of Reagan: The Fall of the Old Liberal Order, 1964–1980* (Roseville, Calif.: Prima Press, 2001), considers Ford from a conservative point of view.

Burton I. Kaufman, *The Presidency of James Earl Carter, Jr.* (Lawrence: University Press of Kansas, 1993), is critical of Carter's overall performance. Peter G. Bourne, *Jimmy Carter: A Comprehensive Biography from Plains to Postpresidency* (New York: Scribner's, 1997), is friendly but has some negative comments about Carter's liabilities. Herbert D. Rosenbaum and Alexej Ugrinsky, eds., *The Presidency and Domestic Policies of Jimmy Carter* (Westport,

Conn.: Greenwood Press, 1994), include many interesting essays about various phases of the Carter presidency, along with comments from many members of the administration. Gary M. Fink and Hugh Davis Graham, eds., *The Carter Presidency: Policy Choices in the Post–New Deal Era* (Lawrence: University Press of Kansas, 1998) provides fresh and insightful perspectives on many aspects of Carter's tenure in the White House.

William E. Pemberton, *Exit with Honor: The Life and Presidency of Ronald Reagan* (Armonk, N.Y.: M. E. Sharpe, 1997), offers a balanced and thoughtful one-volume examination of Reagan's impact as president. Lou Cannon's *President Reagan: The Role of a Lifetime* (New York: Simon and Schuster, 1991) is a thorough study by a journalist who covered Reagan's entire career. Deborah Hart Strober and Gerald S. Strober's *Reagan: The Man and His Presidency* (Boston: Houghton Mifflin, 1998) is based on recollections of major participants in the administration and is often helpful in understanding the development of Reagan's thinking.

John Robert Greene, *The Presidency of George Bush* (Lawrence: University Press of Kansas, 2000), provides a good beginning on a presidency for which much of the documentary record is not yet available. David Mervin's *George Bush and the Guardianship Presidency* (1996; reprint, New York: St. Martin's Press, 1998) is an interesting summary of the Bush years by a British scholar. Herbert S. Parmet's *George Bush: The Life of a Lone Star Yankee* (New York: Scribner's, 1997) is a biography whose author did have access to some private and primary Bush materials.

The Clinton presidency is too recent to have had any scholarly work done based on original sources. Martin Walker's *The President We Deserve: Bill Clinton: His Rise, Falls, and Comebacks* (New York: Crown, 1996) is a lucid narrative by a British journalist who could avoid the partisan tensions that affected most writing on Clinton while he was president. William C. Berman, *From the Center to the Edge: The Politics and Policies of the Clinton Presidency* (Lanham, Md.: Rowman and Littlefield, 2001), provides a brief survey of important issues. Joe Klein's, *The Natural: The Misunderstood Presidency of Bill Clinton* (New York: Doubleday, 2002) is written by a sympathetic but critical journalist. Daniel Benjamin and Steven Simon, *The Age of Sacred Terror* (New York: Random House, 2002), look at how Clinton did and did not meet the challenge of terrorism. For the Clinton marriage, Gil Troy, *Mr. and Mrs. President: From the Trumans to the Clintons,* 2d ed., rev. (Lawrence: University Press of Kansas, 2000), has thoughtful insights. Haynes Johnson, *The Best of Times: America in the Clinton Years* (New York: Harcourt, 2001), is good on Clinton's personal scandal. Bruce Buchanan, ed., *The State of the American Presidency* (Austin: University of Texas System, 2002), provides a variety of comments about the modern institution. No doubt other studies of the Clinton presidency, pro and con, will appear in profusion in the years to come.